The Archaeology of Contact in Settle

Several decades of research into the archaeology of contact in North America have laid the foundations for the global exploration of the archaeology of European colonisation. It is significant, however, that archaeologists, unlike historians and geographers, have yet to develop a global account of contact and its consequences. This edited work presents case studies from nations developed from British settlement so as to allow historical archaeologists to examine differences and similarities between the histories of modern colonial societes world-wide. Written by an international team of experts, the work shows that historical archaeologies can assume marvellously different and suggestive forms when examined from the periphery. Furthermore, the imperatives of the periphery could result in different perspectives on North American and European archaeological contexts. The work also examines the role of a global vision of the historical archaeology of colonialism in providing a new basis for the evolution of the 'nation'.

TIM MURRAY is Professor of Archaeology at the School of Historical and European Studies, La Trobe University. He is the author and editor of numerous publications, including *The Archaeology of Aborginal Australia* (1998), *The Archaeology of Urban Landscapes* (2001) and the five-volume *Encyclopedia of Archaeology*, including *The Great Archaeologists* (1999) and *History and Discoveries* (2001).

NEW DIRECTIONS IN ARCHAEOLOGY

Series Editors

WENDY ASHMORE
Department of Anthropology, University of Pennsylvania
FRANÇOISE AUDOUZE
Centre de Recherches Archéologiques, Meudon, France
CYPRIAN BROODBANK
Institute of Archaeology, University College London
TIM MURRAY
Archaeology Program, La Trobe University, Australia
COLIN RENFREW
Department of Archaeology, University of Cambridge
NATHAN SCHLANGER
Paris, France
ANDREW SHERRATT
Department of Antiquities, Ashmolean Museum, Oxford
TIMOTHY TAYLOR
Department of Archaeology, University of Bradford
NORMAN YOFFEE
Department of Near Eastern Studies and Department of Anthropology, University of Michigan

Recent titles in the series include

The Archaeology of Contact in Settler Societies

TIM MURRAY

La Trobe University

CAMBRIDGE
UNIVERSITY PRESS

PUBLISHED BY THE PRESS SYNDICATE OF THE UNIVERSITY OF CAMBRIDGE
The Pitt Building, Trumpington Street, Cambridge, United Kingdom

CAMBRIDGE UNIVERSITY PRESS
The Edinburgh Building, Cambridge, CB2 2RU, UK
40 West 20th Street, New York, NY 10011–4211, USA
477 Williamstown Road, Port Melbourne, VIC 3207, Australia
Ruiz de Alarcón 13, 28014 Madrid, Spain
Dock House, The Waterfront, Cape Town 8001, South Africa

http://www.cambridge.org

First published 2004

Printed in the United Kingdom at the University Press, Cambridge

Typeface Minion 10.5/14 pt.   *System* LaTeX 2$_\varepsilon$ [TB]

A catalogue record for this book is available from the British Library

Library of Congress Cataloguing in Publication data
The archaeology of contact in settler societies / edited by Tim Murray.
    p.   cm. – (New directions in archaeology)
Includes bibliographical references and index.
ISBN 0 521 79257 6 – ISBN 0 521 79682 2 (pb.)
1. Archaeology and history.   2. Colonisation – History.   3. Acculturation – History.
I. Murray, Tim, 1955–   II. Series.
CC77.H5A7175   2004
970.01 – dc22   2004040762

ISBN 0 521 79257 6 hardback
ISBN 0 521 79682 2 paperback

To Susan, Patrick and Celia

Contents

Figures

Tables

Contributors

Steven Acheson, Archaeology Branch, Ministry of Small Business, Tourism and Culture, British Columbia

Stuart Bedford, New Zealand Historic Places Trust/Pouhere Taonga, New Zealand

Yvonne Brink, Historical Archaeology Research Group, University of Cape Town

Patricia Capone, Peabody Museum of Archaeology and Ethnology, Harvard University

James P. Delgado, Executive Director, Vancouver Maritime Museum, British Columbia

Olga Klimko, Tourism and Recreation Branch, Ministry of Sustainable Resource Management, British Columbia

Rodney Harrison, Cultural Heritage Division, NSW National Parks and Wildlife Service

Tim Murray, Archaeology Program, La Trobe University

Laurier Turgeon, Directeur du CELAT, Université Laval

Christine Williamson, Archaeology Program, La Trobe University

1 | The archaeology of contact in settler societies

TIM MURRAY

Introduction

Although archaeologists (particularly in North America, but to a lesser extent in South Africa, Australia and New Zealand) have for some time been interested in exploring the archaeology of European colonisation (see for example Allen 1969; Deagan 1983; Deetz 1963; Fitzhugh 1985), there is no doubt that the need to celebrate the quincentenary of the voyage of Christopher Columbus fostered a major reassessment of research in this field, and there have been numerous discussions of its impact (see for example Deagan 1998; Wylie 1992).

The three volumes in the series *Columbian Consequences* (D. Thomas, 1989, 1990, 1991), apart from documenting the richness and diversity of contact research being undertaken in the United States, were also intended to right what the editor felt to be a major wrong. For Thomas one of the most significant reasons for embarking on an archaeological exploration of the consequences of European colonisation in the United States was that the role of *Spanish* colonisers had been masked in narrative histories of colonisation, and of life on the frontier. By focusing the three volumes on the consequences of Spanish colonisation, Thomas (and the Society for American Archaeology which backed the project) believed that the dominant Anglocentric or Francocentric views of the European colonisation of the United States would be challenged and replaced. It was a signal achievement and remains so.

This editorial agendum reflects the scale and style of historical archaeology which has been undertaken in North America since the field began to expand rapidly (both inside and outside the universities) in the 1960s. During this time archaeologists, historians and ethnohistorians have charted the extraordinary variety and richness of indigenous American societies, and the equally diverse histories of their experiences of contact. As has often been observed, the European invasion and settlement of the Americas is one of the most significant passages of human history, leading to a fundamental reorganisation of the ecology of two continents and to the lives of their inhabitants (both indigenes and invaders). Documenting, understanding and explaining these impacts in the Caribbean, the United States and Canada have been the primary focus of archaeologists, ethnohistorians and historians who have ranged across the 500 years of colonial history to encompass studies of contact, slavery, frontiers and nation-building that have become disciplinary landmarks of equal importance to *Columbian Consequences* (see for example Crosby 1986, 1994; Deagan 1991; Deetz 1991; Ferguson and Green 1983; Lightfoot 1995; Rogers 1990; Rogers and Wilson 1993; Trigger 1980, 1984).

North American research on historical archaeology in general, and contact archaeology in particular, is characterised by the scale of the enterprise (see for example Miller *et al.* 1996), and the diversity of histories produced, be they of diasporas or migrations or communities created from (among a host of alternatives) slave or free, creole and maroon populations (see for example Farnsworth 2001; Weik 1997). North American historical archaeology also exhibits a strong theoretical focus where practitioners have sought to understand change and variation in historical societies (and the consequences of interactions across boundaries and frontiers – both temporal and spatial) through concepts such as acculturation, dominance, resistance, ethnogenesis, gender, and frameworks broadly described as evolutionary theory and world systems theory (see especially the papers in Cusick 1998 and Rogers and Wilson 1993). Such diversities of problem, data and theory have also required archaeologists, ethnohistorians and historians to reflect on difficult issues arising from the integration of all this variety into coherent analysis. A focus on the methodology of history writing in contact contexts has also required archaeologists to think more clearly about the value of previously strongly drawn boundaries between history and prehistory (see for example Lightfoot 1995; Lightfoot and Martinez 1995) and of the structural relationships between diverse databases (see for example Wilson 1993). Last, but certainly by no means least, has been a long-standing interest in modelling the consequences for American indigenous populations of diseases brought by invaders (see especially Dunnell 1991; Hutchison and Mitchem 2001; Ramenofsky 1987, 1991; but see also Crosby 1994).

These studies have laid the foundations for the global exploration of the archaeology of European colonisation, in that North American approaches and concerns have strongly influenced the development of contact archaeology in South Africa (see for example Hall 1993; Jordan and Schrire 2002; Schrire 1991), Australia (see for example Allen 1969; Birmingham 1992; Murray 1993, Torrence and Clarke 2000a) and New Zealand (see for example Bedford, this volume). However, it is significant that archaeologists, unlike historians and geographers (see for example Crosby 1986, 1994; Daunton and Halpern 1999; Fieldhouse 1982, 1999), have not yet sought to develop a global account of contact and its consequences. Notwithstanding this, it is worth noting that there has been some exploration of the value of case studies derived from analyses of modern colonialism as sources of analogical inference (or just as heuristic devices) for an archaeology of colonialism in the ancient world (see for example Deitler 1995, 1998; van Dommelen 2002). Of course a major topic of debate here is the usefulness of inferences drawn from modern times to understanding the colonial experiences of pre-capitalist societies.

Sketching a global archaeology of contact

The value of comparisons and inferences that might be drawn from generalisations raises important questions. For example, should the development of a global archaeological account of contact in the modern world require us to expand and contextualise this North American inheritance; if this is so, then should this be via the demonstration of differences between North America and other parts of the world, or should it be through a reflection about the applicability of the theories and perspectives that have thus far underwritten the field? Answering such questions is well beyond the scope of this book, as is a thoroughgoing reflection about theories and perspectives. None the less it is possible to create a broad-brush sketch of some of the issues that have come to dominate research in this field around the world, and to document variations in approach and purpose that reflect local contexts and practice.

Thus at this most basic level *The Archaeology of Contact in Settler Societies* presents some case studies (such as those by Turgeon and Capone) that are firmly within the tradition of North American research, others (such as those by Acheson and Delgado) that owe much to those perspectives, and still others drawn from South Africa, Australia and New Zealand that perhaps owe less to North America and more to a need to comprehend the colonial experience closer to home. However, the purpose of these case studies (apart from documenting variation) is to enhance understanding of diversity through comparison, to acknowledge that the foundation of colonial societies in the modern world (and their subsequent histories) allows us to compare and contrast within the overarching framework of the 'settler society', which I shall define below. Of course 'settler societies' (which are themselves highly diverse) are only one kind of colonial society created in the modern world, and it is not intended that the archaeology and history of all colonial and postcolonial social formations either can or should be written within this framework. None the less the virtues of comparison and contrast can be seen here too.

A framework of comparison

The many differences in the histories of colonies and colonisers are the product of readily understood processes and contexts, five of the more obvious interlocking variables of which are: the chronology of colonisation, the types of societies encountered by Europeans, the intentions of the colonisers and the responses of the colonised, the demographics of colonisation, and the chronology of independence and decolonisation. These are readily exemplified.

First European contacts with the indigenes of North America took place over 500 years ago, somewhat later in South Africa, and post-1788 in Australia. However, chronology is more than just the timing of colonisation, in that significant variations in the type and intensity of impact are related to the economic and political state of both indigenous societies and colonising powers. In this analysis the colonisations of the sixteenth and seventeenth centuries differed markedly from those undertaken (especially in Australia and in western North America) during the industrial revolution. Similarly the phase of Dutch colonisation of the Cape differed in important respects from that undertaken in the nineteenth century by the British in southern Africa.

The types of societies encountered by the colonists were crucially important in shaping both indigenous and invader responses at a local level. These varied considerably across the entire range of colonial contexts and interactions, for example in treaty-making, access to land and resources, resistance and its consequences, the impact of disease, the participation by indigenes in the colonial economy and military (whether free or forced), and the role of religion in indigenous and colonial societies. European colonists encountered a great diversity of social and cultural formations that were later to be synthesised (by Europeans) into the classical evolutionary hierarchies. Of course these were also to underwrite the structure of both local and global interpretations of humanity by anthropologists and archaeologists in the nineteenth and twentieth centuries.

The intentions of the colonisers and the responses of the colonised were also crucial. Obviously these were influenced by the first two variables, but other factors such as the nature and extent of local raw materials for extraction and removal to Europe, the growing of plantation crops (such as cotton, sugar, coffee, tea), the strategic importance of the place (for example the Cape and the east coast of Australia), and the suitability of the place for settlement were important too. The primary purpose of many European colonies was purely economic – control over resources for export to the metropolitan and over economies for the subsequent import of European goods to the colonies. 'Settler societies' or settler colonies combined this former purpose with that of very large-scale movements of populations from the metropolitan to the colony. Of course both the intentions of the colonisers and the responses of the colonised could (and frequently did) change over time, as the 500-year history of North America and the shorter colonial histories of the Cape and Australia testify.

The demographics of contact are also a major source of diversity, both within 'settler societies' and in other colonial social formations. These range from the massive population movements of free settlers associated with 'settler societies', through societies with large numbers of slaves (primarily sourced from Africa) who were eventually to be liberated, and on to the frequently catastrophic consequences of dispossession and disease for indigenous peoples. Major population shifts, be they of the African diaspora or of the various European diasporas, are a major source of diversity among settler societies, a factor that is particularly prominent in the Americas, where large creole communities have grown up.

The duration of colonisation is a significant outcome of the chronology of independence and decolonisation, and is a crucial source of differences in colonial histories. In Latin America, 'settler societies' that were founded on blended populations obtained independence from either Spain or Portugal in the nineteenth century. The United States achieved independence by force in the late eighteenth century, at a time when much of the North American continent was yet to be colonised. Australia was not to become independent from Britain until 1901. Outside the 'settler societies' the process of decolonisation in Asia, Africa and the Pacific, while not yet complete, occurred rapidly after the Second World War. These former colonies, especially in India and Algeria, have developed histories that have been highly influential in the construction of postcolonial discourse in literature, art, history, sociology and, of course, politics. Postcolonial discourse has also become important in describing and interpreting the consequences of contact and dispossession among indigenous groups in 'settler societies'.

Settler societies

I have made frequent reference to 'settler societies', but what are their primary characteristics and what are the strengths and weaknesses of this category as a framework for global comparisons between colonial societies? 'Settler societies' were most prominently, though certainly not exclusively, a creation of the British Empire, and are best understood as being the product

of a mass European immigration where people settled on land appropriated by conquest, treaty, or simple dispossession from indigenous groups.
Settler societies, particularly in North America, Australia and New Zealand,
are also characterised by a link between mass migration, major ecological
change, the introduction of new diseases, and a catastrophic impact on the
viability of indigenous populations (see for example Butlin 1993). In these
lands of 'demographic takeover' (Crosby 1994) massive changes in land
use strategies and the introduction of new diseases by settlers collectively
pushed indigenous populations to the margins of viability, and frequently
beyond (Crosby 1994; see also the contributions to Griffiths and Robin 1997;
Russell 2001). British settler societies are also often described as sharing a
common legal and parliamentary inheritance, and many other elements of
British identity which, taken together, provided a framework of stability
and resilience and became the basis of the nations they were to develop into
over the late eighteenth, nineteenth and early twentieth centuries (see for
example Eddy and Schreuder 1988).

  If a common characteristic of British 'settler societies' is the fundamental
realignment of population to a developing numerical superiority of settlers
over indigenes, then there are many other examples of European colonisation
where this was not the case – especially in the case of Belgian, German,
French, Italian and Portuguese colonies in Africa, in Spanish and Portuguese
colonies in Latin America, and of course in European possessions in Asia.
Many of these colonies were not true 'settler societies', in that they were
colonies administered for European economic benefit by a small cadre of
administrators and soldiers, but many were, and these came to an end as a
result of imperial conflicts (for example, the demise of the German Empire
in Africa), through wars of national liberation in the twentieth century, and
of course in the great surge in European decolonisation through somewhat
more peaceful means after the Second World War. Yet prior to decolonisation
(and in the case of South Africa with the end of apartheid – in part a form of
internal colonisation), white settlers were none the less able to function in
much the same way as they could in colonies where numerical dominance
assured political and cultural dominance because 'they were able to gain a
disproportionate amount of power, maintain a viable political constituency,
and assert and defend their strength through explicitly racial institutions'
(Griffiths 1997: 9).

  These variations in the form and structures of 'settler societies' (and
in their colonial and postcolonial histories) underpin their value as a
global framework of comparison and contrast. To my mind this value
counterbalances the quite proper reservations that have been expressed
during the twentieth century about the validity of the 'settler society' model

in developing an analysis of contact and its consequences. Historian Ian Tyrrell (2002: 169) has usefully surveyed the history of the model and found that it had gone out of fashion in the twentieth century, to be replaced by nationalism, especially by United States historians who have focused on the genesis of nation and of the republic rather than European colonial history of that country. Other historians have noted that in the past the 'settler society' model has not been sensitive to race, gender and indigenous resistance, but there is absolutely no reason why this must or should continue to be so now that it is more generally acknowledged that colonial societies are mixtures, ambiguous hybrids that are full of divergent lines of interest and interaction (see for example Stasiulis and Yuval-Davis 1995). None the less Tyrrell is right to insist that if it is to be of much use to historians (and the same applies to historical archaeologists) then the 'settler society' model requires us to integrate our global comparisons with 'the analysis of the systemic relationships between the "new worlds" and the "old". These relationships were determined by the process of European, and particularly British, imperial expansion, and the economic relationships of trade and investment in developing global economy that accompanied that process' (2002: 170).

One final aspect of 'settler societies' needs to be touched on, and this has to do with the notion that 'demographic takeover' translated into the total domination of indigenous societies by those of the settlers. I have remarked that in colonial societies where 'demographic takeover' did not occur (for whatever reasons) domination was effected by control over economies, and institutions such as the courts, the police and the military. This colonial domination began to disappear during the process of decolonisation (whether through warfare or by more peaceful means). However, this was not to be the case in the lands of 'demographic takeover' until the 1970s, during which period 'settler societies' have been confronted with abundant evidence that the domination of indigenous societies, although seemingly total and complete, is not always so (see for example Thomas 1991, 1999). The histories of indigenous societies do not cease with colonisation, with independence or with the creation of new nations, and the realisation of this fact has far-reaching consequences for the nations descended from 'settler societies' ('settler nations'), which have begun to experience the impact of the survival and persistence of indigenous societies.

What will be the consequences for the practice of contact archaeology? The need for contact archaeologists to chart the histories of indigenous societies after contact has been recognised in North America for some time (see for example Deagan 1997). Ruhl and Hoffman (1997: 3) reviewing the history of contact studies observed:

Somewhat less attention has been directed to understanding the emergence of European-American colonial societies. These latter efforts have tended to concentrate on either the initial encounter or established colonial society, leaving much of the immediate post-contact period of adjustment ignored.

Of course Ruhl and Hoffman are right, but there is something more to it than documenting such important transformations. The impact of indigenous survival and persistence also means that explorations of historical archaeologists must have real consequences for the nature and structure of identity formation in these communities. But these explorations can also be taken further for the nations that have developed from 'settler societies', in that new indigenous histories will challenge and contextualise existing national historical narratives. All this goes to demonstrate the value of historical archaeology, both as a vehicle for acknowledging transformations in indigenous societies, and as part of a framework within which we can accept that the task before us is to provide a disciplinary environment where these new 'hidden' historical archaeologies of colonisation can be explored and written. Thus the historical archaeologies of indigenous societies do not cease with contact (or shortly thereafter). Rather they should be understood really to begin then and to continue up to the present, as they do for the colonial societies with which they share landscapes and experiences.

One of the major challenges this new agendum poses is in fact quite an old one for historical archaeology in that it has long been understood that the integration of highly diverse databases (spoken word, written word, observed behaviour, preserved behaviour) is a fundamental objective of the discipline. But the fact of survival and persistence makes this more challenging still. In these new historical archaeologies, issues related to a discussion of the relationships between history and the nation and between material culture and identity, and the notion of dissonant heritage (see Tunbridge and Ashworth 1996), provide three important focal points that connect the existing concerns of the historical archaeology of contact and its consequences with matters arising from the recognition of similarities and differences that might be revealed through comparison on a global scale.

History and the nation

That the histories of 'settler nations' and of the descendants of other colonial formations are likely to be complex and ambiguous, and that previous understandings deriving from imperial and colonial histories written by the European 'victors' will be challenged, has been well understood for some time now, as a result of the work of Said, Spivak and Bhabha, among others. Similarly there has been a thoroughgoing reanalysis of the idea of nation, leading to their characterisation as 'imagined communities' that (by definition) might be (and are) reimagined (see for example Anderson 1982; Eley and Suny 1996). Archaeologists have also not been slow to recognise the implications of these new contexts of history writing, especially the notion that 'subaltern voices' exist and should be heard (see for example M. Hall 1999a) and that many alternative histories exist both in the centre as well as at the periphery (see for example Schmidt and Patterson 1996b). Indeed archaeology itself has become an object of analysis in these new histories (see especially Griffiths 1996) and this has also added a new interest in the history of archaeology, particularly in the links between archaeology and the creation of nations in the nineteenth and twentieth centuries (see for example the many national entries in the three volume *Encyclopedia of Archaeology: History and Discoveries*, 2001). None the less, the role to be played by historical archaeology in the building of new national histories that are both sensitive to the needs of indigenous communities, and capable of enhancing the understanding of others, is still unclear.

However, historical archaeologists working in the 'settler nations' are already playing a significant role in the process of reconciliation between indigenous societies and the nation. This frequently takes the form of investigations associated with making or sustaining claims to land, and of the maintenance or persistence of traditional culture, aspects of which are discussed by Harrison, Bedford and Murray in this volume. Both tasks require archaeologists to begin to describe the roles played by indigenous peoples (passively or actively, overtly or covertly) in the development of colonial nations, and to understand the roles surviving indigenous groups are playing in the development of new identities in the contemporary successors to such societies. These are far-reaching challenges, which have required archaeologists to build on the earlier work of Lightfoot (1995) and others about the ways in which the historical trajectories of indigenous societies can be described and understood (an issue at the heart of Williamson's contribution to this volume).

Material culture and the mechanics of colonisation and identity

If all social and historical analysis can or should involve the study of transformation, inquiry into colonialism cannot avoid doing so. Colonialism is not domination but the effort to produce relations of dominance, to produce social orders that have not previously existed. In many different modalities, it is oriented toward incorporation, exploitation, assimilation and reform; however these operations are understood, they are transformative ones, ones that typically entail not only new forms of government and economic exchange but new perceptions of space and time, new habits and new modes of embodiment as well. (Thomas 2002: 182)

The analysis of material culture in contact situations has been of fundamental importance to the development of contact studies in historical archaeology. Here too the notion that domination is never total, and that cultural forms arise that can both subvert that domination and transform it into new forms of colonial culture, has been particularly influential (see Thomas 1991). Thomas' notion of 'entanglement' is a subtle but highly effective way of demonstrating that contact situations (and their aftermaths) are ambiguous and fluid, where the 'them' and the 'us' are transformed in complex and diverse ways. Archaeology is understood as a way of demonstrating the fact that the acquisition of exotic material culture by indigenous societies does not necessarily imply that indigenes were simply passive receptors, and that agency, control, and the capacity to make meanings lay only with the colonisers.

Many of the studies in *The Archaeology of Contact in Settler Societies* advance this agenda, revealing new evidence to underpin our understanding that 'demographic takeover' did not always entail the total cultural domination of indigenous societies. Turgeon and Capone, working from different perspectives, both explore significant elements of the contexts of production and consumption of material culture within economic systems ostensibly dominated, or at the very least seriously impacted upon, by European colonists. The related theme that social and cultural trajectories of indigenous societies are an important element in the formation of postcontact societies is well exemplified by Acheson and Delgado, Brink, Harrison and Bedford. At a more abstract level, Williamson and Murray consider the value that the idea of cultural persistence through transformation has in characterising these trajectories, and as an element in indigenous cultural revitalisation in contemporary 'settler nations'.

Documenting the many roles played by material culture helps us to understand the mechanics of colonisation and identity formation. Many of the contributors to *The Archaeology of Contact in Settler Societies* seek to integrate a diversity of data to create such documentation. For example Acheson and Delgado use ethnohistories and historical documents (including visual documents) to create their account of the contacts between the Haida and European maritime traders; Brink bases her discussion of San/Khoikhoi/Dutch interactions on a complex integration of highly detailed historical documents and archaeological and ethnohistorical research to create a complex account of the trajectories in human society in the Cape from the late prehistoric to the supplanting of the Dutch by the British; Harrison combines all these data sets with the insights derived from oral history to chart the vectors from past to present in the Kimberley region of northern Australia.

These are important additions to our store of case studies and examples of the transformations of indigenous societies. Discussions of this kind need to be balanced by analyses of processes of cultural transformation in the settler population of these 'settler nations', which have long focused on the influence of architecture, art and material culture of the periphery on the centre, as well as on transformations within peripheral societies driven by internal forces.

Heritage and identity

The many issues raised by the creation of new local, national and international histories, and the idea that the histories of colonies (whether or not they are 'settler societies') are more complex and diverse than has been previously understood, have profound implications for the constitution and management of heritage. Meskell (1998) and others have recognised that archaeology has an active role to play in reconciliation in many societies, but the context of colonialism (especially of 'settler nations') allows us to explore matters beyond reconciliation.

Here we encounter the reality of 'dissonant heritage' – or really dissonant heritages (Tunbridge and Ashworth 1996) – where heritage has profound economic and political consequences (see especially el Haj 2001). Klimko in this volume neatly analyses the heritage agendas of Canadian governments with respect to forts associated with the fur trade, demonstrating that such heritage archaeology has (in the main) not served the interests of the descendants of those indigenous societies that had played such a significant role in that trade. The issues arising from a need to write indigenous interests back into the history of such shared places is also discussed by Murray, who (and this also applies to Rodney Harrison's contribution) takes the matter further to consider the impacts of such new histories on existing colonial narratives about place or heritage.

The recognition of 'dissonant heritages' in the colonial nations does not in any way imply that disagreement and conflict must inevitably arise when it is more widely recognised that cultural landscapes can be seen (often at the same time) as being ones of conflict, sharing and reconciliation (as discussed by Murray in this volume). In an important sense such heritages will become our collective responsibility, flowing as much from archaeological research requested by indigenous communities (see for example Clarke 2002; Greer *et al.* 2002; Marshall 2002 on community archaeology) as from the descendants of the settlers or colonists.

The structure of the volume

The Archaeology of Contact in Settler Societies comprises ten chapters, which are grouped into two sections. The chapters in Part I focus on case studies of various types or aspects of contact history and archaeology. The chapters in Part II take up some broader matters of theory and method outlined in this chapter and seek to develop further the idea of a global historical archaeology of contact in the modern world. Specific attention is paid to early responses to the question 'who is the archaeology of contact in settler societies for?'

Part I, 'Diverse contacts and consequences', contains six chapters arranged geographically and in a sense temporally. It begins with Laurier Turgeon's 'Beads, bodies and regimes of value: from France to North America, *c.* 1500– *c.* 1650'. Turgeon's goal is to develop a more nuanced understanding of the mechanics of contact, one that takes into account the transformative power of exchange between indigenous societies and the French. In this he addresses issues related to our assessment of the value of acculturation theory (see also Alexander 1998; Cusick 1998; Deagan 1998).

In chapter 3 we move across both space and time to the other side of Canada in the nineteenth century. Acheson and Delgado's 'Ships for the taking: culture contact and the maritime fur trade on the Northwest Coast of North America' presents a vivid analysis of the sometimes violent interactions between the indigenous Haida and the fur traders, based on detailed documentary records, diaries and evocative photographs.

Chapter 4 takes us into the Southwest of the USA and back in time, where Patricia Capone's 'Culture contact viewed through ceramic petrography at the Pueblo Mission of Abó, New Mexico' demonstrates the value of highly specific analyses of domestic production in contact contexts. This chapter stands as an example of the ways empirical information about contact interactions can be expanded using using archaeometrical techniques, and continues the great tradition of contact research in the Southwest.

In chapter 5 Yvonne Brink broadens the discussion of cultural dynamics in contact situations in her analysis of the impact of Dutch control of the

Cape of Good Hope during the seventeenth and eighteenth centuries. 'The transformation of indigenous societies in the south-western Cape during the rule of the Dutch East India Company, 1652–1795' presents a comprehensive analysis of San and Khoikhoi societies both in mutual interaction and in separate interactions with the Dutch, which emphasises the value of integrating diverse data sets as a basis for probing ambiguity and in creating contradictory interpretations (see also Jordan and Schrire 2002).

In chapter 6 we cross the Indian Ocean to north-west tropical Australia in the nineteenth and twentieth centuries. Rodney Harrison's 'Contact archaeology and the landscapes of pastoralism in the north-west of Australia' demonstrates the virtues of community archaeology in the broader context of revealing a 'hidden' colonial history spanning the precontact, contact and postcontact experiences of Aboriginal people working in the pastoral industry. Harrison's account is particularly powerful because of its thoughtful integration of archaeological and oral historical evidence with available historical documents, and the fact that it provides an opportunity to contrast the consequences of pastoralism in temperate and tropical Australia during this period.

The consequences of the persistence of indigenous society and culture after the initial challenges of contact are further exemplified in chapter 7. Here Stuart Bedford in 'Tenacity of the traditional: the first hundred years of Maori–European settler contact on the Hauraki Plains, Aotearoa/New Zealand' considers the cultural resilience of the Maori agriculturalists of the North Island of New Zealand and the ways in which exotic material culture and white legal and economic practices could be adapted to support agency among indigenous groups. Bedford's discussion also serves to emphasise the value of taking a longer-term perspective on contact as a means of charting the responses of indigenous communities to settler domination.

Part II, 'Issues and methods', begins with Olga Klimko's 'Fur trade archaeology in western Canada: who is digging up the forts?' (chapter 8). Klimko is mindful of the tendency for archaeologists of European descent to pursue research agendas which may have little meaning to indigenous communities. Klimko asks who this knowledge is for and explores the consequences of a dissonant heritage in fur trade archaeology.

In chapter 9, 'Contact archaeology and the writing of Aboriginal history', Christine Williamson changes our focus to survey the ways in which Aboriginal history has been written in Australia, and to consider the influence contact archaeology is beginning to have on its practice. Following the work of Lightfoot and others, Williamson is keen to establish that reconstructing the historical trajectories of indigenous societies poses significant challenges in integrating divergent data sets and temporalities. To this end she argues that recent work by historians and archaeologists incorporating the perspectives of 'chaos theory' or the theory of dynamical systems can be of great help to historical archaeologists in breaking down the 'barrier between history and prehistory'.

In the final chapter, 'In the footsteps of George Dutton: developing a contact archaeology of temperate Aboriginal Australia', Murray addresses issues related to the practice of contact archaeology in Australia. These range from a consideration of its role in the process of reconciliation, through a focus on the place of historical archaeology in the Native Title process, and on to the development of research into the archaeology of pastoralism in temperate Australia.

Concluding remarks

I began this chapter with a celebration of the North American contribution to historical archaeology in general and to contact archaeology in particular. Part of this celebration was a recognition of the very great influence that the approaches and perspectives of North American historical archaeology have had on our understanding of the historical archaeology of modern colonialism in other parts of the world (especially South Africa, Australia and New Zealand). While accepting the value of these approaches as the means by which archaeologists can comprehend the meanings of contact and its consequences in North America, I made the uncontroversial point that they need not necessarily perform this function equally well in all parts of the globe, and indeed no one has claimed that they should do so. I then discussed some of the more obvious reasons why this should be so, ranging from the chronology and duration of colonisation through to the different social and cultural contexts of colonisation and its aftermath. These points were made to advance the value of 'settler societies' as a framework of an inquiry into the archaeology and history of modern colonialism, to be used primarily as a prism through which comparison and contrast would allow us to explore differences and similarities within the histories of modern colonial societies all over the globe.

Imperial histories have (unsurprisingly) tended to emphasise the overarching significance of great flows of capital, people, technology and ideas as powerful forces in creating the modern world. But it is acknowledged in this volume and elsewhere (see for example N. Thomas 1991) that the experience of colonialism is also local and specific. This might tend to imply that a global approach to understanding the historical archaeology of contact and its consequences should be primarily focused on documenting histories that, if they do not overtly eschew generalisation, mainly emphasise the particular. It should be clear that such histories have a valuable role to play in reaching our goal, but they do not comprise it.

One of the great benefits of a global approach to our subject is that there is no natural geographical point of view (although it is fair to say that in the main such histories have been written by colonisers about the colonised, by the centre about its impact on the periphery). Yet this need not be so, and in *The Archaeology of Contact in Settler Societies* the contributors have sought to demonstrate, amongst all that variety in the centre and in the peripheries, that a broader agenda is possible, and that global archaeologies and histories might take on marvellously different and suggestive forms if they are written from the periphery. Australian historian Tom Griffiths puts this aspect of the issue clearly when discussing new forms of history writing about ecology and empire:

By referring in my title to 'an Australian history of the world', I am not seeking to replace one form of imperialism with another, but drawing attention to the way in which Australians, more conscious now of their indigenous natural and human history and of its depth and integrity, have won back some agency in the global narrative. Furthermore, the Australian experience makes the interactions of ecology and empire a central historical problem and demands a more complex (and distinctive) account of Crosby's ecological imperialisms. Scholars . . . have begun to use the insights of local ecology and history to fragment and overturn the conventional patterns of imperial history. There is much to be gained from an awareness of the parallels and differences between settler societies and the creative dialogues at the edge of empire. (1997: 8–9)

Ecology and Empire (Griffiths and Robin 1997) is full of examples of the transformative power of the local, of the existence of forms that allow us to recontextualise global environmental history in ways that subvert discourse framed in terms of the interests and concerns of the centre. In its focus on issues of history, heritage and identity in both the New and Old Worlds, *The Archaeology of Contact in Settler Societies* provides support for a similar approach to the building of a global historical archaeology of contact and its consequences. In this the imperatives of the periphery may also provide a basis for different perspectives on North American contexts (especially during the eighteenth, nineteenth and twentieth centuries) and potentially new areas to be investigated and compared. Among the many insightful studies that comprise Thomas Bender's *Rethinking American History in a Global Age* (2002), historian Ian Tyrrell observed:

Any plan to internationalize American history must draw on the histories of people from outside of Europe. Atlantic perspectives must be part of this manoeuvre but they, too, are not enough. The importance of southern Africa and the African diasporas for the study of race relations in the United States is already well established. These subjects are heavily researched partly because they are contained within the Atlantic world and within the commerce of those European empires based especially upon the Atlantic region. While it is important not to forget the wider concept of the Americas implied in any Atlantic perspective, it is equally vital to consider 'new worlds' beyond the Americas that can open new questions about American history. These may concern matters currently central to historical debates, such as race and slavery, or other more neglected topics, such as environmental history. (Tyrrell 2002: 168–9)

The same very much applies to the histories of the European colonial powers. The colonisation of the modern world had clear impacts on European societies that went far beyond the great diasporas of the English, Irish, Germans, Russian, Italians or Greeks that have been so much a part of its special character. Notwithstanding the foundation of new nations from the 'settler societies' they created, the experience of colonies either as sources of raw materials or as places of settlement binds them to the metropolitan in ways that have affected society and culture in the centre as well as at the periphery. The experience of sundered families and the struggle for identity among settlers in new lands (see for example Curthoys 2003) are just two examples of the complex and ambiguous consequences of colonialism that await further study by historical archaeologists.

It is now a commonplace that archaeology was an active principle in the forging of the ideology of European nationalism in the nineteenth and twentieth centuries (and in the ethnic nationalisms of the later twentieth century). Global perspectives on the historical archaeology of modern colonialism and its consequences are beginning to provide the basis of a new role in the evolution of the nation. Of course there is no little irony in understanding that archaeology as a basis for the nation can also now be a basis for its deconstruction, and for underwriting the development of new social and cultural formations in the twenty-first century.

I would like to thank Susan Bridekirk for editorial assistance and Wei Ming for preparing the illustrations.

PART I

Diverse contacts and consequences

Beads, bodies and regimes of value: from France
to North America, *c.* 1500–*c.* 1650

LAURIER TURGEON

Introduction

Almost all of the early French travel literature from Northeastern North
America comments on the value Amerindians attributed to beads. In all three
of his reports (1534, 1535–36 and 1541–42), the French explorer Jacques
Cartier remarked on the important role of beads in gift-giving and in forging
alliances with different Amerindian groups. For instance, the Algonquian
group Cartier encountered in the summer of 1534 on the Gaspé Peninsula
'showed great pleasure' upon receiving the beads, hatchets, knives and other
wares that he and his crew members gave to them. He goes on to say that,
as an expression of their gratitude, some of the women sang and danced,
standing in water up to their knees, while others 'advanced freely towards us
and rubbed our arms with their hands' (Cook 1993: 22). The glass beads and
knives he gave to a group of St Lawrence Iroquoians the following year, at
Stadacona, sparked a similar response. Cartier described the women showing
'wonderful pleasure' by dancing and singing 'uninterruptedly' in water up
to their knees (Cook 1993: 51). The Amerindians also presented Cartier
with beads. When the Stadaconians offered him twenty-four strings of shell
beads for the redemption of their captured chief and nine other prisoners,
he recognised that this 'is the most valuable article they possess in this world;
for they attach more value to it than to gold or silver' (Cook 1993: 85).

Likewise, the explorer Giovanni da Verrazzano reported of the Algonquian Indians he met at Narragansett Bay in 1524 that 'azure crystals'
(bright blue glass beads) were among the things they most highly prized; gold
was not valued because of its yellow colour, 'especially disliked by them; azure
and red are those [colours] in highest estimation with them' (Winship 1905:
15–16). The Amerindians (probably the Micmac) the French lawyer Marc
Lescarbot encountered during his voyage to the Atlantic coast of Canada in
1606 prized shell beads more than 'pearls, gold or silver' (Lescarbot 1914:
157–8).

A few years later another French explorer, Samuel de Champlain,
remarked that the Huron of southern Ontario considered beads to be one
of the most precious things they possessed (Biggar 1932, 4: 312–13). Cartier

and most of the other French explorers of the time constantly reminded readers that the objects they gave their Amerindian counterparts were 'trinkets of small value', insinuating that the dialectics of exchange greatly favoured them because they obtained precious information on the geography and the resources of the land in return.

Archaeological research on beads in North America has focused primarily on gathering data to answer questions about provenance, techniques of manufacture and Amerindian exchange networks. Elaborate classification systems of glass and shell beads have been developed, based on method of manufacture, shape, size and colour (Ceci 1989; Kidd and Kidd 1970). Because the assemblages of beads change rather quickly over time, they have been seriated and used for establishing chronologies of sites (Bradley 1983, 1987; Kenyon and Fitzgerald 1986; Kenyon and Kenyon 1983; Moreau 1994; Snow 1995; Wray *et al.* 1987, 1991). This groundwork was necessary to construct a large body of reliable information and to make more general interpretations possible. Scholars have begun to use these findings to study the social and cultural meanings beads had for Amerindians and how they were integrated into their thoughtworlds (Bradley and Childs 1991; Hamell 1983, 1992, 1996; Miller and Hamell 1986). Taking into account the Amerindian perspective has led to a revision of earlier ethnocentric interpretations that promulgated the idea that Amerindians were simply acculturated by the superiority of European material culture. More recent interpretations have stressed the symbolic functions European beads had in indigenous societies and have challenged the purely utilitarian and reductionist approaches which preceded them (Trigger 1991a). These new interpretations have also placed emphasis on continuity between the late prehistoric and the early historic periods of North American history, and the resistance of Amerindians to European imperial designs. Although this 'resistance literature', as it is sometimes called, has contributed significantly to demonstrating the persistence of Amerindian customs and cosmologies throughout the contact period, it has also had a tendency to minimise the disruptive impact of contact, and to simplify the complex forms of native appropriation of European objects. Christopher Miller and George Hamell argue, for example, that Amerindians did not perceive European beads as something new; they viewed them simply as substitutes for native copper, quartz and shell, which were 'assimilated into traditional native ideological systems' (Miller and Hamell 1986: 315). One is left, then, with the lingering impression that the borrowing of these alien objects produced no changes in the culture of reception.

I want to shift the focus of attention to the object itself and to the process of exchange. The exchange of material objects is a privileged means of human

interaction and of identity transformation (Miller 1998: 10–12; Schiffer
1999: 3). Rather than dwelling on the mechanics of 'giving, receiving, and
giving in return', such as outlined in Marcel Mauss's famous essay on the
gift (Mauss 1991: 147–261), I will focus on the act of 'taking'. After the
initial period of contact, characterised by the ritual exchange of gifts nar-
rated by Cartier and other early explorers, exchange became a more regular
and conventionalised practice, aimed at benefiting the participants on both
sides. Amerindians and Europeans alike sought empowerment through the
acquisition of the other's objects. What Goethe has so forcefully demonstrated about language is also true of culture, which draws its strength
by taking elements from the other: 'The power of language is displayed
not in rejecting but rather incorporating what is foreign to it' (cited in
Todorov 1986: 19). Exchanged objects, too, are appropriated things. Once
they have changed hands, they become culturally recontextualised: they take
on other shapes, acquire new functions and undergo changes in meaning
(Thomas 1991: 2–6; see also Bazin and Bensa 1994; Howes 1996). When
an object is transformed, the process also transforms those who are making use of it. Taking possession of new objects brings about not only cultural reconfiguration, but also social reproduction and the regeneration of
individuals and groups. Material and social worlds are continuously being
recreated through the creative hybridity of exchange (Saunders 1998: 225).
Although foreign objects are selected and integrated into the culture according to traditional cosmologies, their appropriation can generate a renewal of
thoughtworlds.

My aim is, more specifically, to examine how regimes of value as 'operators' of identity are constructed through intercultural exchange. I emphasise
the interactive and regenerative aspects of the transmission of culture. My
approach seeks to reconstruct the trajectories of beads and to find out how
they were used in producing value and, ultimately, in the shaping of group
identity. I document the uses made of beads in the culture of origin, track
their transcultural pathways and uncover the new uses developed for them
by the receiving culture. Following the movement of objects through time
and space, from one culture to another, allows us to understand better how
value is acquired and expressed through exchange. I also compare the uses
Amerindians made of beads in the late prehistoric (fifteenth century) and
early historic periods (sixteenth and seventeenth centuries) to evaluate better the impact of contact on the culture of reception.

It was during the period of first contact that power relations were nego-
tiated and interaction was most crucial. When the Europeans first arrived
in North America, Amerindians were very much in control of the territory;
it took some time before European domination was decisively felt (Trigger

1976, 1978a). As Michael Dietler has pointed out, to scholars of encounter studies generally, 'it is a serious analytical error to assume that asymmetrical relations or structures of power that ultimately appeared in later periods were necessarily a feature of the first stages of encounter' (Dietler 1998: 298). I pay special attention, then, to the initial period of encounter to highlight the first responses to contact and the specific processes that resulted in the entanglement of indigenous and colonial societies.

Northeastern North America provides an interesting vantage point from which to study the uses and meanings of beads in intercultural colonial situations. It represents an area for which the archaeological and historical sources are abundant. A large number of Iroquoian and Algonquian sites from the late prehistoric and early historic periods have been excavated, and their collections catalogued, during the last hundred years. The sites excavated for the Iroquoian groups of the Great Lakes region alone are more numerous than for the Aztecs of the Valley of Mexico (Ramsden 1993). Complete villages and their cemeteries have been unearthed; sequences and chronologies of settlements have been established; material culture patterns and mortuary practices have been documented and studied. The archaeological collections allow us to follow the evolution of Amerindian material culture from the end of the prehistoric period into the historic period in order to see how the European presence and the introduction of European goods impacted on Amerindian ways of life. Archaeologists have paid particular attention to beads because they appear on early contact sites, they are found in large numbers and they are well preserved. Additionally, the collection of travel accounts for the northeast region is one of the richest from North America, in terms of the number of published accounts available and the quality of ethnographic description in them (Atkinson 1920; Thwaites 1896–1901). These accounts often provide descriptions of beads and of the uses to which they were put. I supplement these archaeological and ethnohistorical sources with a database of some 6000 French notarial records (Turgeon 1997, 1998),[1] often containing information on the manufacture and the sale of beads, and with a Parisian archaeological collection of beads found at the Louvre, dated to the second half of the sixteenth century (Van Ossel 1991).[2]

Beads in France

France became a major centre for the manufacture and trade of beads in Europe during the sixteenth century. The domestic market for beads increased considerably with the development of the Renaissance fashion of embellishing clothing with precious stones and beads (Boucher 1996: 191–203). Members of the court and wealthy merchants encouraged Italian glass bead makers to practise their trade in France. Glasshouses were established in Lyons, Nevers, Paris, Rouen, Nantes, Bordeaux; by the end of the century, they were present in most of the major French cities (Barrelet 1953: 62–5, 91–5). These glasshouses produced coloured glass and 'enamel' in the form of rods and canes, and sold them to bead makers who worked them into beads of different forms and sizes. France exported large quantities of beads to England and North America (Kidd 1979: 29); they were purchased by merchants for the North American trade at La Rochelle (DACM, 3E 2149, 20 June 1565), at Bordeaux (DAG, 3E 5428, 5 Feb. 1587) and at Paris (NA, MCN, XCIX-65, 3 Nov. 1599). Charles Chelot, one of the most prominent bead merchants (mercer/haberdasher) in Paris, provided beads to Guillaume Delamarre of Rouen, Samuel Georges of La Rochelle and Pierre Bore of Bordeaux, merchants actively involved in the early trade to Canada (NA, MCN, X-13, 21 June 1610).

Many of the beads used in the North American trade were manufactured and purchased in Paris. I have identified thirty-seven bead makers active in Paris and thirty-one post-mortem inventories for the period 1562 to 1610.[3] They were part of a recognised guild (Lespinasse 1897, 2: 96–7) and their shops were clustered just north of the central marketplace (Les Halles).[4] They were still designated as *paternostriers* – a loan word from Italian meaning rosary bead makers – because glass beads had been used in late medieval Italy almost exclusively for making rosaries. Many of the paternosters also manufactured bracelets, earrings and buttons, and identified themselves as haberdashers. Boniface Marquis, an active member of the guild, gave paternoster as his profession in 1562, but was designated as haberdasher in his post-mortem inventory of 1581 (NA, MCN, IX-25, 28 Dec. 1562; IX-162, 14 Feb. 1581). The numbers of bead makers seem to increase during the second half of the century as they become progressively more involved in the clothing industry. Several of the inventories of the last quarter of the century contained sewing goods along with beads: thread, needles, thimbles, scissors, ribbon, lace and cloth. In some cases, gloves, belts and purses are described as being embroidered with beads, which indicates that clients were leaving these accessories in shops to have beads sewn on to them (NA, III-436, 2 May 1569; III-322, 30 May 1570; LIX-27, 19 Feb. 1572). The use of beads to decorate garments became widespread during the sixteenth century; it is this new and growing market that explains the upsurge in the number of bead makers rather than simply the manufacture of rosaries. Beads embellished hats, gloves, boots, belts, shirts and coats, and ever more frequently bed canopies, cushions, altar cloths and chasubles

Table 2.1 Materials of beads from
Parisian post-mortem inventories

Material	Percentage
glass	28.5
faience	23.0
jet	16.3
shell	6.6
coral	4.8
amber	4.8
rock crystal	4.4
undetermined	4.4
cornelian	2.4
wood	1.2
chalcedony	1.2
bone	0.8
horn	0.8
ivory	0.4
copper	0.4

(De Farce 1890: 37; Wolters 1996; 36–9). Costume books attest to the increased association of beads and precious stones with costume during the second half of the sixteenth century (Bruyn 1581; Glen 1601; Vecellio 1590). Amerindian traders probably saw them on the bodies and clothing of ship captains or even ordinary sailors. Mariners often wore shell necklaces or bracelets as proof of their travel to distant lands and also perhaps as a way of identifying themselves with the sea. It was a well-known custom amongst seamen to wear a spiral brass earring to protect against bad eyesight (Witthoft 1996: 205).

The sample of post-mortem inventories is not very large and the information contained in them is sketchy, but they do give a general idea of the occurrences of materials, shapes, sizes and colours. Beads were made from a variety of materials during this period (Table 2.1). Glass, enamel/faience,[5] jet and shell are the primary materials, but there are also references to amber, coral, cornelian, chalcedony, rock crystal, wood, horn, bone, copper and ivory. Glass represents only slightly more than a quarter of the beads listed in the inventories. Beads were worked into all sizes and shapes: oval, round, circular, discoidal, tubular, melon and faceted. Round and oval appear to be the preferred shapes; faceted beads are also prevalent, but there are fewer tubulars.[6] However, tubular beads are present early on: the inventory of Jacques Leroy, drawn up in December 1562, contains large numbers of them (AN, MCN, LIX 25, 28 Dec. 1562). The notaries very seldom designate large or medium-size beads; but small to very small beads are often described by terms like small ('petit'), tiny ('menu') or seed ('semance'). The colour spectrum appears to be restricted to basic colours: black, white, red, turquoise, blue, violet and green, in that order; yellow is the only other colour mentioned and it occurs only once. The presence of polychrome beads is suggested by the expression 'beads of various colours'; however, it does not appear frequently, leading one to believe that the majority of beads inventoried are monochrome.

Some beads are described as imitations of Italian models and others as being imported from Venice or Milan. In 1573, bead maker Jeanne Gourlin had in her shop,[7] located on Grenier St Ladre Street, some 43,000 'turquins' (round turquoise, IIa40)[8] 'of the manner of Venice', indicating they were made in the Venetian style. The same inventory also lists 100,000 'false glass pearls from Venice' (AN, MCN, IX-154, 20 Oct. 1573). Likewise, the shop of Judith Rousselin, wife of the deceased Pierre Rousselin, had in it 17 pounds and 2 ounces of 'daisies' ('marguerites')[9] from Milan (AN, MCN, XCI-130, 22 March 1584). However, these references to imported beads are exceptional. The vast majority were made by the bead makers themselves because the inventories often refer to equipment and tools used in the manufacturing process: marble or clay furnaces to fuse glass, iron pestles and mortars to crush materials for making frit, crucibles to contain the frit, slabs of marble or stone for marvering the molten glass, pincers for drawing molten glass into canes or rods, gathering irons for retrieving molten glass, iron and wooden moulds for shaping enamel beads, lamps and bellows to make enamel and wire-wound beads, drums to tumble beads, tongs to manipulate them, knives and chisels to cut organic beads (jet, shell, bone, etc.), turning wheels to turn and polish beads, files and grindstones to facet them.[10]

Much of the information drawn from these post-mortem inventories is supported by evidence obtained from a collection of some 110 beads representing forty-one different types recently recovered from a site in Paris, dating from approximately 1572 to 1605 (Van Ossel 1991: 354). The site was excavated as part of a salvage archaeology project at the Louvre, one of the official palaces of the French monarchy in the sixteenth century. After the Revolution of 1789 it became a major museum, and it was being renovated and expanded in the late 1980s and early 1990s. The beads were concentrated in ditches which had been used to dispose of human waste. The ditches were dug to extract the sand needed in the construction of the Tuileries Palace during the second half of the sixteenth century when it became part of the Louvre complex (Van Ossel 1991: 356).[11] Varying in depth from 2 to

4 metres, the ditches were progressively back filled with garbage collected seemingly from the Louvre and the surrounding neighbourhoods of this central part of Paris.[12] As with the post-mortem inventories, one of the striking features of the collection is the wide variety of materials, shapes and sizes of the beads. They are made of eight different materials: glass predominates (44 per cent), followed by jet (14 per cent), shell (10 per cent), amber (10 per cent), coral (7 per cent), enamel/faience (5 per cent), bone (5 per cent) and rock crystal (5 per cent).[13] Most of the glass beads (83 per cent) are found on North American contact sites dating from the second half of the sixteenth century or the first part of the seventeenth century. Shell, jet, amber, coral, enamel and rock crystal beads are also found on Amerindian sites. These results confirm France, and more specifically Paris, as the place of manufacture of many of the North American beads. As in the post-mortem inventories, black, white, blue and red are the dominant colours, making up 90 per cent of the collection. The only other colours represented are green, brown and yellow. Furthermore, almost all of the beads are monochrome; only three glass beads and one enamel bead are polychrome. The beads come in an equally large number of shapes: round, faceted, discoidal, oval, tubular, circular, melon and glandular, in that order.[14] Sizes vary from the large black jet beads, measuring 22 mm by 17 mm, to the very small bright blue and black circular glass seed beads, 2 mm by 1–1.5 mm. Although seed beads are not abundant, they are present.

The presence of shell beads in the post-mortem inventories as well as at the Louvre site is an important observation because it has been assumed by bead researchers that shell beads were exclusively of North American origin (Beauchamp 1901; Ceci 1989; Hamell 1996; Sempowski 1989). The marginella and the six discoidal shell beads from the Louvre collection are similar in size, colour, shape and appearance to those found on Amerindian contact sites.[15] Several Parisian bead makers specialised in the manufacture of shell beads, commonly called 'porcelaine' in French, a term derived from the Italian *porcellana* which designates the cowrie shell (Greimas 1992; Hamell 1992: 464). When the word 'porcelaine' is used in the inventories, there is no question that the notaries are referring to shell beads and not frit core enamel beads. Scraps of unused shell ('coquilles') are mentioned, but none of the tools needed to manufacture frit core beads are listed (NA, MCN, III-321, 30 May 1570; XX-128, 7 Jan. 1581; XCI-130, 6 April 1584). Furthermore, the word 'porcelaine' is used to designate shell beads in all of the early French travel literature of North America (Karklins 1992: 13; Vachon 1970–71: 260) as well as in the royal charters (*Lettres patentes*) of the Parisian bead makers (Lespinasse 1897, 2: 109). Some of these shell beads were making their way to North America. Charles Chelot, who had strong ties with many of the merchants outfitting ships to Canada, sold large quantities of shell beads in 1599 to Pierre Chauvin, a well-known Canadian fur trader (NA, MCN, 3 Nov. 1599). Lescarbot also specifies, in his travel account, that the Indians 'make great use of *Matachiaz*, [the Micmac word is employed here to designate marine shell beads] which we bring to them from France' (Lescarbot 1612: 732).[16]

In France, the value of glass, enamel and shell beads was limited, they were simply considered imitations of precious stones such as diamonds, pearls, emeralds, sapphires and rubies (Barrelet 1953: 62, 91). Beads rarely acquired enough status to be worn directly on the body as necklaces or bracelets, a privilege reserved for precious stones. In all of the European portrait paintings of the sixteenth and seventeenth centuries I have examined, the central figure or figures are represented wearing precious stones, primarily pearls. The 1584 painting by Felipe de Llano of the daughter of the king of Spain, *The Infanta Isabella Clara Eugenia* (Prado Museum, Madrid, in Boucher 1996: 426), is the only one where beads are clearly depicted, and they are in the form of a rosary strung around the neck of the Infanta's chamber maid. Beads are not even represented in costume books which claim to portray people of all ranks and of different countries and regions, women as well as men. The only exception is that of an Amerindian from Florida described as wearing a collar and earrings of copper and bone (Vecellio 1860: 503). The beads found at the Louvre site were probably part of the dress of servants, chamber maids and valets – some still had pieces of thread or wire attached to them. Even as a part of costume, they were relegated to the peripheral elements such as boots, gloves, belts and purses. Beads remained inexpensive and apparently decreased in price as their production increased (Palissy 1844: 307). A Basque mariner and trader, Johannes Hoyarsabal, purchased 50,000 turquoise beads in Bordeaux in 1587 for the price of 40 French pounds (*livres tournois*), the wage a seaman could make on a transatlantic voyage to Canada at the time (DAG, 3E 5428, 5 Feb. 1587).

Precious stones acquired greater symbolic forms of value because they were considered to have intrinsic properties superior to beads. Harder and shinier, they could not be easily altered by grinding or firing, and expressed immutability better than most other objects. Diamonds were the hardest and the most brilliant of precious stones and were therefore considered the most precious. They represented incorruptible and indestructible virtue in Renaissance culture. As stated by Physiologus, the source of most Renaissance nature emblems, 'death does not rule it [the diamond]. He [the diamond] destroyed death and trampled it under foot . . . Nor can fire do anything to this rock' (Physiologus 1979: 64). Diamond rings expressed the faithfulness of lovers and the beauty and durability of their union. The French emblematist Gilles Corrozet illustrates a diamond, set in a gold ring, under the inscription: 'Beaulté compaigne de bonté' ("Beauty the companion of goodness") (Corrozet 1543: H. 82). In the aristocratic circles of Italy, men wore diamond rings as a protective talisman that was thought to give courage (Tervarent 1997: 181–2). Moreover, diamonds symbolised the immortality of the human soul and even Christ himself. In an English emblem book, the durability topos is expressed in an image that portrays the hand of God holding a hammer and striking a diamond, which 'shines in the dark like Christ' (Simonds 1992: 280–3). In the Christian tradition, light was the metaphor for cosmic order, moral health and life. Light shaped and energised the world; Christ was incarnated light, and the 'light of the world' in the Gospel of St John (Saunders 1998: 242).

However, hardness and brightness seem to be relative and secondary properties. Attributing intrinsic qualities to precious stones was a convenient way of essentialising and naturalising their value. Value appears to be more directly related to geographical and cultural distance. The eighteenth-century French specialist on precious stones Louis Dutens judged the few stones that came from South America and Europe to be of less value even though they are as bright and as hard as those from the Orient (Dutens 1776: 3–5). Oriental stones had always been considered the most precious, for they came from far away and often unknown places, were acquired through exchange and were brought back to Europe at great risk. Diamonds came from the region of Golconda in India, pearls from the Persian Gulf and the Indian Ocean, topaz from the island of Topazion in the Red Sea, sapphires, emeralds and rubies from Burma and Ceylon (Lach 1970, 2: 117; Tavernier 1678, 2: 139–55). Even though smaller in size, the diamonds of India were judged heavier in weight, finer in clarity, and higher in virtue than the diamonds of Arabia, Scythia, Macedonia, Ethiopia and Cyprus (Lach 1970, 2: 116). By the seventeenth century, most precious stones were also being imported from Brazil and Peru, but their value remained inferior to the oriental ones. Traders even exported South American emeralds to Europe by way of China or India and sold them as oriental in order to get a better price (Dutens 1776: 41). Not only did these stones travel great distances, they were acquired from people with cultures and religions (Hindu, Moslem) fundamentally different from those of the Christian people of the West. Europeans also generally considered these civilisations equal or even superior to their own. It is probably for these reasons that glass beads, a product unique to Europe, became so highly valued by Indians, Asians, Africans and Amerindians (Sciama 1998: 7).

Precious stones from the Orient had been imported to the West since the Greco-Roman era and were deeply rooted in cosmology and astrology. Western cosmology was based on the idea that there was a correspondence between the position of the planets and the signs of the zodiac on the one hand, and events occurring on earth on the other. Each planet was identified with a precious stone: the topaz represented the sun, the pearl the moon, the emerald Venus, the ruby Mars, the sapphire Jupiter and so on. In Renaissance Europe, it was taken for granted that the planets dictated, by radiating light, the fortune of earthly things; like God himself, they were considered immutable themselves, yet able to cause change in all things (Tillyard 1965: 52). It was believed that precious stones served as mediating devices between men and the stars and brought good fortune to those who owned them. Precious stones were given medicinal, antidotal and talismanic virtues. After being totally extinct during the Middle Ages, the art of gem engraving was revived during the Renaissance and jewellers began once again to make pins, brooches, buckles, necklaces and rings for personal ornament (Lach 1970, 2: 114–15).[17] Gems were associated with power and inlaid in the crowns of kings and queens as well as in the mitres and chasubles of bishops and cardinals. They also served to ornament the garments of members of royal families. For example, the queen of France, Marie de Medeci, wore for the baptism of the children of France in 1606 a dress embellished with 32,000 pearls and 3000 diamonds. It was so heavy and awkward that she wore it only once (De Farce 1890: 37). Madame Blanche de Montferrat, duchesse de Savoie, was even more sumptuously attired to receive the king of France, Charles VIII. In his account of the lives of the noble women of France published in 1655, Pierre de Bourdeille Brantôme described her as being 'that day in magnificent state, dressed in a grand gown of crinkled cloth of gold, edged with large diamonds, rubies, sapphires, emeralds, and other precious stones. Round her neck she wore a necklace of very large Oriental pearls, the value of which none could estimate, with bracelets of the same' (Brantôme, edition of 1899: 293–4). If Brantôme went to the trouble of specifying that the pearls were 'Oriental' and spelling the word with a capital 'O', it is certainly because he attached importance to their exotic provenance.

Beads in America

Like precious stones in Europe, beads in North America acquired symbolic and ideational value because they were appropriated foreign objects. Jean Baudrillard reminds us that one of the primary functions of the material

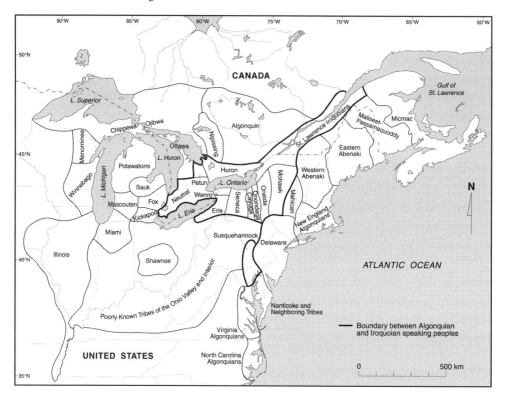

Fig. 2.1 Map of the tribal territories of Northeastern North America.

object is to express ownership (Baudrillard 1968: 104). From the time of contact, the vast majority of beads circulating amongst Native American groups, whether of shell, copper or glass, were not local to the cultures which used them. Beads were displaced cultural artefacts, produced in faraway places by other peoples, and gained through exchange.[18] Like all exchanged objects, they carried with them a history, a narrative of their acquisition and displacement, and therefore a unique identity. Beads embodied the tension of foreign appropriation and, as a result, bestowed strength upon their owners. Their potency and value increased as they moved through the exchange network.

Marine shell beads are one of the first exotic objects to appear on Amerindian sites of the interior.[19] They are all but absent from the archaeological record during the late prehistoric era (1000 to 1500 AD), a period of profound localism showing little if any archaeological evidence of trade or contact between groups (Bradley 1987: 25). Most of the beads found on these sites are made with local materials: freshwater shell, animal bone, deer phalanges and mammal teeth (Ceci 1989: 68; Lennox and Fitzgerald 1990:

423; Ramsden 1990: 370–1; Wray *et al.* 1987: 147). The late prehistoric sites where a few marine shell beads have been excavated are, in fact, so late that they could be considered to date from the early historic period. One bead on the Seneca Alhart site (1440–1510) (Hamell 1977), another on the Mohawk Elwood site (1475–1500) (Kuhn and Funk 1994: 78–9), three on the Huron Kirche site (*c.* 1495–1550) (Pendergast 1989: 98), ten on the St Lawrence Iroquoian Mandeville site (*c.* 1500) (Chapdelaine 1988: 109) and a dozen on the Onondaga Barnes site (*c.* 1500) (Bradley 1987: 42) are examples. Since marine shell has been assumed to be of Native American origin and the presence or absence of European trade goods has been the primary criterion for dividing the prehistoric from the historic periods (Hamell 1992: 458), there has been a tendency to push the dates of sites containing shell beads back into the prehistoric period. However, if the introduction of marine shell was a contact-related phenomenon, these sites could just as easily be placed in the early historic period.

The Iroquoians may have acquired shell beads from Europeans or, while waiting for them, from coastal Algonquian groups who began manufacturing beads at about the time of these first contacts (Ceci 1989: 72; Fenton 1998: 226). Native groups encountered Europeans during the very first decades of the sixteenth century, when English, French and Portuguese fishing vessels began establishing shore stations to dry cod (as early as 1501) and when explorers such as Gaspar Corté Réal (1501) and Thomas Aubert (1509) not only encountered Indians along the coasts, but also brought some back to Europe to be sold as slaves or exhibited as curiosities (Quinn 1977: 123–31). These voyages were followed by those of Verrazzano (1524) and Cartier (1534–42). During his last two voyages Cartier sailed up the St Lawrence River as far as Hochelaga (the present-day site of Montreal) and bartered with various Amerindian groups along the way. In both cases his crews and vessels wintered in the Quebec City area and left precipitously the following year, abandoning ships and buildings. Even though the French were forced to leave the St Lawrence owing to the hostilities of the Indians, they had established contacts and traded intensively with them (Bideaux 1986: 29–30).[20] Narratives of the European presence certainly circulated quickly and widely, and Indian groups must have travelled to the coasts to see these strange creatures. The St Lawrence Iroquoians encountered by Cartier on the Gaspé Peninsula in 1534 had probably come with this intention. Indeed, the absence of Iroquoian material culture in the archaeological record of the area points towards a recent and sporadic occupation, and not a long-lasting seasonal migratory movement (Tremblay 1998: 116). The small amounts of marine shell beads that appear on early sites may very well be the first tangible signs of migratory movements to the eastern seaboard which do not necessarily imply direct contact with Europeans. Many of the early journeys must have been fruitless; shell beads or pendants may have been the only means for these travellers of showing that they had made the voyage to the sea.

The occurrence of marine shell beads increases considerably during the second half of the sixteenth century and peaks towards the middle of the seventeenth century (Bradley 1987: 97). For example, the Seneca Adams site (1560–75) contained more than 1700, whereas the later Seneca Power House site (1635–55) had over 120,000 specimens (Wray *et al.* 1987: 137; Ceci 1989: 9). This upsurge in consumption is very probably related to the introduction of French discoidal shell beads. These types begin to occur in large quantities, strung into bracelets and necklaces, during the second half of the sixteenth century. The consumption of tubular marine shell beads developed with the appearance of the wampum belt, strings of these barrel shaped beads woven together several inches wide and 2 to 3 feet long, made up of hundreds, sometimes thousands of beads. The first European descriptions of wampum belts appear in the historical record at the beginning of the seventeenth century. It is likely Lescarbot was referring to wampum belts when he wrote about the 'collars' and 'scarves' of shell beads used by the Micmac; Champlain also uses the term 'collars' of shell beads in connection with his dealings with the Huron (Vachon 1970–71: 255). The first detailed text, however, is provided by the Recollet priest Gabriel Sagard, during his sojourn with the Huron in 1623–24: 'Some coloured ones, three or four fingers broad, are like the saddle girths of a horse which would have the pack threads all covered and threaded with them . . . These collars are about three and a half feet in circumference or more, which they put in quantities on their necks according to their ability and wealth' (Sagard 1990: 224; author's translation). The use of wampum belts spread quickly to all Iroquoian groups and to some of the northern Algonquian groups as well (Heidenreich 1990: 486; Vachon 1970–71: 254; Whitehead 1993: 43, 67, 77). The tubular beads employed in their manufacture rapidly replace the round flat discoidal beads in earlier archaeological collections (Ceci 1989: 72).

The upsurge in consumption also appears to be related to the sharp increase in the production of tubular shell beads. During the second quarter of the seventeenth century, Dutch and English colonists began providing the Algonquian groups of Connecticut and Long Island with iron awls so that they could manufacture larger quantities of shell beads. The colonists acquired these beads through barter and then used them to buy furs from the Iroquoian groups of the interior (Ceci 1990: 59; Fenton 1998: 227; Peña

1990: 28). It was not long before the Dutch and English colonists themselves started manufacturing them. The demand for shell beads among the Iroquois was so great that they became a form of currency in the beaver trade. They even acquired legal tender in New England – in 1637 their value was established at four beads for one penny (Beauchamp 1901: 351). It is significant that the only Amerindian groups not to consume shell beads were the Algonquians of southern New England who produced them (Beauchamp 1901: 342; Ceci 1989: 72). Marine shell beads could not acquire symbolic forms of value amongst these Algonquian groups because they were manufactured locally with indigenous materials.

Marine shell beads were transformed and put to new uses by native groups of the interior. To make these foreign objects more familiar and to appropriate them even more thoroughly, they reworked some beads to adapt them to specific aesthetic designs. The presence of iron awls, grindstones and debitage provides archaeological evidence of on-site reworking of marine shell (Ceci 1989: 72). In some necklaces, the beads appear to have been tapered: the largest ones are strung in the middle and the size gradually decreases toward the ends (Sempowski 1989: 91). In other cases, tubular beads have been split and used to form an inlay on wooden objects (Wray *et al.* 1987: 145).

European copper beads and scrap pieces of brass show up on Iroquoian sites towards the middle of the sixteenth century, slightly before glass beads. This characteristic artefact assemblage found on numerous sites spread over a large part of the Northeast, is coincident with the development of trade with French fishermen and Basque whalers on the Atlantic seaboard in the 1540s and 1550s. The number of codfishing and whaling vessels outfitted for the Strait of Belle Isle and the Gulf of St Lawrence rose in earnest during this period (Turgeon 1998: 590). Vessels would have had on board copper and brass kettles for cooking meals and for rendering whale blubber into train oil, and ships' officers could have worn glass beads on suits, hats, belts and gloves. These substances were not completely new to Amerindians, for they had equivalents in their cultures: native copper and quartz crystals are found in small quantities on sites of the late prehistoric and early historic periods (Bradley 1987: 42; Fitzgerald 1990: 429; Miller and Hamell 1986: 316). The Mohawk became major suppliers of quartz crystals to other Amerindian groups of the Northeast and were called by the Huron *Agnié*, a cognate for 'People of the Place of Crystals' (Snow 1994: 86). It is possible that glass beads appear a little later than European copper because in America, as in Europe, they simply became more abundant as a trade item during the second half of the sixteenth century. Whatever the reason, glass beads gained in popularity towards the end of the century and became extremely widespread during the seventeenth century.

Like the marine shell beads, these types show signs of modification: copper beads were rolled into round or tubular shapes from small pieces cut out of copper kettles, and glass beads were sometimes ground down to make certain colours salient (Kenyon 1986: 58–9). Glass, shell and copper are juxtaposed in necklaces and bracelets to form assemblages of mixed bead types radically different from the European ones (Sempowski 1989: 87; Wray *et al.* 1987: 248). Glass beads are even incorporated with shell beads in wampum belts, and many of the most prominent belts have one or more glass beads discreetly woven into them (Hamell 1996: 47; Snow 1994: 4).

Amerindians selected colours of glass beads that corresponded to the values they wanted to express. While the vast majority of beads in the Paris collection are monochrome, the archaeological assemblages in North America appear to have a higher proportion of polychrome beads, including appliqués, strips, eyes and stars of different colours (Kenyon and Kenyon 1983: 59–66; Whitehead 1993: 66, 164; Wray 1983: 42). The exchange of polychrome beads must have been consumer-driven by Indian interest because they were more difficult to manufacture and generally more expensive than monochrome beads. Although the same basic colours (white, black, blue and red) predominate in the collections on both sides of the Atlantic, there is a major difference in the way the colours evolve. In France, the colour categories remain stable throughout the period, whereas in North America there appears to be a shift from white to black and then from black to red (Bradley 1983: 30–4; Hamell 1992: 459–62; Kenyon 1986: 53–9). These colour shifts may have reflected the changing social and political contexts Amerindians experienced at the time. As George Hamell has brilliantly demonstrated, colour was for the Northeastern Iroquoian and Algonquian speaking people an organising principle of ritual material culture (Hamell 1992: 456). White expressed social states-of-being – it was the metaphor for light and life itself. White represented positive states of physical, social and spiritual wealth and well-being, in short, abstractions of greatest cultural value.[21] For this reason white marine shell was, in the words of Jesuit priest Paul Le Jeune, 'the pearls and the diamonds' of the country (Thwaites 1899, 44: 287–91). On the other hand, black expressed asocial states-of-being, negative aspects of life and, ultimately, death. Red was the colour for antisocial states-of-being, animacy and war, although it could have positive connotations, if consecrated to socially constructive purposes, or negative ones if consecrated to socially destructive functions. The predominance of white during the initial period of contact may have corresponded to an expression of optimism and hope for a better well-being through the encounter with Europeans, the predominance of dark-coloured beads to a generalised pessimism generated by the epidemics which decimated Indian populations in the 1620s and 1630s, and red to the period of bloody inter-tribal warfare that ensued and led to the demise of many groups in the 1640s and 1650s.

Although the exotic shell, copper and glass beads introduced in the historic period had antecedents in Amerindian prehistoric cultural schemes, they did not merely act as substitutes for native substances or express a continuation of the prehistoric value system. On the contrary, the use of these objects represented a break with the past. Foreign beads were given special attention and invested with ritual and ceremonial value. They rapidly outnumbered their prehistoric antecedents, freshwater shell beads, bone beads, deer phalanges, perforated teeth, and lithic and ceramic discs, which tend to appear in fewer numbers or completely disappear from the archaeological collections of the second half of the sixteenth century (Lennox and Fitzgerald 1990: 423; Ramsden 1990: 371–2; Wray *et al.* 1987: 254). At this time Amerindians also began creating forms of beads and objects from beads that did not have antecedents in earlier periods: shell crescents, wampum belts, copper spirals, cones, rings and hoops (Bradley and Childs 1991: 7; Wray *et al.* 1987: 250). Not only did new beads and beaded objects replace local ones, they were used in new ceremonial contexts – as a privileged means of body adornment, of negotiating treaties, of redeeming captives, of compensating for lost lives, and of recording important historical events.

Beads and the body

In Amerindian cultures beads were considered more valuable than most other foreign objects because they could be associated with the body and efficiently express abstract social and political values. The polished surface of beads conveyed the notions of finish, brilliance, aliveness and action.[22] Sagard conveys more vividly than anyone else the importance Amerindians attributed to hardness and brightness, when describing a scene in which he and some French traders attempted to substitute ivory for marine shell beads: 'we had tried to pass ivory for marine shell but to no avail for they consider marine shell much harder, whiter and brighter than ivory' (Sagard 1866: 253). The hardness of beads denoted permanence, durability and control. Unlike foods and other perishables, beads could neither decay nor wear out; they could not even be divided into separate parts without being destroyed. Immutable, they were icons of completeness, wholeness and immortality. Shell, copper and glass beads were also reflective substances signifying light, mind and knowledge for the Iroquoian and Algonquian groups of the Northeast (Hamell 1983: 5). White shell and glass beads were associated with the hair of grandfathers and connoted the cognitive aspects of life: visibility, transparency, harmony and purposefulness of mind. They were also metaphors of vision. In his dictionary of the Huron language, Sagard specifies that the Huron use their word for eye (*acoinna*) to designate the French glass bead (*rassade*) (Sagard 1632). The cognate is expressed not only in language but also in material culture: glass and shell beads are sometimes inlaid as eyes in smoking pipe effigies from Seneca Iroquois sites of the seventeenth century (Hamell 1983: 24, 27). The bead resembled the iris and its line hole the pupil, through which light and perception passed. Eyes mediated between the inside world of the mind and the outside world of life, and finally the soul and the spirits. Beads as metaphors of eyes and light had the power to activate the memory and serve as mnemonic devices for remembering important events or for determining culturally encoded actions.

Beads were used first and foremost for body adornment. Using the body as a site of display was an effective means of showing ownership and making it visible (Comaroff and Comaroff 1997: 178; Graeber 1996: 4–5). The body, and more particularly the skin, has always been considered the first canvas of the art object and of conspicuous consumption (Sciama 1998: 15; Turner 1995: 147). There was an apparent desire amongst Amerindians to transform European goods into beads or other objects of bodily adornment. Heavy iron axe heads have been found on or around the chest area of skeletons in burials, suggesting they were worn as necklaces (Fitzgerald 1979: Whitehead 1993: 41). In his *Relation* of 1657–58, Le Jeune claims to have seen 'a Huron wear at his neck a boat-pully, and another some keys' (Thwaites 1899, 44: 91). Unlike the practice in France which relegated beads primarily to the embellishment of fabric, Amerindians attached beads to practically all the joints of the body: the neck, the hips, the knees, the ankles, the elbows, the wrists and the fingers. Le Jeune points out that: 'In France, bracelets are worn on the wrist; but the Savages [in Canada] wear them not only there, but also above the elbow and even on the legs above the ankle' (Thwaites 1899, 44: 289–90). During excavations of cemeteries, archaeologists have recovered bead bracelets still attached to arm bones, and rings with glass bead inlays found *in situ* on finger bones (Kidd 1953: 369–70). Glass beads as well as shell beads were also worn in the form of knee garters, waist belts, shoulder belts and headbands (Karklins 1992: 68). They were threaded together and made more resistant, 'hardened' as it were. Beads literally tied the different limbs to the body and empowered them.

Beads were worn by all members of the community, men, women and children, to ensure its social regeneration. Beads offered strength, courage and protection to men at war. Champlain encountered Montagnais warriors in 1603 who were dressed with fur garments adorned 'with beads and cords of various colors' (Biggar 1922, 1: 179). Iroquois and Huron warriors similarly 'hardened' themselves by wearing beaded necklaces, headbands and armbands (Thwaites 1893, 13: 39; 22: 279). Sagard specified that the Huron men wore 'their most beautiful collars and *matachias* at war' (Sagard 1990: 240). Beads extended beyond the warring body to give agency to war clubs and tomahawks. The 300 reworked marine shell beads found in a male burial at the Seneca Adams site were probably used as inlay on a wooden warclub (Wray *et al.* 1987: 145). Two Iroquois tomahawks identified by Brasser as dating before 1650 suggest a widespread use of beads for this purpose – both are elaborately decorated with marine shell and glass beads set in gum (Brasser 1978: 87). Beads served in initiation rites of young warriors so that they would harden their souls (Radisson in Skull 1967: 40). In this period of devastating epidemics and intense inter-tribal warfare, warriors played a crucial role not only in protecting but in regenerating the community. The capture and adoption of men and especially women and children constituted practically the only way to counter the onslaught of disease and rival war parties. It was only through the adoption and integration of captives that certain groups like the Mohawk managed to maintain their populations (Snow 1994: 76, 81).

Beads also bestowed powers of sexual attraction and performance upon women. Associated with fertility and reproduction, they symbolically represented the nipples, the clitoris, the ovaries and, in the case of the marginella shells, the vagina (Sciama 1998: 15). Acquired by men from French, Dutch or English traders, they were assembled and worn by women at feasts, dances and other ceremonies. Champlain describes the great pains parents took to provide their daughters with the exotic finery of necklaces, belts, bracelets and earrings of shell beads: 'in this manner, gaily dressed and arrayed, they like to show themselves at dances where their fathers and mothers send them, sparing nothing to beautify and adorn them; and I can assure you that at dances I have seen girls who had more than twelve pounds of shell beads on them' (Biggar 1932, 4: 313). Beads not only enhanced seductive parts of the body, such as breasts, arms, legs and waist, but also aroused sexual instincts by their swaying movement and their jingling sound.[23] They were the aesthetic vehicle for a young woman wanting to attract a spouse for herself and a son-in-law for her parents, and ultimately to produce new members of society through birth and child-rearing.

Beads were used especially to strengthen and protect the youngest and most vulnerable elements of society. The vast majority of beads found in early Seneca burials are associated with sub-adults. At the Adams site (1560–75), for instance, more than 70 per cent of the glass beads were in the graves of infants, children and adolescents (Wray *et al.* 1987: 114). The first copper and glass beads found in Neutral and Huron burials are also associated with sub-adults (Lennox and Fitzgerald 1990: 429; Ramsden 1990: 380). The young were more susceptible to famines and epidemics, and infant mortality rates were extremely high (Wray *et al.* 1987: 398). Champlain explains that the Huron bedecked cradleboards with beads and put them around the necks of children, 'however small they may be' (Biggar 1932, 4: 318). Sagard also points out that beads embellished the decks of cradleboards and the ears and necks of infants (Sagard 1990: 205–7). The jingling sound of beads on infants and cradles was believed to frighten away the spirits calling the infant to rejoin them. The placing of beads on ears was perhaps a way to prevent foreign and evil elements from penetrating the body. It was often from this body opening that the illness of the child was first expressed. Beads were a means of preserving these precious beings and keeping them within the community of living souls.

Whereas the hardness of beads evoked resistance and the full maturity of adulthood, their smallness represented the infinitely fragile and the innocence of childhood. It is significant that the most highly prized of exotic objects was also the smallest. Furthermore, beads were themselves evaluated according to size: small was best. Assemblages from archaeological sites indicate that glass beads became progressively smaller. For example although they are rare on sixteenth-century sites, seed beads become more frequent on those of the seventeenth century. These minute objects had to be handled with great care for they could be easily lost. Like the smallness of infants, the smallness of beads had the capacity to create a reverie of life, a type of transcendent time that negates change and mortality (Stewart 1993: 65). Through the manufacture and consumption of these objects, Amerindians also expressed a desire to miniaturise the foreign and the distant: copper kettles were broken down into strips of metal and made into round and tubular beads, tinkling cones and disc pendants (Bradley 1987: 70; Wray *et al.* 1987: 48–60). Beads walled in the culture of origin and, at the same time, reflected the outside world, creating an enclosed exteriority; they interiorised in an infinitesimal space the outside and the foreign.

Beads placed upon the body served as signs of the progressive socialisation of individuals into the community. The strings of beads wrapped around the neck and sometimes the wrists and ankles of infants was a way of giving them status and expressing the desire to integrate them.[24] Adolescents were again adorned with beads at puberty. Young men were given necklaces, garters, armbands and headbands to mark their entrance into warrior society (Skull 1967: 40). These were intended to provide added vitality, but also to help them to make use of their judgement in combat. Young women received beaded necklaces, wristbands and waistbands. Sagard remarked that some wore 'great plates [of beads] in front over the stomach' (Sagard 1990: 224), like an apron, to cover the pubis. Apparently worn by women with spouses, the beaded aprons seem to express the need to contain the potentially disruptive forces of sexuality. As men and women grew older, their use of beads diminished. The Jesuit missionary Joseph-François Lafitau noted that the elder in Iroquoian societies 'no longer wear[s] any superfluous adornments or anything that is not worn out, since he wants to indicate that his mind is on serious things' (Lafitau 1977, 2: 44). The inner selves of the more securely socialised members of the community had become sufficiently firm for their outer bodies to go without beads.

For adult men, beads were associated with roles of leadership and public oratory. It was, for example, hard and wise middle-aged men who were designated to go on diplomatic missions and who carried with them the wampum belts used to objectify and seal verbal agreements. From the beginning of the seventeenth century, perhaps even earlier, these beaded belts became central objects in diplomatic encounters. Wampum belts were made up of several hundred and even thousands of shell (and sometimes glass) beads, tightly woven together by women to express the 'words' or 'voices' of the group (Hamell 1996: 46–7; Karklins 1992: 66–9). When a diplomatic action was agreed upon, individuals and family clans contributed beads and, once assembled, the belts metaphorically signified the assembly of these people and their voices (Vachon 1971: 182). The person designated to speak in the name of the group reminded listeners, during his speech, that he was speaking for the group as if they were speaking with one voice. The Iroquois spokesman Kiotsaeton, sent to Three Rivers to negotiate a peace treaty with the French in 1645 begins: 'Onontio [the name used to designate the Governor], lend your ears to my words, I am the mouth of my country. You hear all of the Iroquois when you hear my words' (Marie de L'Incarnation 1971: 254). Kiotsaeton had arrived, in the words of Marie de L'Incarnation, 'covered with beads', carrying seventeen wampum belts, some on his body and the others in a bag, made from some 30,000 shell beads. The highly staged gathering took place in the courtyard of the fort: the French Governor and his delegation seated to one side, with the five Iroqouis Ambassadors just in front of them; on the opposite side the Algonquian groups allied with the French; the French and Huron delegates adjacent to them; and, finally, Kiotsaeton, placed centre stage. He not only spoke but also literally played out the meanings of the belts, 'like an actor at a theater making all sorts of gestures' (Marie de L'Incarnation 1971: 254). The first belt was given to the Governor for having saved the life of an Iroquois warrior, the second to bear witness to the return of a French captive, the third to calm the anger of the Algonquians, and so on. The most beautiful and most important of the belts, the tenth, expressed the desire of the Iroquois to make peace with the French. While he spoke, he presented each belt in his outstretched hand so all could see. They were then individually hung from a rope strung across the courtyard; as he unfolded the belts, Kiotsaeton was opening his heart and the hearts of his people. Suspended, free of creases, concealing nothing, they expressed the sincerity of the spokesman, the words of the soul (Vachon 1971: 188). Kiotsaeton was, according to the French, 'eloquent' and successful, for the following day the Governor replied by offering fourteen gifts and accepting the terms of the peace treaty. For Iroquoians, oratory represented the epitome of political action. It was through the manipulation of words that one could persuade and control other people, and extend the influence of the community beyond its boundaries.[25] Oratory was considered the ultimate form of symbolic capital; it was through the circulation of structured discourses that social and political reproduction could be engendered. More than just words and voices, wampum belts objectified the polity and the politics of the nation (Fenton 1985).

Not only did beads invigorate the biological and social reproduction of the community, they also followed the dead into the grave to serve them in the afterlife. As with other European trade goods, almost all beads circulating in North America ended up in burials (Bradley 1987: 110; Lennox and Fitzgerald 1990: 429–31; Ramsden 1990: 380; Whitehead 1993: 23–82; Wray et al. 1987: 115–37, 239; 1991: 393). Mortuary offerings appear to be a European-contact related phenomenon, for burials at the end of the prehistoric period included almost no material objects. The interment of beads and most other exotic objects appears at the time of the arrival of Europeans and progressively increases with the development of trade; furthermore, the vast majority of beads buried are of European origin (Fitzgerald 1990: 113; Hamell 1992: 458). In the case of the Huron and the Neutral, for example, almost all of the exotic beads, whether of European or North American origin, show up in burials, whereas beads made of local materials are found exclusively on village sites (Drouin 1993: 3–4). Beads were used by the dead in ways similar to the living: they were again placed directly on the body as ornamentation. The inclusion of beads in graves represented an extension of the exchange system into the afterlife and a way of giving the beads added value. As grave offerings, beads were 'traded' for the last time as they passed from the living to the dead, from this world to the other world. The idea of exchange is clearly expressed by a Micmac leader who explains to a French colonist, Nicolas Denys, that provisioning graves with European goods is to make them 'of service to the deceased in the other world . . . because they are newly introduced objects . . . with which the other world is not yet supplied' (D'Entremont 1982: 259). The act of interment expressed the intention to withdraw beads from economic circulation, to guarantee a continued demand, and, at the same time, to make this visible object of display invisible, to appropriate it radically by putting it out of the reach of its creators and other living beings. Inaccessible, beads became sacrificial objects destined to strengthen the gods or reincarnated beings. No longer operative on earth, they could now produce enduring souls in the afterlife.

Conclusion

More than mere substitutes for local materials, exotic beads are, in North-eastern North America, an expression of a new inter-cultural dynamic. The contact period brings about significant changes in the use of beads: they now come from external instead of internal sources, serve in ceremonial contexts, appear more frequently and abundantly in new forms and configurations. It is probably the contact situation that generated these changes in the objectification of value, rather than any internal transformation of Amerindian thoughtworlds or cosmologies. During the profound localism of the late prehistoric period, native groups expressed value and identity with beads made of local materials. With the subsequent increased exchange of goods, movement of populations and intercultural tensions, Amerindians adapted their forms of representation to the changing context and reconstructed their identity with beads of the other, for incorporating the other was a means of regenerating the self. Contact brought about a fundamental shift from an identity grounded in the self to one constructed from the (re)sources of the other.

Exotic beads acquired value in North America because they were displaced and appropriated foreign objects. It was the act of appropriation as much as the nature of the object itself that endowed beads with value and made them 'operators' of identity. As expressed by the wampum belt, beads wove the members of the community together, so that, once unified, they could draw others in. Exchange was aimed not at capital accumulation but at social regeneration; the magnitude of the value of beads was proportional to their power to bind people together. Further, their regenerative potency extended beyond the body and the body politic to the afterlife. The inclusion of beads in graves represented an extension of the exchange system into the other world: the intention to withdraw them from earthly circulation, to appropriate them radically and, in so doing, to give them added ritual value.

In Renaissance France, precious stones and metals were prized for the same reasons Amerindians valued beads: they were shiny, hard and small acculturated objects worn as body adornment to express durability and individual as well as collective identity. Diamonds, pearls, sapphires and rubies were inlaid in gold crowns of kings and queens to symbolise the inde-structibility and prosperity of the realm. The value of precious stones also extended into the metaphysical domain: they represented the immortality of the human soul and of Christ himself.

Although Amerindians and Europeans produced precious objects in the same way and for similar reasons, the objects themselves remained fun-damentally different because they were the vehicles of different identities. French and other European travellers continuously compared and con-trasted Amerindian valuables with European ones, using wealth objects as templates to express the opposing natures of the two cultures. What Euro-peans considered to be baubles and bangles were to Amerindians objects of ideation, and what was to Amerindians mundane appeared to be highly val-ued by Europeans. During Jacques Cartier's final voyage to the St Lawrence region, in 1541–42, the newly appointed chief of the Stadaconians offered the French explorer his leather headband edged with shell beads, 'in stead of a crowne', and two shell bracelets in the hope of forging an alliance with his European counterpart. Cartier declined the gifts and returned them to the chief. The explorer was, however, overwhelmed by the diamonds and the 'leaves of fine gold as thicke as a mans nayle' (Cook 1993: 101) that he and his crew discovered on a nearby cliff, which bears to this day the name 'Cape of Diamonds' in memory of the event. Moved by personal ambition, he abandoned the colony and returned to France, hoping to cash in on his precious finds. It turned out that the diamonds were false and the yellow metal was fool's gold. Cartier had given up the first French colony in America for an illusion.

Acknowledgements

Much of the research for this chapter was carried out while I was a Mellon Fellow at the Newberry Library in Chicago. A first draft was presented at the workshop on interdisciplinary approaches to modern France at the University of Chicago. I would like to thank the professors and students of the seminar, more particularly Robert Morrissey, Michael Dietler, François Hartog and Daniel Nordman, for their stimulating comments. I am very grateful to Martha Sempowski and Dean Snow for providing me with very helpful archaeological comments on the second draft, and to Carla Zecher and Margot Finn for their assistance in refining the ideas and the language of my text.

Notes

1. I generated this database with the assistance of a group of graduate students as part of a team project financed by the Social Sciences and Humanities Research Council of Canada and by the *Fonds pour les chercheurs et l'aide à la recherche* of the Province of Quebec. The research was carried out over a ten-year period, from 1985 to 1995.
2. A collection of 110 beads was found during salvage excavations at the Louvre, the French national museum, in the late 1980s and early 1990s, and these are presently preserved at the *Direction régionale des affaires culturelles de l'Ile de France, Service régional d'archéologie*, at Saint-Denis, a northern suburb of Paris. I would like to thank Jean Chapelot for informing me of the existence of this invaluable collection, Fabienne Ravoire, Nicole Meyer and Dominique Orssaud for showing it to me and Paul Van Ossel for giving me permission to use it for my research.
3. The post-mortem inventories were drawn up by notaries after a person's death at the request of the inheritors. They contain a detailed list of all of the deceased person's material possessions: land, buildings, furniture, tools (in the case of artisans), merchandise, clothing and other personal belongings, including account books and bills in the case of merchants and shopkeepers. The post-mortem inventories of the Parisian bead makers provide descriptions of workshops, lists of tools, inventories of beads on stock (often specifying type, shape and colour), and sometimes even itemised bills giving names and place of origin of clients. Post-mortem inventories were not necessarily drawn up each time someone died; they were needed only when the value of the estate was uncertain or contested.
4. In order to make research manageable in the several thousand Parisian notarial registers for the second half of the sixteenth century, secondary sources and

published inventories (which exist for some notaries) were used to find the names of bead makers and references to some of their post-mortem inventories. It soon became apparent that the bead makers' shops were clustered just north of Les Halles. A systematic search was then carried out in the records of the notaries residing in this area; most of the post-mortem inventories were located in the records of four notaries: Filesac, Chazeret, Peron and Thevenin. I am very grateful to my research assistant, Bernard Allaire, for carrying out this research for me.

5. The Parisian notaries use the term 'enamel' to designate these faience or frit core beads. In order to avoid complicating the terminology, I have kept the same term and used it throughout the chapter.

6. Parisian bead makers used specialised terms to designate the shapes of the beads: olive ('olive') for oval, flute ('flute') for tubular, strawberry ('fraise') for melon, cut ('taillé en mirroir' or 'taillé en plein') for faceted, and blackberry ('mure') for the corn bead.

7. It was not uncommon for women to own shops. Many women inherited the shops of their husbands, and either remarried and kept them, or remained widows and passed them on to their sons or daughters. The workers in the shops were often women, as illustrated in Denis Diderot's and Jean d'Alembert's encyclopedia (1751–65) (see 'paternôtrier' and 'émailleur'). In Italy, women were also often employed by bead makers (Sciama 1998: 1–15).

8. This is certainly the IIa40 of the Kidd classification. The word 'turquin' or 'turgyn' is defined in dictionaries of the time as a 'Turkish [hue] between blue and azure' or 'Venetian blue': Claude Desainliens, *A Dictionarie of French and English* (1593) (London: Menston, 1970); Randle Cotgrave, *A Dictionarie of French and English Tongues* (1611) (London: Menston, 1968).

9. The daisy ('marguerite') very probably designates the opaque white round or oval glass bead (IIa13 or IIa15 from Kidd). The Huguet dictionary of sixteenth-century French describes the 'marguerite' as white and round, and more commonly called a pearl (Huguet 1961). In his dictionary of medieval French, Godefroy defines the 'marguerite' as a fine white and round pearl (Godefroy 1982).

10. The techniques involved in the manufacture of glass beads have been described by Kenneth Kidd (1979), by Marvin Smith and Mary Good (1982), and by Marie-José Opper and Howard Opper (1991). The most recent and thorough study is that of Italian historian Francesca Trivellato (2001). For descriptions and illustrations of the tools used, see Diderot and D'Alembert (1751–65), entries 'paternôtrier' and 'émailleur'. The enamel or frit core beads were made in the same manner as faience. A cold ceramic paste was moulded to the desired shape in a 'presse' and fired; once cooled, the bead was glazed and fired a second time. Motifs could be painted on to the bead before or after glazing. The firing of enamel beads demanded less equipment and labour than glass beads, made from molten glass and drawn into canes.

11. It was impossible to have any grasp on stratigraphy because the deposit had been continuously stirred, mixed and levelled. However, the distribution of artefacts

points towards a deposition spread out over time. The 213 coins recovered helped narrow down the chronology: some coins had the year of manufacture stamped on them, which ranged from 1581 to 1599; those bearing only effigies were given approximate dates running from 1572 to 1603. From this information, Paul Van Ossel has hypothesised 1590 to 1605 as the period of formation of the deposit (Van Ossel 1991: 354). It seems reasonable to assume that the chronology of the coins can be applied to the beads.

12. During the excavations, survey trenches were dug in three different areas; water screening with 2.5 mm and 0.5 mm mesh screens was undertaken for two of the trenches. It was in these trenches that most of the beads and other smaller artefacts were found (Van Ossel 1991: 351–2).

13. The enamel frit core beads appear much less frequently than in the post-mortem inventories. However, the characteristic enamel blue oval bead with raised white appliquéd lines and dots is present in the Louvre collection. In North America, it is considered a unique bead type and a good time-marker because it is only found on a few early Amerindian contact sites (Fitzgerald, Knight and Bain 1995: 119).

14. Tubular beads represent less than 10 per cent of the collection.

15. I would like to thank Martha Sempowski for giving me this information. Only two of the seven shell beads of the Louvre collection were found together, which indicates that they were deposited at different times and came from different sources. Many Parisians must have worn shell beads at the time. One cannot rule out that the shell beads of the collection were of North American origin, because French explorers and traders frequently brought American products to the French court. However, the notarial records clearly demonstrate that shell beads were being manufactured in Paris and traded in North America, which strongly suggests that they are French. Shell sourcing on a sample would answer the question more definitively.

16. Shell beads remained an important French trade item throughout the colonial period. The king's stores in Quebec City always kept large quantities of shell beads on hand and they were much more expensive than glass beads. According to Nathalie Hamel's calculations, one shell bead was worth 1224 glass beads during the period 1720–60 (Hamel 1995: 13–14). Likewise, shell beads always far outnumber glass beads in the inventories of trade goods from the trading posts of the Chesapeake during the seventeenth century (Miller, Pogue and Smolek 1983: 127–30).

17. It is interesting to note that most oriental precious stones were cut and faceted once they arrived in Europe (Lach 1970, 2: 114–15). Europeans generally considered the oriental techniques of faceting archaic. Jewellers faceted and engraved precious stones and even accepted great reduction in their size in order to increase their brilliance. The faceting of precious stones and gem engraving could also be interpreted as means of transforming and appropriating these foreign objects, in the same way that Amerindians would rework European shell, glass and copper beads.

18. Ian Cook and Philip Crang have convincingly argued that cross-cultural consumption represents the appropriation not only of culture but of space and territory as well (Cook and Crang 1996: 132). Mary W. Helms also explores the ideological nature and political significance of geographical distance and long-distance contacts. Dealing with people more than with things, she argues that 'geographical distance from a given cultural heartland may correspond with supernatural distance from that centre; that as one moves away from the *axis mundi* one moves toward places and people that are increasingly "different" and, therefore, may be regarded as increasingly supernatural, mythical, and powerful, the more distant they are from the heartland' (Helms 1988: 4). I would like to thank George Hamell for pointing this work out to me.

19. Some exotic stones (chalcedony, catlinite, steatite) and minerals also occur early (Martha Sempowski, personal communication).

20. During his first voyage in 1534, Cartier presented the Micmac Indians he encountered in Chaleur Bay with hatchets, knives, beads ('paternostres'), and other wares; a few days later, he gifted the group of Iroquoians at Gaspé with 'knives, glass beads, combs, and other trinkets of little value' (Bideaux 1986: 112, 114). The following year, during his second voyage, he gave the women of Stadacona (present-day Quebec City) knives and glass beads, and the chief two swords and two large brass wash basins; on the way to Hochelaga (present-day Montreal), he distributed knives and beads (in one of the three instances Cartier specifies that the beads were of tin); at Hochelaga, he gifted the men with hatchets and knives, the women with beads and other 'small trinkets', and the children with rings and tin *agnus Dei* (Bideaux 1986:139, 143, 149, 150, 155). Upon returning to Stadacona the same year, he gave the men knives 'and other wares of small value', and a tin ring to each of the women; throughout the long winter spent there, Cartier exchanged knives, awls, beads and other 'trinkets' for foodstuffs (Bideaux 1986: 159, 162). As James Axtell has pointed out, Cartier gave the Stadaconans the hull of an old ship when he returned to France in 1536 so they could make use of the nails. Cartier's lieutenant, Roberval, left behind three towers and four court buildings in 1543 (Axtell 1988: 175).

21. White shell beads were associated with beauty, moral excellence and social status in other parts of the Americas. In Inca culture, for example, light bright shell beads represented the celestial complex and served as icons of religious purity and moral integrity for the upper nobility, whereas dark-coloured objects represented the terrestrial complex and connotated evil, illness and death (Mester 1989: 164).

22. This is true of the Americas (Mester 1989: 160; Saunders 1998: 226), as well as of Africa (Comaroff and Comaroff 1991: 185–6; Drewal and Mason 1998: 78; Roberts and Roberts 1996: 31).

23. Catherine Howard has remarked, with regard to the Waiwai of Amazonia, that beads beautified the body to stimulate the reproductive mechanisms and overcome the mortality of the human life-cycle (Howard 1998: 51). They contributed

to the hardening of female as well as male genitals which, in turn, hardened affinal relationships and ensured human reproductivity – the only real form of control over the death of the individual and the group.

24. With the Waiwai studied by Howard (1998: 55), beads placed on the extremities of the limbs (head, hands and feet) represented the demarcation of the boundaries of the child's autonomous identity.

25. I wish to thank Kay and Franz Scaramelli for giving me this idea based on their work in Middle Orinoco, Venezuela (personal communication and Scaramelli and Scaramelli 1999: 11). Many of the ideas in this section of my text stem from my discussion with them.

3 | Ships for the taking: culture contact and the maritime fur trade on the Northwest Coast of North America

STEVEN ACHESON AND JAMES P. DELGADO

Culture contact for the indigenous peoples of the Northwest Coast, a region encompassing coastal British Columbia and adjacent states of continental USA, is synonymous with the development of the maritime fur trade. Representing an intense, albeit brief and unique, chapter in native–European contact relations, the maritime fur trade period is seen by many historians and ethnographers to have entailed barely more than a simple exchange of goods, resulting in little real impact on the indigenous community.

The maritime fur trade was a complex, international and multicultural activity, often intensely focused on the decks of the ships themselves. These interactions could be hazardous. Loss of profit, vessel or life itself was an inherent risk, either through bad business, shipwreck or misadventure. Loss by misadventure attracted considerable attention in the trade from financiers back home, as well as public interest, particularly when it entailed stirring accounts of captivity in strange and distant lands.[1] The loss of the *Tonquin* in 1811 and the famous narrative of John Jewitt concerning the seizure of the *Boston* eight years earlier thrilled readers and instilled a particular view of the perils of the trade.

While the day-to-day affairs of the trade were often a mundane activity, violent incidents, including vessel seizures and hostage taking, were frequent enough. Encounters such as these, though not always as dramatic as the tales of *Boston* and *Tonquin*, nevertheless attest to the fragility of trade relations between the parties. The fact that these were not isolated events argues for a substantially different view of the impact of the trade, one involving a complex, volatile history that had very real socioeconomic consequences for the participants. The maritime fur trade itself, with its primary focus on the sea otter, lasted only until around 1825, a little earlier for some regions of the coast, a little later for others. By then, the sea otter was near extinction and the trade had begun to diversify to include a wide range of resources for export to Euro-American markets. While still a coastal trade, the content and form of the trade on the Northwest Coast was changing, to include timber for ships, salmon, dogfish oil, whale oil and bone, and seal skins. Native productive relationships were also being restructured, with some

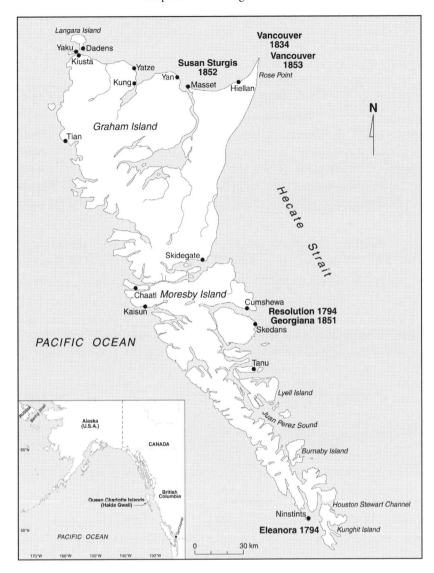

Fig. 3.1 Map of the Queen Charlotte Islands, Northwest Coast of Canada, showing major Haida settlements of the nineteenth century and the approximate locations of the six trade vessels lost to the Haida between the years 1794 and 1853.

native groups having a progressively smaller role in the trade, while others served as wage labourers, hunting or harvesting resources on a piecework basis.

The Haida of the Queen Charlotte Islands[2] can be credited with seizing at least six of some dozen or so vessels lost on the Northwest Coast during this trade period, dating from the late 1700s to the mid-1800s. The plundering

of the American schooner *Susan Sturgis* at the hands of the Masset Haida
in 1852 received much attention in its day, with the convening of an official
inquiry (see Gough 1982). Others, including the brigs *Eleanora* (1794) and
Resolution (1794), the schooner *Vancouver* (1834), a brigantine of the same
name seized in 1853, and the sloop *Georgiana* (1851), received little attention
in their day, and slipped into historical obscurity. Numerous other violent
incidents, failed attacks, the cutting off of shore parties and indiscriminate
killings appear throughout the record, and, although not reviewed in detail
for this study, are seen to have contributed in no small way to the loss of
these ships (see Table 3.1; see also Howay 1925).

This chapter examines the volatile nature of these trade relations from
the perspective of both European and native interests through a detailed
reconstruction of the events surrounding the loss of several of these vessels,
drawing on both published and unpublished accounts.[3] Sources include the
journals, logs, letters, drawings and charts of traders in the region. Particular
attention is given to a previously unpublished account on the loss of the
Hudson's Bay Company schooner *Vancouver* in 1834. The stranding and
seizure of the *Vancouver* left a rich record, and though neither the first
nor the last vessel to be lost to the Haida, it is seen as archetypal of these
encounters.

Troubled waters

When a people meet who owe each other nothing yet presume to gain from each
other something, peace of trade is the great uncertainty. (Sahlins 1972: 302)

Within only a few years of the trade beginning in 1787, the southern or
Kunghit Haida attempted to seize the American sloop *Lady Washington* in
1791. Their attempt failed at a cost of some forty Kunghit lives, including
the wife and two children of the leading chief, as well as the serious wounding of a number of others (Ingraham 1971: 204). After a three-year hiatus,
the Kunghit struck again. Though little is known of the circumstances surrounding the capture of the American brig *Eleanora* in 1794, the event marks
the first successful seizure by the Haida, and the first on the Northwest Coast
(Bartlett n.d., 1925: 320–1; Hoskins n.d.; Ingraham 1971:141, 145). Within
weeks of the loss of *Eleanora*, the American schooner *Resolution* was seized
by a neighbouring Haida group at Cumshewa. Only one crew member from
each vessel was spared, living in slavery among the Haida until being released
a year later. A year after *Eleanora*, the Kunghit Haida attempted to seize John

Boit's *Union*, but were repulsed, with a heavy loss of Haida lives (Boit 1981: 49–50). The Haida then made two unsuccessful attempts at capturing a ship in the early 1800s, one a Russian vessel and the other American (Howay 1933: 124; Clinton n.d.). Haida fortunes were to improve, however, when the Hudson's Bay Company (HBC) schooner *Vancouver* sailed into these troubled waters.

While sailing from the Haida village of Kaigani to the Tsimshian village of Sebassa on the mainland coast, *Vancouver* ran aground off Rose Point, the north-easternmost point of the Queen Charlotte Islands on 3 March 1834. The vessel was abandoned to the local Haida, who laid claim to it after a tense stand-off over possession of the wreck. Captain Duncan (n.d.a) later explained to his superiors that:

from the hostile state of the Indians, I was reluctantly compelled by the officers and crew to abandon the vessel. As I am perfectly certain that my courses were sufficiently ample to go clear of said point, I can attribute the cause of my getting there to a strong current or some other cause to me unaccountable.

George Simpson (n.d.), reporting to the Governor and Committee of the HBC on the wreck, explained that:

It does not appear that any blame can be attached to Mr. Duncan, the master, for the loss of this vessel, nor are we in a condition to bring the natives to account for the seizure of the property, indeed we rather feel they behaved well in permitting the crew to escape with their lives.[4]

Duncan (n.d.b) explained the circumstances of *Vancouver*'s stranding and seizure in a letter addressed to the company's 'Chief Factors and Chief Traders', dated Fort Simpson, 6 March 1834. His account, signed by his mates and crew, is a compelling document that offers a European perspective as well as his own unique view from the deck of the unlucky and ultimately ill-fated schooner *Vancouver* during the tense hours of 3 March 1834.

Captain Duncan's account of the loss of the *Vancouver*

It is with much regret that I have to give you an account of the loss of the Honble. H. B.Co's schooner Vancouver. Having received on board a trading outfit from Fort Simpson, with instructions to proceed to Kygarny,[5] Tongass or Sebassa, I accordingly sailed from Nass on the 19th February, the wind being favourable. Got down to Kygarny the same night, where I remained as long as I could procure a few skins.

On the 1st March the brig Convoy, Capt. Pickens, arrived from Woahoo, and on the 2nd I paid him a visit. He informed me that there would be, to my knowledge, three American vessels on the coast this season which information made me very anxious to proceed to the Sebassa tribe as early as possible in order to procure the skins of the place before the arrival of the American vessels, or intelligence of the information to be conveyed to them.

I got underweigh at 5 the same evening . . . I then had every reason to suppose that we were sufficiently to the northward to go clear of Point Rose.[6]

A careful & vigilant lookout was kept both by myself & crew. We had run about 10 minutes, when we perceived breakers ahead. I immediately hauled by the wind and tacked, but the vessel paying off before the wind with the heavy sea, struck before she came to the wind or had time to drop anchor, and was immediately driven by the sea high onto the beach. It being nearly high water at the time, & the surf great, the vessel struck heavily on the sand.

Fortunately she was strong, & able to resist the force of the sea, which at times made a complete breach over us. When the tide fell it left us high & dry. Found that she had worked and imbedded herself about 4 feet into the sand. Point Rose bearing SE 1/2 E about 2 miles & the outer point of sand NNW about 1 mile. Carried out an anchor to the Eastward. and commenced to lighten the vessel by heaving overboard all the heavy articles, such as provisions, water and ballast, which was completed by 10 A.M., & was done in the expectation of getting her off next high tide.

About this time the Indians began to collect round the vessel in great numbers, all armed either with pistols, muskets or knives. The chief when he came alongside used every endeavour he possibly could to induce me to come on the beach with the intention I believe of securing me. When first invited on board he pretended sickness, said he could not walk, and such frivolous excuses, but was at length prevailed upon. Very generous offers were made to him & his tribe if they would give their assistance, but that would not satisfy them, for they wished me to deliver the vessel & cargo to them, which they considered as their right, as it was on their lands.[7]

The chief appeared to have very little influence over his people or was unwilling to use it on our behalf, for they soon began to plunder & cut away everything which came within their reach in the most daring manner, although strong remonstrances were made at the time. Seeing an Indian taking away the boat hook in this manner, & thinking that they would attribute it to fear if we did not attempt to check this, I went on the beach to prevent him, upon which he drew his knife & brandished it before me, and had it not been for the interference of the chief on board, whose safety depended upon mine, I am fully convinced would have stabbed me.

After this they appeared a little more peaceably inclined until about 2 P.M. when I proposed to clear away the sand from the vessel, to which the chief and his people appeared willing to give their assistance. The shovels were given to them, but they did not begin to work. Mr. Heath went on the beach with the view of setting an example to the crew, was instantly seized by the Indians, but fortunately made his escape by running into the water, or perhaps he owed his safety to the chief who was still on board. The crew however had their arms pointed at the Indians, and this also might have had some effect on them.

Mr. Heath got safe on board with the loss of his hat, which they afterwards iron-ically offered for sale. Soon after this they became very troublesome & audacious, presenting their muskets & pistols at several of the crew – marking out parts of the vessel as their already obtained portion – using threatening language – indeed they did everything they possibly could to provoke a quarrel or induce us to commence, which left us no doubt of their hostile intention. They did not think themselves sufficiently strong to take the vessel at this time.

At 4 P.M. they dispatched a canoe for a reinforcement, which they said was not far off, and about the same time they sent away all their women to a place of security. At the time Mr. Heath was taken I thought it prudent not to fire into the Indians, as the safety of the crew depended on my forbearance, yet I must have been under the necessity of doing so had they done him any injury, and if we had fired, I am perfectly convinced we must all have fallen victims to their savage barbarity, for our vessel was on her beam ends, which rendered her helpless, and completely exposed our deck to their fire.

Our cannon were of no advantage, as they could not be made to bear on them. At 5 P.M. the tide began to flow over the beach. The Indians left us, and as I was in hopes of getting the vessel off the same tide, I did not think it prudent to detain the chief, as it might cause an open rupture at the moment. Just before leaving they attempted to break or stove the boat by throwing stones at her, but fortunately she received no injury.

At 6 it was high water, which was not sufficient to move the vessel, she being deeply imbedded in sand. The crew came aft to me in a body, and told me it was their determination to leave the vessel. I told them I had no intention of leaving her, and was resolved from the commencement to remain as long as their [sic] was the least prospect of getting the vessel off – and as I would not comply with their resolution they left me, but appeared not to be perfectly satisfied.

At 7 the Indians began to collect on the beach in great numbers, & made several fires. The crew seeing this came aft to me a second time, and insisted on my leaving the vessel with them, as the only chance of saving their lives; but as I still entertained hopes of extricating ourselves from our perilous situation, I used every argument I could think of to induce them to remain at least another tide longer, but all to no purpose, for both officers & crew were resolved to leave her & hazard their lives in the boats rather than fall into the merciless hands of the Indians. They said that if the boats were lost or taken from us, our retreat would be cut off, and that there would not be a possibility of escaping, & this was the only alternative we had of saving our lives.

Finding them determined, and all my endeavours to persuade them to remain a little longer of no avail, I was reluctantly forced to comply with their resolution. My next consideration was whether I should return to Kygarny & procure assistance from the brig Convoy, which was a doubtful point; or proceed directly to Nass where I expected to find almost certain assistance from one of the Compys. vessels which I hoped to find there on my arrival. And if assistance could be speedily afforded that at least great part of the cargo, if not the vessel, might be saved.

The wind having shifted to the SE a fresh gale with snow & sleet, at 8 P.M. we left the vessel, and so eager were the crew to leave that they did not take any clothing except what was on them & a few blankets, & I forget to take any water or provisions, with the exception of about 10 lbs. biscuit & a little tea. After getting clear of the breakers, which we did with great difficulty & danger, we set sail on the long boat, & took the jolly boat[8] in tow, as I was anxious to make all dispatch I possibly could.

The aftermath of *Vancouver*'s seizure and loss

After learning of the loss of *Vancouver*, Captain Benjamin Pickens of the brig *Convoy* sailed to Graham Island. According to George Whitemore, a 'half breed' who visited John Work, a Hudson's Bay Company official aboard the Company's brig *Lama* in February 1835, Pickens found no one at the wreck, 'and the vessel was broke up'. Work was told that Duncan's abandonment was unfortunate, 'for the next tide she floated off to her anchor & might easily have been saved' (Dee 1944a: 141, entry for 23 February 1835).

The Haida who had plundered the wreck, whom Work identified as the Massets, also claimed to Pickens that 'a great deal of the danger . . . apprehended from the Indians was imaginary for the Natives . . . affirm that only 8 were on the ground, and that in order to intimidate the crew, they kindled a great number of fires in the night to make it be believed that their numbers were greater than they really were' (Dee 1944a: 141, entry for 23 February 1835). Work also blamed the Naikun, or Point Rose Haida, as well as the Skidegate Haida for the 'plundering' of the schooner. In June 1835, he reported that the 'old chief, the old scoundrel Kinsly', of the Masset, 'was the head and active hand at pillaging the Vancouver' (Dee 1944c: 311, entry for 8 June 1835).

Work was told that 'since the wreck the Indians who have obtained the property have enriched themselves buying slaves &c.' He fumed:

It is a pity there were not the means of compelling them to give back the property or something in lieu of it and at the same time of punishing them effectually for what they have been guilty of. But were we to go there we would not be able to do anything by force, and until we [can] do so it is deemed better to say nothing on the subject further than it will not be dropped. Should the Steam boat come, they might probably be punished effectually. (Dee 1944a: 141, entry for 23 February 1835)

Work was vexed by the lack of action, because he felt, from his observations and discussions along the coast, that the Haida and Tlingit were emboldened by the lack of response; 'we are much lessened in their estimation and our power looked upon with very little respect' (Dee 1944a: 143, entry for 1 March 1835). Yet, a few months later, during a visit to Graham Island, Work concluded that the power of the European traders was still feared when he encountered a group of 'shy' Haida.

Their shyness arose, from the loss of the Vancouver last year, as they are connected with the tribe who inhabit where she was lost, and who plundered her. We learn from them that 25 canoes of that tribe and these people are off now at the fort Simpson for the purpose of making up matters, and that the Chief means to exculpate himself & his people by stating that it was not their fault, but the fault of the waves that occasioned the loss of the vessel. This appears to be their way of reasoning on the subject. (Dee 1944b: 239–40, entry for 10 May 1835)

On a visit to Naikun near Rose Point, Work noted that 'I have not been able to observe any of the articles belonging to the vessel about them. So that it is probable they have not come in for much share of the plunder' (Dee 1944b: 240, entry for 11 May 1835).

Captain Pickens and John Work were the only traders who followed up on the loss of *Vancouver*, albeit unsatisfactorily in Work's view. With their visits to the islands, the matter was indeed dropped, and thus passed out of memory, though not entirely forgotten by the Haida. Three other vessels, beginning with the *Georgiana* in 1851, the *Susan Sturgis* a year later, and lastly a Hudson's Bay Company brig with the same ill-fated name of *Vancouver*, would suffer similar fates.

On the afternoon of 18 November 1851, the American sloop *Georgiana* arrived off the east coast of the Queen Charlotte Islands near Cumshewa

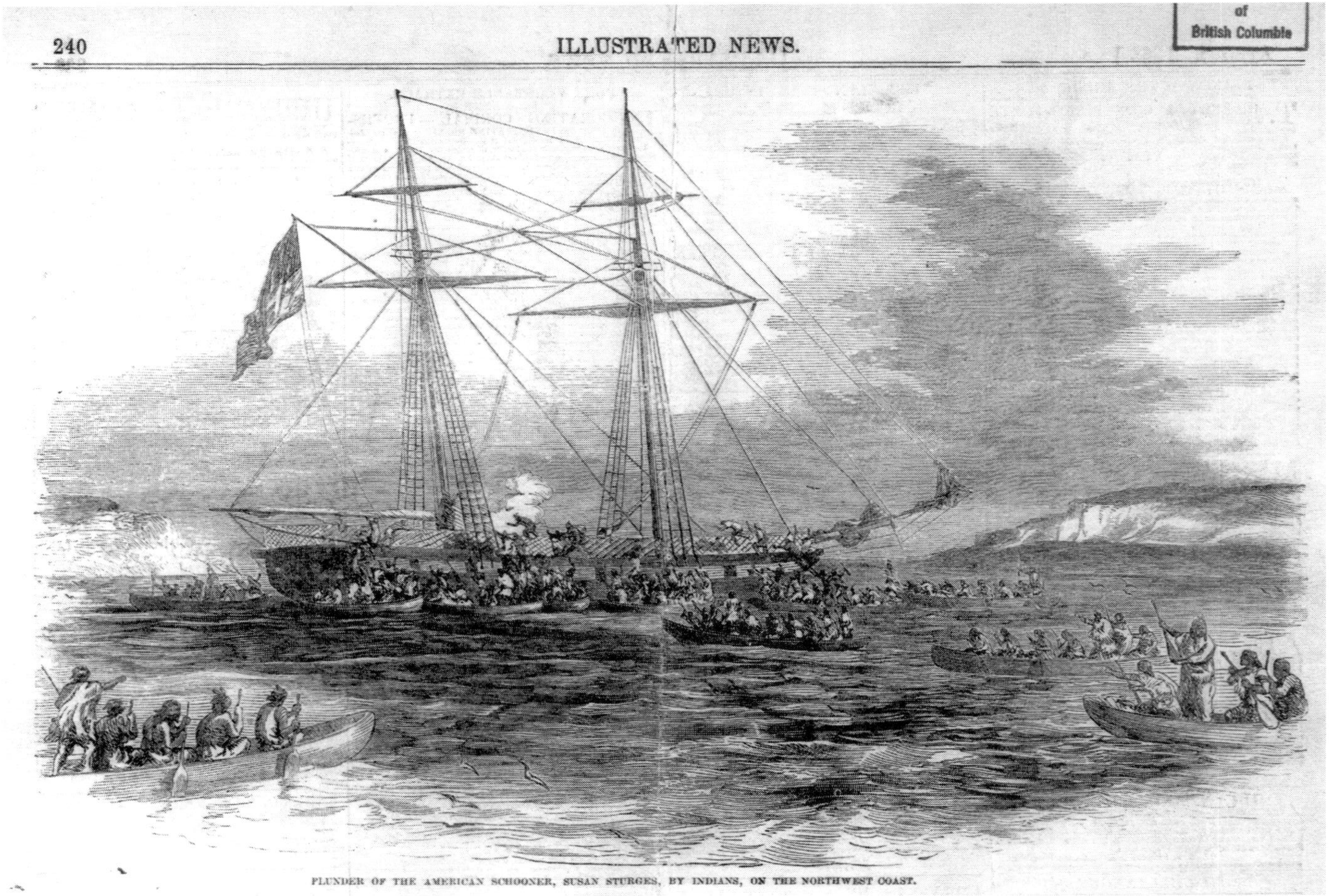
240
ILLUSTRATED NEWS.
of
British Columbia
PLUNDER OF THE AMERICAN SCHOONER, SUSAN STURGES, BY INDIANS, ON THE NORTHWEST COAST.

Fig. 3.2 The seizure of the schooner *Susan Sturgis* in 1852 by the Haida at Masset as depicted in the *Illustrated News* of New York, 1853.

Inlet. The vessel was transporting a group of hopeful gold miners to the site of a recent discovery on the rugged west coast of the islands. Ignoring the advice of his Haida pilot, 'John', and a chief of Cumshewa village, to seek safe anchorage inside the inlet for the night, the captain, William Rowland, chose to anchor offshore. A severe storm in the night drove the vessel on to the rocks. What then ensues, according to a passenger's account, shows close similarities to the 1834 loss of *Vancouver*. Charles E. Weed (1868: 2) wrote:

Nearly abreast of where she [Georgiana] was grounded was another [Haida] camp, and on the beach Indians were assembling from all quarters . . . At first they received us with great show of friendship . . . but we soon learned that those demonstrations of kindness were but affected to induce all our party to abandon the wreck, which they indicated to us unmistakably was now their plunder . . . [I]t so happened that but few of the people from John [the Haida pilot] and Charley's band (our companions on the sloop of the night previous) could reach the wreck, and it was already evident there was a jealousy about their first having made our acquaintance . . . [A] contention had started between the two camps as to the distribution of the plunder . . . We gave our sympathy to John's party, and by assuring them that if good care was taken of us, and we were carried over to Fort Simpson, a large ransom would be paid, a compromise was effected by which the beach party received the sloop and we became the prisoners of John's camp.

The scene now changed. The Indians flocked aboard the ill-fated sloop, stripping her completely . . . [but] no bodily harm was inflicted, and we were soon satisfied that plunder was their primary object, and that our argument that their reward was to be proportionate to our safety and report of their treatment, was thoroughly appreciated by them.

Indeed all twenty-seven of *Georgiana*'s crew and passengers gained their safe release for a price after '54 days of captivity' (Weed 1868: 2). The Fort Simpson journal for 1852 gives some indication of John's new-found wealth when on 6 July, 'two or three Canoes of Cumshewas people arrived headed by "John" etc. . . . [who] brought lots of property which they obtained from the wreck of Georgianna [*sic*] and the American Vessels who have visited Q.C.I. this summer' (Hudson's Bay Company n.d.a).

The subsequent capture of the American schooner *Susan Sturgis* on 26 September 1852, led by Chief Wiiaa [Weah] of the Masset, received considerably more attention, official and otherwise. The incident was investigated by the Royal Navy, seeking to know what role the Haida pilot, Albert Edward Edenshaw, chief of the *S'dast'aas* lineage, and town chief of nearby Kiusta on the north-west coast of the Queen Charlotte Islands, had played in the seizure. That the schooner's master, Matthew Rooney, ignored prior warnings of possible hostilities by both Chief Nestecanna of Skidegate and Captain Kuper, master of the British frigate *Thetis* (Kuper to Moresby, 4 February 1853, in Lamb 1942: 202; Prevost 1853), says something of the arrogance or naïveté of the ship's master and crew. The *Susan Sturgis* continued north to Masset with a crew of only seven and Edenshaw as pilot, calling in at various points to trade for fish.

The vessel rounded Rose Point, whereupon it was met by a canoe with Chief Wiiaa. A conversation ensued over the side between the Masset chief and Edenshaw in Haida. What was said between them was never determined, but on the following day Chief Wiiaa with 150 Masset, faces blackened, in twenty-five canoes came alongside the *Susan Sturgis*. The significance of the blackened faces, along with the absence of women in the trading party, was lost on Captain Rooney. Not long after trading commenced over the side, the Haida boarded the vessel *en masse* and overpowered the crew. The captain later wrote, '[I] was immediately covered by five or six muskets . . . and was only saved by the chief's [Edenshaw] wife forcing herself between the Indians and myself. The chief then came up to me, and by dint of force dragged me away from them towards the cabin.' Edenshaw is credited with having saved the lives of the crew, persuading the Masset that they could be ransomed to the Hudson's Bay Company at Fort Simpson. Matthew Rooney later wrote of the incident, 'However anxious chief Edenshaw, and his party, may have been to preserve our lives, they appeared equally anxious to share the plunder with the Massett tribe' (Rooney 1853: 240). Another Haida chief by name of Scowell from Chatsina (Kaigani) offered to protect the captain and took him off the vessel in his canoe. *Susan Sturgis* was 'captured, pillaged, and burned . . . and her crew enslaved', Edenshaw later told the missionary, the Reverend William Collison (n.d., 1915).[9] As it had in the case of the *Georgiana*, the Hudson's Bay Company did pay the ransom in blankets for their safe delivery to the fort. Aside from the ransom, the Haida recovered some $1500 in gold and silver from the ship's strongbox, 'besides several amounts of private cash, amounting to about $200' (Rooney 1853: 240). Scowell was as good as his word and brought both Captain Rooney and his Mate to Fort Simpson, receiving '17. 3 pt Blankets & Shirts, Powder, Tobacco, and Cotton' for his efforts. But it did worry John Work, the Chief Factor (Hudson's Bay Company n.d.a), who wrote on 4 October 1852, 'Our own Indians [Tsimshian] are much excited seeing the Chatsema [Haida] obtaining so much property . . . and the affair may cause us troubles.' Over the next two months the remaining four crew members were brought to the fort with the assistance of Edenshaw, Scowell and Robert Peel, another Kaigani Haida. Various goods and money from the vessel began showing up in trade at Fort Simpson in the months following. On 5 February 1853 Robert Peel arrived with the bell 'formerly belonging to the "Susan Sturgis". We will purchase it of [sic] him if possible' (Hudson's Bay Company n.d.a). Other chiefs had a hand in the affair. An Eagle lineage chief named Stilta, and a close relative of Wiiaa, was awarded the eagle carving off the sternboard of the *Susan Sturgis* (Harrison 1925: 173). It was affixed above the entrance way to Stilta's house at Masset, displayed prominently in a manner typical of a Haida 'war trophy' (MacDonald 1983: 146).

In 1853 the Hudson's Bay Company lost a second ship of the same name, the brigantine *Vancouver*, when it foundered off Rose Point. Despite the arrival on the scene of the Hudson's Bay Company steamer *Beaver*, the *Vancouver* could not be saved. In a futile bid to free the vessel from the sand bar, the crew began jettisoning goods overboard when 'a number of Indians arrived and commenced pillaging the Cargo and using threatening language pointing their Guns and flourishing knives . . . A quarrel ensued between the Chief and the Interpreter which was very nearly ending seriously.' On returning to the vessel the following day James Reid, master of the *Vancouver*, 'observed the Indians plundering the ship'. Seeing that nothing more could be done:

'Officers and Crew embarked on board the Steamer having just before leaving set fire to the wreck in order that the large quantities of Spirits and Wine on board might not fall into the hands of the Indians who had threatened their lives and hindered their exertions to save the vessel and arrived safely at Fort Simpson' (Reid 1853).

The Edenshaw name is linked to this last incident, though it is not entirely clear whether it was the old chief or his nephew, Albert Edward, then reportedly residing with his uncle at his village of Hiellen near Rose Point (Collison 1915). The elder Edenshaw apparently died before 1850 (Dalzell 1968: 72), and the title passed to Albert Edward (*c.* 1810–94),[10] who became town chief of Kiusta. Albert Edward Edenshaw went on to establish two villages in succession along the north coast of Graham Island. Kiusta was abandoned for Kung, built and settled within a year of the loss of the *Susan Sturgis* (Inskip n.d.: 625), and undoubtedly financed by the wealth it provided. Yatza or Yatze ('knife') village, situated closer to Masset and more accessible to the centres of trade on the north coast, followed sometime around 1870. Described as a small temporary settlement or campground (MacDonald 1983: 184), Yatza was never permanently occupied, and Edenshaw abandoned the site shortly after in favour of Masset. To what extent the fate of the ships and crew lost in these waters was inextricably intertwined with the changing demographics and internal rivalries on the Queen Charlotte Islands becomes evident when considering Haida culture and contact. As for these encounters, the loss of the brigantine *Vancouver* in 1853 marks the last year the Haida carried out such attacks on maritime trade vessels.

The other half of the equation: the Haida

The taking of these vessels by the Haida not only serves to illustrate the complex, volatile nature of coastal trade, but also provides us with a very real measure of the socioeconomic role and impact of trade on the indigenous community. From these encounters it is abundantly clear that the Haida were not simply passive victims of trade. This is not to say they, or maritime traders, could control its direction or outcome. By the time of *Vancouver*'s arrival on the Queen Charlottes in 1834, the population of the islands was in serious decline (Boyd 1991; Duff 1964) with many of the islands' smaller villages already, or in the process of being, abandoned (Acheson 1998). This trend would continue until just two large multi-lineage settlements, Masset and Skidegate, remained at the close of the nineteenth century, representing the combined surviving membership of all the northern and southern Haida respectively. These were unsettling times for the Haida, as fiercely autonomous kin groups gravitated towards the centres of trade and consolidated to create larger multi-lineage settlements. The Haida's stake in the trade and shifting demographics created its own volatile social mix for which these ships would pay the price. Desperate times lent themselves to desperate measures.

The politics of wealth

The supernatural beings around Rose Spit once had a contest as to who could give away the largest amount of property. (Swanton 1905a: 214)

A persistent element in the accounts of these attacks was the limited, and at times conflicting authority of the chiefs present at the scene, not to mention the ambiguity surrounding the identity of the group involved. Rank and authority were liable to change, and were intimately bound up with the ability to amass and distribute wealth. Haida society embodied a historically well-defined socioeconomic class structure characterised by socially complex and elaborate institutions such as the potlatch and slavery. The basic social unit was the kin group or lineage, a social unit defined by rules of descent and residence. Lineages were self-sufficient and autonomous, with inter-group relations based on alliances through marriage and the reciprocal exchange of goods. Titles to productive resources were controlled by the lineage chief, who coordinated the political and ceremonial affairs of the lineage group as trustee for the jealously guarded territory and resources owned by the lineage. Proprietary rights included sea otter and fishing grounds, as well as stretches of coastline and all that might wash up on its shores (Barbeau n.d.; Niblack 1890: 335). Dawson (1880: 117–18) was clear on this point, observing among the Haida in 1878:

So strict are these ideas of proprietary right in the soil, that on some parts of the coast sticks may be seen set up to define the limits of the various properties . . . [where] a stranded shark, or seal or sea-otter which has died from its wounds [may come ashore]. Along the shores the principle berry-gathering grounds are found, and thus divided.

Albert Niblack (1890: 335) remarked upon the extent to which the Haida recognised property rights in the late nineteenth century. Travelling to the region in the late 1880s, he remarked that 'the ownership of a tract of land by a family . . . through being vested in an individual or in the head of that family, [meant] practically individual ownership'. By the same reasoning, such rights were extended to stranded vessels, as the Haida endeavoured to impress upon the masters and crew of *Vancouver* and *Georgiana*.

While John Work blamed Chief 'Kinsly' of Masset for what happened to *Vancouver* in 1834, Captain Duncan was quick to note in his report that the chief's authority on the beach that day had been limited. Although the position was inherited, a lineage chief's power was 'a varying one, dependent on, and at the same time, limited by, the number and power of his house chiefs' (Swanton 1905a: 69; see also Swanton n.d., 1905b). Deference to lineage chiefs was thus highly variable, largely personal, and achieved 'according to the amount of his property and number of his people' (Dawson 1880: 116). The authority of the chief in the highest-ranking house, in turn, was recognised by consent of other house chiefs as 'town' chief, or *lana-oka* ('people's mother') (see Curtis 1916: 119, 187; Dawson 1880: 118–19; Murdock 1934: 237, 238; 1936: 16; Swanton 1905a: 69).

Kinsly's identity may be that of Chief Sigai or Segai, the leading town chief of Masset during this period. Masset itself became home for most of the northern Haida groups throughout the region by the close of the 1800s. Sometime in the 1840s, Sigai bestowed the chieftainship to his son, Wiiaa (Weah), and not to his eldest maternal nephew, violating traditional practice.

Fig. 3.3 Chief Wiiaa's Monster House at Masset, c. 1887–89. Wiiaa was one of several chiefs who benefited from the seizure of trade vessels on the northern Queen Charlotte Islands. Appearing in the photograph with Chief Wiiaa is Henry Edenshaw, the great nephew of Chief Albert Edward Edenshaw who had a hand in the seizure of the schooner *Susan Sturgis* and brigantine *Vancouver*. Note ship's cannon in right foreground.

Fig. 3.4 Interior view of Chief Wiiaa's massive Monster House 1884, revealing the obvious wealth of the owner along with the trappings of historical contact.

Despite the personal popularity of Wiiaa, the decision was not universally accepted by the community, adding to the dynamic tension between Wiiaa and the aspiring Edenshaw for which '[t]he resulting split in Masset remains unresolved to this day' (MacDonald 1983: 136). Chief Wiiaa, and Eda'nsa (Albert Edward Edenshaw), who would later rival Wiiaa for pre-eminence at Masset, were leading players in the plundering of the *Susan Sturgis* in 1852. According to Collison (1915), Albert Edward, who was by then chief of Kiusta, was also involved in the aborted plundering of the *Vancouver* in 1853, in the year he and his followers moved to Kung.

For the Haida, rank and privilege were inextricably bound to the ability to amass and redistribute wealth. Preferential access to new sources of wealth was a means to increased social standing and authority, but remained subject to close scrutiny by community members, particularly those of rival families. The influx of new wealth, coupled with a declining population, left fewer contenders for vacated positions amongst high-ranking members, and this in turn gave rise to greater competition and disputes over the legitimacy of some claimants.[11]

Although a lineage chief could usually, but not invariably, count on the support of house chiefs, he could not 'command their obedience or punish insubordination', a circumstance which proved disastrous in Anglo-American/Haida trade relations (see Murdock 1934: 237; Dawson 1880: 118–19; Dixon 1789: 227). As some chiefs bitterly experienced, they were all too often held accountable by mariners for the behaviour of kins- men whom they had little vested authority to control or reprimand. This act alone was repeatedly played out in the late eighteenth and early nineteenth centuries with tragic consequences for both native and European alike. A graphic case in point was the Kunghit Haida's failed attempt to capture the *Lady Washington* in 1791, and consequent loss of life, followed by the Kunghit's success in capturing *Eleanora* three years later with the killing of all hands save one (Bartlett n.d.; Hoskins n.d.; Howay 1929a: 114–23).

This chronic lack of understanding concerning the limits of political authority was compounded by the fact that, as Captain Inskip of HM Steam- Sloop *Virago* observed in 1853, 'They never forgive an injury until ample retribution has been made . . . their children or relative considering it a point of duty to revenge an insult.' Captain Kendrick of *Lady Washington* failed to appreciate the significance of his actions when in 1789 he detained and humiliated Xo'ya, a senior-ranking Kunghit chief, along with a second chief, on account of their kinsmen having pilfered some goods while trading aboard the ship. A Haida recounted the affair to John Hoskins (n.d.) aboard the ship *Columbia Rediviva* in 1791:

[Kendrick] took Coyah, tied a rope round his neck, whipt [sic] him, painted his face, cut off his hair, took away from him a great many skins, and then turned him ashore. Coyah was no longer a chief, but an 'Ahilko,' or one of the lower class. They have no head chief, but many inferior chiefs.

Chief Xo'ya's bid to redress this affront and loss of face, aside from the loss of an undisclosed number of valuable furs, culminated in a bloody exchange between these two protagonists when *Lady Washington* returned in 1791 (Bishop 1967: 97).

A contributing social ingredient in these encounters was the existence of class among the Haida. Although chiefly authority and rank were highly variable, Haida society was stratified with descent groups containing members of two strata – *yahit* ('nobility') and *'isa'gida* ('commoners'). Nobles seldom associated with commoners and had superior legal rights to those of commoners (Murdock 1934: 245–6, 247–8; see also Dawson 1880: 119). That a noble class existed was clear to Dawson in 1878, for 'in no case . . . does the chieftaincy pass from the royal clan to any of the lesser men of the tribe' (Dawson 1880: 119). Nobles were quick to avenge an affront to one's name or erase a slight or loss of status through the hosting of the potlatch. The potlatch served a crucial function in witnessing and acknowledging, or refuting for that matter, the continuity of a lineage's rights over territory and resources, aside from being a mechanism for the redistribution of goods among kin groups (Murdock 1936). Potlatches were held to mark a number of events, the most important being the building of a house, and, upon the death of an individual of high rank, the subsequent raising of a mortuary or memorial pole. They were also given in answer to a challenge from a rival, to regain face after a personally embarrassing event ranging from a small public mishap to the calamity of having been taken captive and enslaved. The event required enormous economic activity, calling upon one's descent group for the accumulation of goods on behalf of the intended host.

For the commoner, access to resources was conditional on their commitment to amassing goods for redistribution by senior-ranking kinsmen through the institution of the potlatch. A leader's 'sphere of influence' was relative then to what resources were being distributed, the amount and to whom. A third stratum, *xAlda'ngats* ('slaves'), existed as a form of property attached to each descent group. Slaves were highly valued and, as a social class, were comprised usually of captives taken in raids on distant groups.

The strength of the kin group and that of the chief rested then on the ability to arrange successfully lucrative alliances through marriage, manage the lineage's resources, and wage war. These imperatives placed an enormous

Fig. 3.5 Skidegate village in 1884 is one of only two Haida settlements to survive the contact period with the in-migration of numerous families from surrounding villages.

premium on maintaining large, stable kin groups and access to lucrative resources, both of which were being eroded by events of the contact period.

The contact period

From a projected precontact population of over 14,000 the Haida steadily declined in numbers through the trade period (Boyd 1991: 144). The first 'census' commissioned by the Hudson's Bay Company in 1836 tallied 8342 Haida (Douglas n.d.), six decades after European contact and the smallpox epidemic(s) of the late eighteenth century on the north coast. They numbered only a tenth of that figure in 1881, reaching a mere 588 individuals for the Queen Charlotte Islands by 1915 (Bishop 1967: 70–1, 83, 91–2; Canada Census n.d.; Duff 1964: 39; Fleurieu 1801: 294; Green 1915: 39; Swanton 1905a: 105).

This demographic trend, together with the massive infusion of new wealth, worked towards realigning traditional productive relationships and village organisation. Certain chiefs were able to enhance, if not redefine their authority, through preferential access to new sources of wealth and the propensity for European and American traders to deal with 'chiefs'. For a senior-ranking chief, the newly emergent multi-lineage community offered a greatly expanded labour pool to forge lucrative alliances using the same general mechanisms and principles that ordered social relations among lineage and house chiefs.

Greater prosperity was both the result of and the means to successful alliances. This process, and the changing conditions of warfare with the introduction of firearms, translated into ever greater advantages with the joining of even more followers to a community – a trend which ran counter to the inherent sectional autonomy of the traditional segmentary lineage. The creation of large multi-lineage settlements was both the means to and the end result of an emerging system of hereditary political unification (Sahlins 1961).

Although adhering to the form and idiom of kinship, ruling lineages and their chiefs could transform positions of rank into divisions of class with the adequate accumulation and redistribution of wealth. The fur trade fuelled the inherent tendencies towards inequality with new opportunities for the seizure and transfer of surpluses beyond those available within the traditional social order (Wolf 1982: 96). Groups strategically located to exploit the maritime trade had the means to expand and consolidate their sphere of influence, as Edenshaw attempted with his establishment of Yatze in the twilight years of the trade. In effect, chiefs who gained access to arms and valuables outside of indigenous productive relationships, and 'hence to a following outside of kinship and unencumbered by it', were then able to extend their authority over lesser leaders, including some in other communities (Wolf 1982: 96). Traditional relations were thus being recast to enable certain chiefs, such as Blakow-Coneehaw of Kiusta (died 1793), Chiefs Skedans and Skidegate, Eda'nsa (the name of the first Edenshaw), and his successor, Albert Edward Edenshaw (c. 1810–94), to strive for, if not realise, ever greater authority (Meares 1790: 367; see also Bartlett n.d.; Ingraham 1971: 129; Poole 1872: 108). Such aspirations were not without controversy and the influence of internal checks and balances. Albert Edward Edenshaw's bid to become the 'greatest of the Haida chiefs' (Gough 1982: 132) is still a matter of debate within his adopted community of Masset. For some, his overtly aggressive search for power and prestige, and the manner in which he went about amassing and demonstrating his wealth, stepped beyond the bounds of acceptable Haida behaviour.[12] His rise to chiefly status began when he asserted his suitability as village chief over that of Itltine, the intended heir of Kiusta on north-western Graham Island, and chief of a closely related lineage. It is no coincidence that Edenshaw's rise to power was closely bound to the shifting fortunes and competition among the various lineages with the seizures of the ships *Vancouver* [1834] and *Susan Sturgis*.

Both the volume of trade and the type of goods sought by the Haida further illustrate the strategic importance of trade in the context of their own social and economic imperatives. At the outset of the maritime fur trade, iron for weaponry and tools and to a lesser degree copper for decorative use proved to be lucrative trade items. These were soon eclipsed by firearms and then later by clothing and foodstuffs. Muskets were a standard article of trade on the Pacific Northwest Coast by 1790–91, and the demand for shot and powder never diminished as native groups became increasingly reliant upon their use (Možino 1970; Colnett 1940).[13] But by the close of the eighteenth century, the Haida were sufficiently armed so that muskets 'would not sell unless they were the best of the King's arms' (Sturgis n.d.b; see also Sturgis n.d.a; 1978: 121). Clothing, blankets and foodstuffs, such as bread, sugar, rice and molasses, became equally important as staples by the end of the century. Foodstuffs particularly could be profitably traded during the winter months for use in potlatches and at a time when staples were often scarce (see Furgerson n.d.).

Sturgis (1978: 121) remarked in 1799 on just how reliant the Haida had now become on the trade, while believing 'that the supplies furnished them would continue to be as liberal as at present'. But by 1835 the numbers of fur bearing animals in the Queen Charlottes were so depleted that the Haida's share of the market represented less than 1 per cent of the total volume of furs being traded at Fort Simpson that year (Galois 1993).

Another contributing factor in the diminishing trade for the Haida was geography. Geography dictated that the Haida would not have the benefit of the lucrative middleman role enjoyed by their mainland trading partners. The Tsimshian, Niblack (1890: 265) remarked, 'seem to have acted as the middlemen, for most of the trade and intercourse of the Haida with the other tribes has been through them'. Whereas both the Tlingit and the Tsimshian could tap the fur wealth of their interior neighbours, once their own stocks were exhausted, the flow in furs to outer coast groups could be and was easily intercepted by maritime traders. William Sturgis (1978: 88) astutely remarked how at the close of the eighteenth century:

one after another are discovered the great resources of the port tribes that inhabit this coast – formerly all the Skins that were collected were got at Nootkah [west coast of Vancouver Island] where some vessels purchasing inland to the Northward of them [Kwakiutl] met that tribe on their trading expeditions. Panick [sic] struck at the discovery they scarcely made any exertions to keep the trade in their hands, and in one or two seasons sunk to nothing. It was next transferred to the Islands [Queen Charlotte Islands] who still keep a considerable share of it; but not half the skins are now got from them that formerly was, and we now have an evident proof that the greatest part of those they have are got from the Main by the chief part of Cumshewah's tribe being at this place [Skeena] for the purpose of trade.

The loss for the Haida became acute following the establishment of the land-based fur trade with the building of the Hudson's Bay Company fort at the mouth of the Nass River on the mainland coast in 1831. It is telling that on the eve of this development, Scouler (1841: 219) observed the Haida's declining fortunes in unquestionable clarity in 1825:

In former times, when the sea-otter abounded, the Massettes, Skittegas, Cumshewas, and other (Haidah) tribes inhabiting the eastern shores of Queen Charlotte's Island, were among the most wealthy on the coast: since the sea-otter has been destroyed, the Haidahs have become poor, and have been reduced to other plans in order to procure blankets. They fabricate most of the curiosities found on the coast, but their staple article is the potato, which they sell in great quantities to the mainland tribes. In the autumn, there is quite a competition among the Haidahs who shall carry early potatoes to the mainland. Fleets of from forty to fifty canoes arrive in September, and proceed to the different villages of the Chimmesyan nation, and the potato fair seldom ends without more or less fighting. They also manufacture and export canoes . . . When Europeans began to frequent the N.W. coast for the collecting furs, especially those of the sea-otter, the shores of Queen Charlotte's Island afforded an abundant supply of this valuable article, and the Haidah tribes carried on an extensive commerce with the English and Americans. During the period when this trade was flourishing, a taste for European commodities was created, which still continues, although the sea-otter, the sole article for which those foreign luxuries could be obtained, has been almost extirpated. In the meanwhile, the Haidahs had learned to cultivate the potato, and to supply the continental tribes with provisions. They now obtain their blankets from the latter, who in turn procure them from the fur traders in exchange for their beaver skins.

John Work's (1945: 39) remarks a decade later mirror those of Scouler's when he describes the Haida near Skidegate as:

wretchedly clothed and apparently badly off for everything. This formerly used to be one of the best places for Sea Otters on the coast, but now scarcely any is to be found among them. They grow a considerable quantity of potatoes they have several patches under cultivation about their villages.

Both Work's and Scouler's assessment of the situation for the Haida at this point in the trade is entirely credible. For the Haida, the vacuum created with the falling sea otter trade was filled by a rapidly growing 'potato trade'. Potatoes provided much needed starch in the heavily salted diet of both maritime and land-based traders. Haida from Skidegate, Cumshewa, Masset and Kaigani were trading potatoes regularly at Fort Simpson, usually crossing over in large flotillas of canoes between March and September. Within a span of ten days in the spring of 1840, for example, the fort acquired 1119 bushels of potatoes from the 'Queen Charlotte Islanders', arriving in 'no less than 48 Canoes' (Hudson's Bay Company n.d.a: B 201/a/4; see also Howay 1929b). The potato trade is testimony to the Haida's industry and adaptation to changing economic circumstances, as well as their growing social and material dependency on trade. Certain trade foodstuffs distributed at potlatches had come to hold enormous social value. The Haida's economic position in the trade was devolving to one of a service role, though this was not a socioeconomic station they would readily acquiesce to, as the officers and crew of the *Vancouver* found in 1834.

Haida trade relations with Anglo-Americans and with neighbouring indigenous coastal groups were predisposed to conflict as sea otter stocks declined and competition escalated. At the onset of historical contact, trade partnerships between Haida and Anglo-Americans were acknowledged through traditional Haida practices of exchanging names and the bestowing of gifts. Chief Blakow-Coneehaw of Kiusta, for example, took the name of Douglas Coneehaw, after Captain Douglas of the *Iphigenia* in 1788 (Meares 1790: 305). Transactions were also sanctioned with song (see Ingraham 1971: 101, 121). Such courtesies were soon dispensed with, however. Mistrust and misunderstandings over conduct accorded to alien trading parties exacerbated the uncertainties of the trade. The practice by mariners of sending boat parties ashore for wood and water without the consent of the respective lineage chief, for example, ran counter to Haida notions of proprietary rights, and would have undoubtedly been seen as a challenge. What appeared as vacant stretches of coastline to the mariner were not unclaimed lands to the Haida.

Contributing to the growing friction between these parties was the maritime fur trader's inability to control the native fur production process. For his sea otter pelts, the merchant relied on the skill and endurance of the native hunter, while the commodities desired in exchange, and their relative value to the Haida, were independent of European markets. Writing of his experiences on the coast at the turn of the nineteenth century, Sturgis (n.d.c) found the trade:

liable to great fluctuations. In carrying it on the law of demand & supply were frequently disregarded, and prices consequently were often unsettled I have seen prime Sea Otter skins obtained in exchange for articles that did not cost 50 cents at home, and I have often seen given for them articles that cost nearly twice as much as the Skins would sell for in China.

Similarly, Joseph Ingraham (1971: 119) observed in 1791 that 'things cannot always be estimated at their real value but at their price in the country they are in or the price they will fetch'. Continual renegotiation and increased demands made by the Haida, the competition between Anglo-Americans themselves, and at times the seemingly contradictory indifference of the Haida to trade at all, were a continual source of frustration for merchants who sought profit through nonequivalent or unequal exchange. The drive for a profitable venture, in a highly competitive and increasingly unsure market, encouraged desperate measures among maritime fur traders. While trade could be inadvertently jeopardised through an ignorance of social protocol, the conduct of some maritime traders can only be described as rapacious and often brutal, even by the standards of the day. Often the only constraint for the trader was one of self-interest and whether or not his conduct could jeopardise future trade if he intended to return to the coast.

Trade relations thus quickly deteriorated from the outset of contact in 1787. Indeed, 'peace of trade' was the great uncertainty as transactions became increasingly tense, often violent affairs. Nefarious practices of holding chiefs hostage to force the natives to trade, or simply to extort furs for some perceived transgression, were all too frequent (see Table 3.1). As early as 1792, Robert Haswell (n.d.), aboard *Adventure*, learned from the Haida

Table 3.1 Attacks and hostage takings involving fur trade vessels and the Haida 1787–1853

Year	Vessel	Captain	Campany/Owner	Nationality	Comments
1787	*Queen Charlotte* (snow 200T)	George Dixon	King George's Sound Co.	British	Haida attempt to steal some furs from the ship, to which the crew respond by firing 'several musquets after them, but did not perceive that they were attended with any fatal effects' (Dixon 1789: 221).
1787–89?	*Princess Royal* (sloop 50T)	Charles Duncan	Nootka Sound Co.	British	Reported attempt by the Cumshewa to capture the vessel, which 'obliged Captain Duncan to fire on them' (Ingraham 1971: 204).
1789	*Iphigenia Nubiana* (snow 200T)	William Douglas	–	British	An attempt to capture the vessel near Langara Island is foiled (Meares 1790: 366–7).
1791	*Lady Washington* (sloop 90T)	John Kendrick	Burrell, Brown *et al.*	American	In a bid to settle an earlier altercation between Chief Xo'ya and Captain Kendrick in 1789 the Kunghit Haida attempt to seize the vessel in the vicinity of Houston Stewart Channel. Forty Kunghit lives are lost (Ingraham 1971: 204).
1791	*Columbia Rediviva* (ship 212T)	John Gray	American	–	Three crew members killed by the Kaigani Haida in what may have been revenge for Crowell's action at Massett, 'thinking us all of one tribe' (Boit in Howay 1941: 227, 337) (see next entry).
1791–92	*Hancock* (brigantine 157T)	Samuel Crowell	Cravell & Creighton	American	Crew kill four Northern Haida 14 July for 'some trifling offense.' Crew member wounds a Northern Haida at Langara Island (Ingraham 1971: 194–5).
1793	*Amelia* (brig)	Trotter	–	American	Crew member killed by the Kunghit Haida (Magee n.d.).
1794	*Eleanora* (brig 190T)	Simon Metcalfe	Metcalfe	American	Captured by the Kunghit Haida near Houston Stewart Channel with the loss of all hands except one who is kept as a slave (Boit 1981: 74–5).

Year	Ship	Captain	Owner	Nationality	Notes
1794	*Resolution* (schooner 90T)	Robert Burling	J. & T. Lamb & Ass.	American	Captured by the Cumshewa with the loss of all hands except one who is kept as a slave (Bishop 1966: 97).
1795	*Despatch* (ship 160T)	Elias Newbury	Dorr & Sons	American	Detained Chief Cumshewa in exchange for the one survivor from the *Resolution* in July while in the company of the ship *Mercury* (Bishop 1966: 96).
1795	*Phoenix* (barque)	Hugh Moore	–	British	Shore party attacked and one crew member killed at Cumshewa. The ship fires on the village with cannon in retaliation, which the village returns in kind (Bishop 1966: 95).
1795–96	*Prince William Henry* (schooner)	William Wake	London or Newcastle Merchants	British	Holds a Kaigani chief for ransom (Howay 1930: 121, 123).
1795	*Union* (sloop 98T)	John Boit	Crowell Hatch & Caleb Gardiner	American	Attempted capture of the vessel 1 July results in the death of 50 to 70 Kunghit Haida (Boit 1981: 49–50).
1796–97	*Sea Otter* (brig)	Stephen Hill	R. Sturgis, Lamb, Magee & Hill	British	Captain and two crew members killed at Cumshewa (Howay 1931: 124).
1798	*Alexander* (ship)	Asa Dodge	Bass *et al.*	American	Three of the ship's crew wounded and ten (two?) Haida killed in a skirmish at Cumshewa (Howay 1931: 126; Sturgis 1978: 54).
1799	*Cheerful* (ship)	Beck	from Macao	British	Shore party is attacked 'with daggers & muskets', killing the 2nd officer and two men at Cumshewa (Howay 1931: 128–9; Sturgis 1978: 115).
1799	*Eliza*	James Rowan	J. & J. H. Perkins	American	Scotseye, a Cumshewa chief, and his brother are captured and delivered to the Kaigani for execution (Sturgis 1978: 90–2).
1801	*Globe*	Bernard Magee	Perkins, Lamb *et al.*	American	Captain killed by the Skidegate in October (Howay 1931: 135; Sturgis 1978: 118–19).
1802	*Hetty*	Briggs	–	American	Detains chiefs for the purpose of trade (Sturgis 1978: 122).

(cont.)

Table 3.1 (*cont.*)

Year	Vessel	Captain	Campany/Owner	Nationality	Comments
1806	*Lydia* (brig)	Samuel Hill	–	American	Six Massett Haida are held hostage for furs and the village fired on for an infraction that occurred days earlier with the Kaigani Haida at Kasaan (Walker n.d.).
1806	*Vancouver* (ship 285T)	Ebenzer Clinton	–	American	An attempt by the Skidegate Haida to seize the vessel is foiled (Clinton n.d.).
1815	*Constantin* (sloop)	–	–	Russian	Haida attempt to capture the vessel at Kaigani (Howay 1933: 124).
1821	*Hamilton* (ship 232T)	William Martain	–	American	'fired 4 broad sides' into Skidegate village with the loss of at least three lives following the Haida's attack on the ship's shore party (Martain n.d.; Cross n.d.).
1834	*Vancouver* (schooner)	Alexander Duncan	Hudson's Bay Co.	British	Runs aground on Rose Spit and subsequently plundered by the Haida, 3 March.
1851	*Georgiana* (sloop)	William Rowland	–	American	Founders off Cumshewa Inlet. Ship is plundered and crew and passengers held for ransom (Rowland n.d.).
1852	*Susan Sturgis* (schooner 150T)	Matthew Rooney	–	American	Seized and plundered by the Massett Haida. The crew is spared and ransomed to the Hudson's Bay Company at Fort Simpson (Gough 1982; Prevost 1853).
1853	*Vancouver* (brigantine 184T)	James Reid	Hudson's Bay Co.	British	Founders on Rose Spit and subsequently is fired by the crew to avoid seizure by the Haida.
1853	*Virago* (steam-sloop)	George Inskip	Royal Navy	British	Kunghit Haida attempt to capture the ship's two long-boats with crew on 20 July (Inskip n.d.).

at Dadens that 'others come, kill us, and take our property by force, You come, bartered with us and hurt not a man' (see also Sturgis 1978: 53, 62, 90). Also, attempts to cheat on the quality or quantity of goods exchanged for furs were not uncommon. Captain Hill of the brig *Lydia*, for example, was discovered by the Kaigani in 1806 putting 'roapyarns into the bottom of the kass & take part of the powder out and the Natives found it out & was very angry about it' (Walker n.d.). The same individual, commanding the brig *Otter* four years later, traded molasses diluted with sea water to the Cumshewa in the winter of 1810 (Furgerson n.d.). In apposition to this pressure was the temptation, a growing desperation even, on the part of some native communities for the wealth that could be gained by seizing a ship. Seizure of a ship was an enormous temptation for an aspiring chief, or one needing to regain lost status. For a careless ship's company, the combination of a laden vessel and the social imperatives of revenge, material need and property rights among the Haida courted disaster. The seizure of vessels like the schooner *Vancouver*, as it lay stranded on Rose Spit, offered simply another opportunity to serve these ends.

Conclusion

Attacks on maritime vessels were surprisingly commonplace. Captain Wallace Houston of HMS *Trincomalle* wrote a sobering account of the fragile balance between the native community and Anglo-Americans in the 1800s after investigating the seizure of the *Susan Sturgis* in 1852: 'all vessels with small crews attempting to trade with these Indians . . . will end in the loss of the vessel and cargo . . . The different tribes are in a perpetual state of warfare, shooting and robbing each other, taking prisoners for slaves, etc. Why should the white stranger expect any other treatment unless he goes amongst them well armed and prepared?' (Houston 1854). It was a highly pragmatic view that, while seemingly passing moral judgement upon the native community for its proclivity towards raiding, Houston was acknowledging the fact that they were a force to be reckoned with. Such occurrences did not happen in a socioeconomic vacuum. This was a turbulent time for the Haida, driven as they were by the compulsions, struggles and relationships of the day. As MacDonald (1983: 136) writes, 'the turmoil of mixing together the chiefs of formerly fiercely independent families' alone pressed for increasingly desperate actions to assert or maintain chiefly status. The indigenous population became increasingly reliant on a trade, punctuated by bitter conflict and disease. Traditional practices were giving way, pressed by the shifting fortunes of the maritime trade and a plummeting population. The stories of the *Eleanora*, the *Resolution* and the others are a measure in very human terms of the complexity and interdependency of native–Anglo-American relations, embodying the elements of revenge, opportunism, material need, and at times respect, if not friendship.

Acknowledgements

We are indebted to a number of individuals and institutions for their assistance. Our thanks to Donald Mitchell, who reviewed and provided insightful comments on a very rough first draft, and to Laurie Williamson for her invaluable editorial comment. Drew Crooks of the Lacey Museum in the State of Washington generously provided historical sources on the loss of the *Georgiana*. The services of the Archaeology Branch of the Government of British Columbia, the Hudson's Bay Company Archives and the British Columbia Archives are gratefully acknowledged.

Notes

1. For a time, cheaply produced personal accounts of such adventures, dubbed 'mendicant books', flourished in nineteenth-century America and were a source of an often meagre, if not the sole, income for the aging author.
2. The preferred local name for this island group is *Haida Gwaii* ('islands of the people'). The archipelago is comprised of some 150 islands, the largest of which, from north to south, are Graham, Moresby and Kunghit Islands.
3. See M. Malloy (1998) for a historical review of the scholarly research and some of the issues surrounding the topic of native–Euro-American maritime fur trade relations.
4. No serious effort was made to retrieve the schooner or its cargo. The Company had acted quickly to suppress the Clatsops in 1829 when *William and Ann* was lost at the mouth of the Columbia River. Acting on rumours that the Indians had murdered the wreck's crew and plundered the cargo, an HBC force, including the crew of the *Vancouver*, had attacked the Clatsops and killed several to retrieve a few barrels. Now, the survival of *Vancouver*'s crew, coupled no doubt by a pragmatic consideration that the well-organised and well-armed Haida were formidable foes, compelled the company to write off the loss. The wreck did underscore the HBC's determination to employ a steamer on the coast instead of more susceptible sailing craft. In 1834, the company ordered a steamship for the Northwest Coast trade, and in 1835 the sidewheel steamer *Beaver* arrived at Fort Vancouver.

5. Kygarny, also known as Kigarnie, was Kaigani ('pretty village'), a former Tlingit village at the southern end of the Alexander Archipelago on Dall Island, Alaska. It was a prominent and popular fur trade rendezvous (Gibson 1992: 30, 206–7).

6. Rose Point, on Graham Island in the Queen Charlottes, was named by Captain William Douglas of the brig *Iphigenia* in August 1788 for a prominent British politician. The point was known to the Haida as 'Naikun' or 'Long Nose' (Walbran 1909: 430–1).

7. Although not accepting the Haida's view of the matter, Duncan none the less understood the nature of the dispute.

8. A jolly boat is the ship's smallest boat, usually carried at the stern, and rowed with four to six oars.

9. William Henry Collison was the first missionary to work on the islands, arriving at Masset in 1876.

10. Alfred Edward Edenshaw's birth date is variously given as 1810 or 1812 (Gough 1982: 132, 1990: 289), while his monument which stands in Masset reads 1822 (Dalzell 1968: 63, 68).

11. It is a legacy continuing to this day for the Masset community with the assertions and counter-assertions of who is the rightful heir as town chief (see Sparrow 1998).

12. See K. Sparrow (1998) for one perspective on the continuing debate about the role, motives and benefits of his actions.

13. In 1795 the Kaigani entreated Charles Bishop, should he trade with the Cumshewa, 'not to sell them Powder Musketts and Ball', given their intention to attack the village (Bishop 1967: 84). A party of Haida were so desperate for ammunition while at Fort Simpson in 1841 that they traded quantities of potatoes to the Tsimshian 'for a mere triffle of powder and shot' (Fort Simpson Journals, 1832–66, Hudson's Bay Company Archives n.d.a, B 201/a/6). Musket fire could pierce aboriginal slat armour, as repeatedly demonstrated to both Tlingit and Haida groups by early traders, the significance of which was not lost on either party (Colnett 1940; de la Pérouse 1798: 372). Aside from its tactical value, the musket itself symbolised power, and could be and was used in a manner designed to intimidate the enemy. The intent was clear in 1794 when the Cumshewa placed an American captive with a musket in hand at the head of a flotilla of canoes on a war expedition against the Skidegate (Bishop 1967: 98).

4 | Culture contact viewed through ceramic petrography at the Pueblo mission of Abó, New Mexico

PATRICIA CAPONE

This chapter illustrates and offers explanations for the construction and reconstruction of social identity in the culture contact situation of early Franciscan missionisation of Southwestern Pueblos at the case study pueblo, Abó, New Mexico. Through comparing pre-mission and mission period ceramic production–exchange interaction networks, an understanding of continuity and change in the construction of Pueblo identity can be reached. Petrographic analyses reveal aspects of continuity and change in production and exchange. The results of the analyses indicate the maintenance of strong Pueblo ties to premission identity and active Pueblo involvement in the transformation of some aspects of society. The factors that appear to be most transforming are those that were met actively and were blended with pre-mission practices. Other factors related to the economic programmes of the mission appear to have been transforming. The religious and sociopolitical programmes of the missions did not overcome the persistence, and probably resistance, of Pueblo identity. The view of culture contact shown through petrographic analysis is an active meeting of worldviews on the part of indigenous people, as well as missionaries and colonisers, rather than passive collapse of indigenous society and traditional ideals.

I have two goals in exploring the nature of Pueblo–Spanish interaction. The first is to reconstruct the protohistoric Pueblo interaction networks that are evident in ceramic production–exchange between AD 1500 and 1680, just before and during the earliest phase of the missionisation of the Southwest. This reconstruction of protohistoric production–exchange helps to fill a general gap in cultural historical knowledge of the protohistoric period in Southwestern anthropology. The second goal is to use the new information on ceramic production–exchange to contribute to an understanding of cultural continuity and change in the construction of Pueblo identity. Both of these goals lead to the illustration and explanation of general theoretical questions regarding the construction and reconstruction of social identity as a result of culture contact. Protohistoric Rio Grande glaze ware ceramics at Abó Pueblo and other Salinas, New Mexico, pueblos provide the empirical record through which these issues are explored (Fig. 4.1). In this study, the

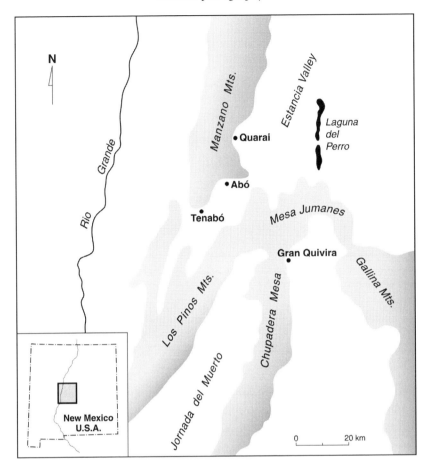

Fig. 4.1 Study area in New Mexico.

glaze wares are divided into two groups following Mera's (1933) Rio Grande glaze ware typology, pre-mission ceramics (1500–1630) and mission period ceramics (1630–80).

During the reconstruction of the two periods of ceramic production–exchange, the empirical record exhibits elements of both continuity and change. Aspects of production which change include features of context, concentration, scale and intensity (as defined by Costin (1991)). Regional and sub-regional exchange continue with similar general levels of organisation, but the specific arrangements of production centres and trading partners become reoriented (see Table 4.1).

During the exploration of continuity and change in the construction of Pueblo identity, the continuity of traditional aspects of Pueblo identity is supported by indigenous ceramic production–exchange. One

Table 4.1 Summary of change and continuity in aspects of glaze ware production–exchange over the protohistoric period

Aspect of glaze ware production–exchange	Change from pre-mission to mission period	Continuity from pre-mission to mission period
context of production – independent specialists	less independent	
concentration of production – dispersed	more dispersed	
intensity of production – possibly seasonal or part-time	may increase	
scale of production – at or below village level	smaller	
raw material choice		associated belief system
organisation of sub-regional production–exchange	specialisation somewhat reduced	specialisation still evident
organisation of regional production–exchange	directionality somewhat reoriented	specialisation and directionality still evident

major change, that of Pueblo accommodation at the mission at Abó, was accompanied by continuities and transformations. These transformations, although dramatic, have their origins and the strength of their continuity in pre-mission production–exchange and sociopolitical organisation. Because of strong traditional values, and strong links to sociopolitical functions, Pueblo ceramic production–exchange played an important part in transforming Pueblo identity into mission Pueblo identity, with its significant roots in pre-mission identity.

Exploring Pueblo identity through ceramics is possible because ceramic production–exchange transmits cultural information, as it continues to do into the present (Guthe 1925; Wyckoff 1985). In particular, the use of ceramics in ceremonial communal feasting, which relates to Pueblo worldviews, had a large impact on Pueblo identity, as suggested by the art compiled by Goldfrank (1970). Another example of aspects of production, which through ethnographic analogy (Guthe 1925) can be shown to relate to Pueblo identity, comprises symbolism in the types of raw materials chosen, including clay and inclusions or temper, and how they are processed. Mission challenges to these aspects of ceramic production, which are imbued with tradition, would have seriously threatened Pueblo identity.

Ceremonial feasting and the use of ceramics in those contexts provides another window into the changes to Pueblo identity among various subsets of people within a Pueblo village, for example within a clan, kiva, moiety or entire village (Hill 1982; Ortiz 1969; Parsons 1932). In general, various feasts are all necessary parts of a whole, and gifts are common at such feasts, even today. Studying the likely role of ceramics as prestige gifts at ceremonial feasts also provides another opportunity from which to examine protohistoric Pueblo identity. Provenance of glaze wares in both domestic and ceremonial contexts within pueblos suggests that most of the types of serving ceramics used in feasts also would have been used in domestic contexts. The mission's attempt to control ritual meant that feasts could not take place as they did before the mission's presence, and that use of ceramics in traditional practices associated with feasting that competed with Catholicism would have been challenged. This known prohibition of Pueblo religious dances, which are among the important feasts, would have challenged Pueblo identity.

To set the stage for the results of this analysis, I will outline a view of pre-mission ceramic production–exchange in terms of mission period factors that could have reproduced or transformed pre-mission patterns. This discussion of the organisation of production is framed in terms of Costin's (1991) descriptive model of the production process. Briefly, the descriptive parameters of her model are: context of production, concentration of production and scale, and intensity of production. This discussion of the organisation of exchange follows the models by Brumfiel and Earle (1987) and Renfrew (1977), with focus on directional exchange versus down-the-line exchange.

The context of pre-mission glaze ware production appears to be that of independent specialists. In general, the distribution of pre-mission production of glaze wares appears to be dispersed and it is present in most communities. However, nucleation is apparent for certain areas, such as the Galisteo Basin area. Pre-mission scale of production is not known. Pre-mission intensity of production may have been part-time and seasonal rather than full-time. In terms of pre-mission exchange, most pueblos appear to have produced some ceramics; however, the products of certain pueblos appear to have been traded in larger volumes than others, or in larger volumes than down-the-line exchange would predict. Some specialisation and directionality of exchange are suggested.

Mission period factors

A review of existing literature (archaeological, ethnohistorical and historical) on protohistoric Pueblo society illustrates a number of specific factors that could have led to continuity or change in ceramic production–exchange during the mission period. For the Salinas area, eight main factors can be identified:

1 introduction of new political officers and associated transformations of sociopolitical organisation,
2 transformation of aspects of prestige associated with feasting and gifting,
3 transformation of prestige associated with the control of marriage,
4 demands on Pueblo labour by mission and civil personnel,
5 mission supply networks as an exchange-structuring factor among mission pueblos,
6 demand for certain ceramics owing to changes in their use,
7 the mission programme goal of producing mission pueblo economic autonomy,
8 creation of new social alliances (e.g. traditionalist and progressive factionalism).

The relationship between aspects of ceramic specialisation and directionality of exchange, context, concentration, scale and intensity of production, and production technology, along with factors listed above, is explored for elements of continuity and change throughout this analysis.

Description of the results of the petrographic analysis

Petrographic analysis involved descriptions of the ceramic fabric as well as identification and sourcing of inclusions for each sample (Capone 1995); 171 protohistoric ceramic samples of glaze wares from the Salinas area form the sample set. The results presented here have implications for the organisation of ceramic production–exchange through time.

Discussion of the results of the fabric descriptions

Fabric descriptions shed light on aspects of ceramic technology such as processing of raw material, raw material choice, and firing and construction techniques. Most aspects of technology appear to become more expedient during the mission period. Particular fabric characteristics addressed here, which are informative about technology, are listed in Table 4.2. Fabric description terminology follows Whitbread's (1989) thin section description system.

Table 4.2 Aspects of technology and their associated petrographic characterstics used in this study

Aspects of technology	Petrographic characteristic
processing of raw material or choice of raw material source	average grain size of large fraction coarse:fine distribution (C:f) inclusion grain size frequency
choice of raw material	inclusion (temper) composition
firing of raw material source	optic state colour (oxidation/reduction)
construction technique	birefringence void frequency

Processing of raw material or raw material choice

Three characteristics, as listed in Table 4.2, suggest that there were changes in either the source or the processing of raw materials. First, average grain size of the large fraction; second, coarse:fine distribution, and inclusion grain size frequency. The changes in each of these characteristics suggest that inclusion and clay processing technology probably became more expedient and less standardised during the mission period when compared to the pre-mission period. The average grain size of the coarse fraction increases notably, which suggests more expedient processing of raw materials such as clay and temper. The coarse:fine distribution and the frequency of inclusion grain sizes show higher density of coarse grains in the mission period, which also suggests that raw materials were not processed at the same intensity to remove coarse material.

The choice of temper material remained the same from pre-mission to mission period. The distinction is made here between inclusion and temper material because temper refers only to material that is added by the potter, while inclusion material may be naturally occurring in the clay. Hornblende diorite material that was not naturally occurring at Abó continued to be the choice of material to be added as temper, which suggests that the reasons for which the material was chosen continued to be important into the mission period. The inclusions added as temper are distinguished by their angularity. Hornblende diorite would not have been the most expedient temper choice because it was not the nearest available functional material. This indicates that, even with the pressures for expedient production during the mission period, some aspects of technology and choice were consciously maintained.

Table 4.3 Summary of technologically informative petrographic characteristics of pre-mission and mission sherds from Abó

Petrographic characteristic	Pre-mission period sherds	Mission period sherds	Technological significance
average grain size of large fraction	400μ	600–800μ	change in processing of raw material or choice of material
coarse:fine distribution (c:f)	single-spaced	close-spaced or single-spaced	"
inclusion grain size frequency (c:f10μ)	50:50	60:40	"
inclusion (temper) composition	hornblende diorite	hornblende diorite	continuity of choice of raw material
optic state	slightly active	moderately active	change in firing or choice of raw material
colour (oxidation/ reduction)	more consistent	not consistent	change in firing or raw material
birefringence	undifferentiated	undifferentiated	continuity of construction technique
void frequency (average)	4 %	7–10 %	change in construction technique

Firing or choice of raw material

Two characteristics, optic state and colour (oxidation/reduction), suggest that there were changes in either firing or choice of raw material (see Table 4.3). Changes in these characteristics suggest that firing technology may have become more variable during the mission period. More optically active micromass and less consistent oxidation and reduction colour patterns show that mission period firing produced less consistent results and suggest that mission period firing technology was more expedient than pre-mission firing technology.

Changes in labour activities or work practices during the mission period may have altered pre-mission schedules, so that firing schedules may have been made more varied, or perhaps left up to the individual, and perhaps the attention to previous standards was no longer possible. Ethnographic information indicates that firing may have been undertaken cooperatively when potters were given the choice (Hill 1982). Cooperative firings may have resulted in more consistent firings because less chance would be left to individual idiosyncrasy. If an accepted standard was recognised by the group, and accomplished each time, consistent results could have been achieved.

Changes in labour activities or work practices during the mission period may have changed group schedules so that firing was more varied, or perhaps left up to the individual, and attention to previous standards was neglected.

Construction technique

Two characteristics, birefringence and void frequency, elucidate construction techniques through time. The continuity in birefringence pattern suggests that coiling techniques continued from the pre-mission period into the mission period. However, the notable increase in void frequency suggests that the fabric was not as compacted during the construction process. It also suggests that while the basic construction techniques continued through time, they were applied in a more expedient manner.

In sum, technology appears to have become more expedient during the mission period in several ways. Processing of clay and temper, firing, and construction techniques all suggest changes towards a more expedient production process. This behaviour may be due to the different pressures of the mission period, which included the increased demand for ceramic products and labour. Overall, the technology results directly and indirectly address aspects of continuity and change in the organisation of production. More expedient technology during the mission period indirectly implies change in context (towards more attached specialisation), concentration (towards more dispersed production) and scale (towards smaller scale of production). More expedient technology directly addresses the intensity of production, and may imply either its continuity or increase in intensity.

Continuity in choice of temper raw material stands out as a significant aspect of technology that remained unchanged during the mission period. In particular, the choice of a raw material which was not the most expedient material choice indicates that some aspects of technology were conserved even under the pressures of the mission period, while others were foregone. The continuity in use of this material may be related to a decision to maintain aspects of a belief system associated with the symbolic meaning of ceramics. The use of the same temper material in Spanish-introduced forms, such as soup-bowls, may represent some changes or syncretism in the symbolism of food consumption for those people using the Spanish forms. In sum, there may be more behavioural significance to temper than is immediately apparent, and this merits further study.

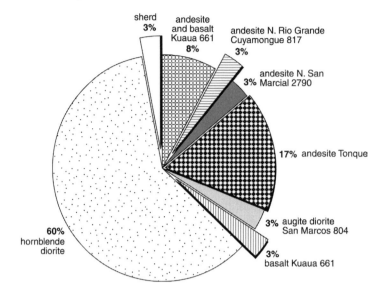

Fig. 4.2 Temper types in Abó pre-mission sherds (Glazes D and E); $n = 36$.

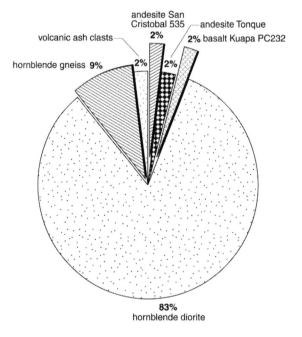

Fig. 4.3 Abó mission period sherds (Glaze F and soup bowls); $n = 56$.

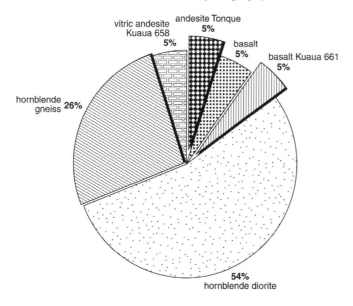

Fig. 4.4 Quarai pre-mission period sherds (Glazes C, D and E);
$n = 20$.

Implications of the inclusion identification results for the organisation of production–exchange

The identification of characteristic inclusion types indicates the source pueblo or sub-region of nearly all Rio Grande glaze wares because of the diverse geology of the Rio Grande. Petrographic determination of the sources of ceramics found at Abó as well as neighbouring Salinas pueblos offers insight into sub-regional and regional production–exchange patterns. The results of these identifications are summarised here with a focus on their implications for the organisation of production–exchange. Detailed descriptions of each sample and its source area may be found in Capone's (1995) presentation of the raw data.

Pie chart summaries of temper types in sherds found at the Salinas pueblos of Abó (Figs. 4.2 and 4.3) and Quarai (Figs. 4.4 and 4.5) for the pre-mission and mission periods present a visual impression of the patterns of inclusion types through time.

The analysis of sub-regional production–exchange demonstrates aspects of continuity and change. The dominance of Abó Pueblo in production–exchange within the Salinas sub-region, evidenced by the frequency of hornblende diorite temper, decreased to about 20 per cent from nearly

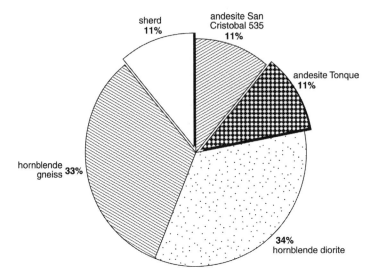

Fig. 4.5 Quarai mission period sherds (Glaze F); $n = 9$.

60 per cent, from pre-mission to mission period at pueblos other than Abó. At Abó the frequency of its own products increased from 60 per cent to 83 per cent. The increase in local ceramics during the mission period may be due to the increased demand by new consumers attached to the mission. The concurrent decrease in imports may be due to the mission programme of economic autonomy. However, the frequency of imports at other Salinas sites remains about the same.

Quarai's circulation of glaze wares, evidenced by the frequency of hornblende gneiss at other Salinas pueblos, increased from about 3 per cent during the pre-mission to about 20 per cent during the mission period. However, Quarai does not approach the degree of dominance that Abó previously held. Therefore, some centralisation and dominance continued although relocated and contracted. Aspects of missionisation such as the supply caravans and the goal of mission pueblo autonomy may have been involved in relocating and reducing the degree of sub-regional centralisation.

Regional long-distance exchange shows evidence of both continuity and transformation. Evidence of continuity is reflected in the specialisation and preferential trade which is demonstrated by the continuity of the Galisteo district's dominance of long-distance exchange into the mission period. The Galisteo district is represented by sherds from the Tonque and San Marcos areas. This evidence supports the continuity of a sociopolitical organisation related to this specialised system, into the mission period, despite the mission efforts to force change. However, the disappearance of the Southern Rio Grande Socorro district, represented by sherds in San Marcial, from the mission period regional long-distance exchange network, suggests transformation. Such a transformation may be due to factors related to missionisation such as supply caravans which came to the Salinas area from the Galisteo area to the north and their intense impact on the Southern Rio Grande.

The shift at Abó, away from dominance in production and frequency of regional imports, suggests that Abó's position as a central node of ceramic production–exchange during the pre-mission period changed during the mission period, and at the same time that Quarai's role as a node of ceramic production–exchange increased. A factor in Abó's pre-mission dominance may have been its location as a gateway between the Plains and South Central Rio Grande pueblos, which was an active trade route during that time. The activity along that route may have waned during the mission period with the increased impact of mission programmes at the Southern Rio Grande pueblos. A factor in Quarai's increased role may be that Quarai's location functioned as a mission period gateway to the northern concentrations of missions along the eastern side of the mountains in the Galisteo area and at Pecos Pueblo.

A basic level of sub-regional production–exchange and regional exchange in the Salinas sub-region continues through time despite the impositions of mission programmes. The accommodation of new groups of people, who were associated with the missions, in the glaze ware exchange system was accompanied by transformations in some aspects of production–exchange, along with significant continuity in the specialisation and the organisation of exchange. Transformations have been shown to have roots in the pre-existing organisation of exchange and sociopolitical groupings.

The addition of new consumers and their goals affected existing techniques and organisation of production–exchange in various ways. Incresed demand on Pueblo labour by mission and civil personnel, mission supply caravan routes, and the creation of new social alliances, appear to have been factors involved in the transformation of glaze ware production–exchange based on the evidence examined here. Conversely, the introduction of new political officers and attempted changes to sociopolitical organisation, the transformation of prestige associated with the control of marriage, and the mission goal of Pueblo economic autonomy, do not appear to have been as effective in changing glaze ware production–exchange. In this way, production–exchange shows that mission Pueblo identity, with strong links to pre-mission identity, was created and re-created while being challenged by the mission programme.

Acknowledgements

The National Science Foundation provided primary funding for this research. Sigma Xi, the Scientific Research Society, funded the pilot study. The following institutions and agencies supported this research by allowing loans of ceramics and sampling of geological materials: the Laboratory of Anthropology at the Museum of New Mexico, Salinas Pueblo Missions National Monument, the University of Colorado Museum and the United States Department of Agriculture Forest Service. I thank Robert Preucel, Katherine Spielmann and Ian Whitbread for their valuable advice and guidance.

5 | The transformation of indigenous societies in the south-western Cape during the rule of the Dutch East India Company, 1652–1795

YVONNE BRINK

The VOC (Dutch East India Company) governed by the word. Textuality was a major factor in its world. In the process of acquiring a surfeit of things, the Company employed a surfeit of words. Rhetoric, discourse, language, writing, all played a crucial role in realising the mercantile dream of worldly riches: 'As far back as 6 December 1621 . . . the Council of seventeen issued an order requiring a Journal to be kept at every one of the Company's stations. In this Journal a careful record had to be kept of everything that happened there' (Thom 1952, I: xxvi). What this means is that, except for the time covered by a few lost records, we know something of what happened at the Cape on every single day of the almost 150 years of VOC rule.

Analysis of VOC writing can therefore yield a great deal of information about Cape colonial history, but analysts need to be aware that even 'historical' documents inhere in language and cannot simply be read as direct reflections of reality. The strangeness, the problematic nature of language, must be taken into account. For example, its polysemy (language is always open to more than one interpretation); its narrative drive (language always desires to tell a story); the existence of a gap between sign and referent (there is no precise overlap between word and thing). Derrida (1977) sums it up when he speaks of the impossibility for language to be clear and precise. What is more, meaning often resides as much in the not-said as the said. This is illustrated by an old joke about a ship's captain who, after explaining to his first mate and good friend that he had no option but to report the latter's being drunk on duty, duly entered in his log: today the first mate was drunk. Some days later the mate took over command when the captain was ill. His log entry read: today the captain was sober. A silly story, perhaps, but it underlines the creative role of the listener or reader in the construction of meaning – a role which readers of historical documents often suppress in attempts to read 'objectively' and 'scientifically'. Allowing reader creativity free play, however, can reveal the rhetorical strategies, ambiguities, outright contradictions and inconsistencies hidden within the seemingly very ordinary language of official documents and other forms of historical writing. The less obvious meanings of such texts can thus be brought to light.

Two documents are of special interest for this chapter: an Oath of
Allegiance, and a list of instructions issued to the first Commander at the
Cape. Ironically, the main focus will be the history of people who did *not* take
the oath and the ways in which their story is linked to the duplicity inherent
in contradictory instructions during the Dutch colonial period. The chapter discusses the attitudes of the VOC towards the indigenous people of the
Western Cape, emphasising the ambiguous relationship between Company
officialdom and the Khoikhoi herder population. The aim is to explain the
injury done to the latter, and to show how this resulted in the transformation
of local communities prior to the British occupation in 1795.

Before the VOC established a halfway station at the Cape under Commander Jan van Riebeeck in 1652 the indigenous inhabitants of the region
had already been stereotyped and categorised as totally inferior outsiders by
a travel discourse in circulation in Europe (Hall 1999b; Ritchie 1990; Ross
1994) – a discourse which did much to reinforce the superior view Europeans
already had of themselves compared to the populations of all other continents. The age of exploration had brought with it a tremendous European
interest in all manner of strange objects, plants, animals and natural phenomena gathered together from reports of ships' crews and elaborated upon
imaginatively by authors in Europe. Included in the exotica were the hitherto
unknown people of far-flung regions of the globe. Not least among those
given attention were the so-called 'Hottentots' and 'Bushmen' of the Cape:
'Writer after writer referred to them in exceedingly denigrating terms . . . Stories of their drunkenness, their grease-covered dirtiness, and their language,
always compared to the gobbling of turkeys (hence the word "hottentot"),
became current in Europe' (Ross 1994: 81). Perhaps the most interesting
references, considering the VOC's fascination with rhetoric, are those which
deal with their deficiency in language, as they suggest an inability to master
'human' articulation so that their speech purportedly resembled natural
sounds. Ritchie has gathered together some examples: 'they clocke with the
tongue like a brood hen (1598)'; they have 'a very strange speech, clucking
like turkeys (1601)'; 'when they speak they fart with their tongues in their
mouths (1649)'. This supposed deficiency in speech must have played a part
in raising doubts, even in as eminent a scientist as Linnaeus, as to whether
such inferior beings could justifiably be classified as human (Ross 1994).

Nevertheless, it is important that they were, in the end, classified as
humans by anthropologists because, as Coetzee (1989: 120) points out, in
order for the differences between indigenes and Europeans to signify, the
type needed to be 'perceived and conceived within a framework of sameness'.
If they were not human, 'savage' behaviour such as smearing themselves with

animal fat or dung, never washing, wearing stinking skin garments, eating uncleaned animal entrails, and so on, would have been meaningless for purposes of reinforcing otherness.

It was precisely their underdeveloped form of humanity which enabled the VOC to consolidate further the established discourse by incorporating the same principles into its rhetorical strategies as it proceeded to structure a textual identity for the underclass within its own ranks. As part of their methods to control the poverty-stricken, mostly illiterate, often rumbustious employees recruited from the streets of Amsterdam and other European cities, all employees were made to swear an Oath of Allegiance to the VOC before embarkation in Holland. Analysis of the oath has revealed its discursive devices for fashioning and maintaining a status hierarchy within the circle of the 'civilised', that is, Christian people from Europe. The oath stresses the necessity for those who swear to honour abstract, civilised, biblical qualities: loyalty, faithfulness, obedience, good conduct. But only those who were aware of and appreciated the value of such qualities, that is, the civilised, were worthy of taking the oath. By gathering Europeans together within the circle of the civilised, where a separate sub-division into high and low could be fashioned, the oath simultaneously drew a line between colonists and indigenes, thus cordoning off the unoathed heathen savages who had no understanding of its biblical values (Brink 1992). In fact, it was not until 1819 that it became customary 'to administer oaths to slaves, Hottentots, and persons of similar condition on account of their ignorance of all religious obligation' (Ross 1994: 178). This means that exclusion (setting apart) of indigenous inhabitants was achieved symbolically through an oath that was not said before it was ever striven for in a physical, material or practical sense.

It did not take long, however, for symbolic separation to be made real and visible at the Cape. The fort constructed by Van Riebeeck and the thick, thorny hedge with which he surrounded it mirrored the unspoken division in the oath, marking the invisible line drawn between civilised and savage, Christian and heathen, those inside and the excluded.

The Khoisan people of the south-western Cape

'Khoisan' is an umbrella term for people who had been living at the Cape for centuries before the advent of European colonisation. It conveniently links two groups of people with physical and linguistic affinities and appears to be the term used most frequently by historians writing mainly about the nineteenth-century Cape colony (Elphick 1977; Ross 1994; Watson 1991; Worden and Crais 1994). Possibly this is because by that time the history of the two societies had converged to a large extent, but perhaps also, as we shall see further on, because some scholars believe that the two groups had already converged by the time the Europeans arrived. For most archaeologists, however, the blanket term is unsatisfactory, as archaeological research in the Western Cape, mainly by Parkington on Later Stone Age sites and Smith on herder sites, reveals two distinct groups: one which existed by hunting and gathering, the San, or 'Bushmen' in colonial terminology; and another, the Khoikhoi or 'Hottentots', who were pastoralists.

The prehistory of central and southern Africa is dominated by the belief that aboriginal hunter-gatherer groups occupying the land were displaced through time by iron-using communities moving southwards in streams, the directions of which vary according to the views of the scholar (Phillipson 1977; Maggs 1980; Huffman 1981). Before the arrival of the Iron Age people, however, some hunter-gatherer groups had long been in contact with stone tool using pastoralists and suffered the consequences of pastoralism on their traditional hunting grounds (Smith 1992). Domestic stock put pressure on wild animals through competition for grazing and water. According to Smith, studies on modern pastoralist groups have demonstrated that when hunter-gatherers and food producers compete in environments where both economies are potentially viable, it is the hunter-gatherers who lose out. The latter can react in three ways – first, by becoming pastoralists themselves. Although Smith believes that some hunter-gatherers must have resorted to this option at various times, it is a slow and difficult process. More often the strategies are for hunter-gatherers either to take refuge in marginal areas not of interest to pastoralists where they can exploit lower-ranked resources, or to enter into client/patron relationships with pastoralists, even though this means entering pastoralist society at the very lowest level (Smith 1992). Both Smith and Parkington (1984) believe that this was the situation in which Cape hunter-gatherers found themselves during the seventeenth century.

Although early agropastoralists never occupied the south-western Cape as the Mediterranean climate of the region was unsuitable for their summer rainfall crops, both Parkington and Smith believe that San society experienced a major disruption at the hands of pastoralists. Herders of small stock usurped San territory, forcing them to subsist largely on snared or collected animals and plant foods supplemented with stock stolen from their pastoralist neighbours when the opportunity arose. Parkington (1984) goes so far as to liken this protohistorical disruption of their world to the later disruption of Khoikhoi society by the Dutch. The later event lowered the carrying capacity of the land 'in the same way as the intrusion of pastoralism into a hunters' world had reduced the viability of an exclusively foraging economy'. He sees aboriginals as 'residual hunter-gatherers who had survived the appearance of pastoralism by a combination of economic and distributional responses while none the less living in the interstices of pastoralist society' (Parkington 1984: 164). Living in the interstices of pastoralist society covers client/patron relationships whereby Khoikhoi granted patronage to destitute San people, paying in kind for services which took the form of acting as messengers, watchers over stock, spies, and assistants in raids on the stock of other Khoikhoi groups. In exchange for their keep, clients were prepared to be incorporated into Khoikhoi society on the fringes of the bottommost level of the social hierarchy (Smith 1992).

Driven, as they frequently were, to stealing, the seventeenth-century San who continued to exist as foragers in the mountainous areas after the arrival of the Dutch did not discriminate between Khoikhoi and Dutch farmers when robbing them of stock. While the Khoikhoi despised and feared them, the Dutch reacted with angry revenge, often shooting them on sight. The crisis conditions under which the San were already existing when the Dutch arrived were thus exacerbated by vengeful attacks and the diseases – most notably smallpox – which the colonists brought with them.

Not all researchers agree that there was still a clear San/Khoikhoi distinction during the seventeenth century. Elphick (1977) and Schrire (1980) feel that what distinctions there once had been had long been obliterated by that time. They maintain that members of these communities could easily switch back and forth between the two modes of living. In an effort to resolve the issue Parkington (1984) looked to archaeology. His aim was to find out whether there was evidence for a different hunter-gatherer pattern for disrupted San communities, which he called *Soaqua* – a name derived from historical documents.

First he found that evidence for a Soaqua pattern is suggested by a change in site distribution. Before 1800 years ago, when the only inhabitants of the region were hunter-gathers, there appears to have been a preference for open sites on the coastal plain, where windbreaks were probably built for shelter. Some caves were utilised, for example Klipfonteinrand (for sites mentioned in the text see Fig. 5.1), which shows occupation to around 5000 years ago. In these lower levels there is evidence for the hunting of fairly large game.

From about 2000–1800 years ago there is a shift in favour of rock shelters in mountainous regions. De Hangen is an example of an excavation which Parkington believes to be typical of many rock shelters in the area. Regular

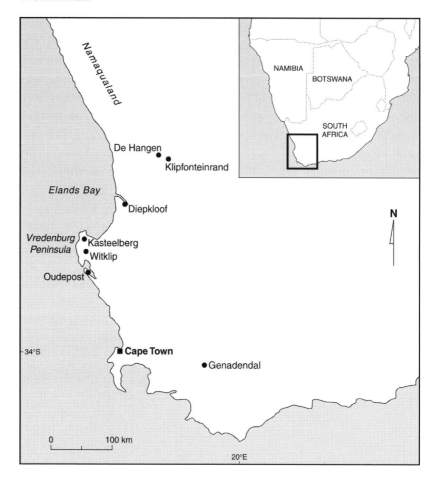

Fig. 5.1 Location of sites mentioned in the text.

occupation only dates back about 1800 years. Faunal evidence in these sites shows a clear shift away from the hunting of larger game (eland, hartebeest, zebra) to an emphasis on snared or collected smaller animals (tortoise, hare, rock rabbit, and shellfish in coastal sites). The toolkit substantiates this type of shift and also points towards greater exploitation of plant food. Very significantly, two elements associated with pastoralism are also found at sites like De Hangen, namely sheep bones and potsherds. It is also significant that in sites with deep deposits such as Klipfonteinrand and Diepkloof the Soaqua pattern does not show until levels of the same date as De Hangen, that is, around 1800 years ago. Elands Bay Cave and Tortoise Cave which have deep coastal sequences exhibit the same type of change when domestic animals appear (Parkington 1984).

While not considering this evidence to be unequivocal proof of his hypothesis, Parkington nevertheless feels justified in concluding that 'the Soaqua pattern of greater emphasis on gathering than on hunting arose at least in part as a response to the appearance of pastoralism in the landscape' (Parkington 1984: 172). In contrast to Elphick (1977) and Schrire (1980), who see 'more continuity between the stock-owning and Soaqua lifeways and less between aboriginal hunter-gatherers and those referred to as Soaqua', Parkington sees Soaqua lifeways as different from herding, 'while not denying the shadowy quality of intercommunity boundaries' (Parkington 1984: 168).

I find Parkington's conclusions convincing enough to believe that, by the time the halfway station was established at the Cape, disruption of the hunting and gathering way of life had already been taking place for over a thousand years. Dispersed and living in inhospitable refugia, it was, then, only the remnants of aboriginal San communities who came into contact with the colonists. Their numbers had been depleted in the Western Cape by fighting, disease and emigration – northwards towards Namibia, and eastwards towards the arid Karoo. In addition, many might have abandoned their traditional way of life to live in servitude among the Khoikhoi.

The San had nothing to offer the VOC. The Company considered them a nuisance to be eradicated, while occurrences of stock theft led to open animosity resulting in many deaths. As far as the San are concerned, the contact experience can be seen as a rapid and particularly vicious intensification of a process of undermining originating in prehistoric times. What had remained of San society in the Western Cape when the Dutch arrived had been almost totally destroyed by the time the VOC handed the government over to the British.

Khoikhoi pastoralists and Dutch colonists

The disruption of Khoikhoi herder communities was a more complex process, partly because of the more complex nature of pastoralist societies in general and of Cape pastoralists in particular, but also because the relationship between the Company and the Khoikhoi was more complex. The Khoikhoi had something vital to offer the Company. The success of the lucrative Dutch trade with the East depended in no small measure on a mundane product: meat. The Company therefore had at least to appear to be more careful in its dealings with the Khoikhoi than was necessary with the San.

The official policy towards the Khoikhoi is set out in the instructions to Van Riebeeck, but analysis of VOC documents which, as I have demonstrated elsewhere (Brink 1992), together constituted a whole discourse of domination shows that VOC words and VOC actions did not always coincide. For example, in the Official Prayer recited when Council of Policy meetings were opened, the top Cape officials prayed for guidance in upholding justice and in bringing the Christian teaching to the *wilde en brutale menschen* (wild and unrefined people) of the Cape. They saw themselves as specially called by God to convert the uncivilised heathen (Brink 1992). As Coetzee (1994) has remarked, however, the Dutch never undertook any official mission work during their stay at the Cape, while Schoeman (1997) describes open VOC animosity towards Moravian missionaries.

An example of VOC duplicity comes to light from free burgher land grants. Free burghers were employees contracted out of Company service to farm or pursue trades on their own account. The deeds grant land 'in full ownership', yet in the same document the Company reserves the right to repossess the land if the free burgher does not behave in keeping with his promises in the oath. Evaluation of free burgher behaviour resided solely with the Company.

The duplicitous contradiction which concerns us here is found in two sets of instructions issued to Commander Van Riebeeck on 25 March and 12 December 1651. In the first document Van Riebeeck is instructed not to 'injure [the natives] in person or in the cattle which they keep' (Moodie 1960: 8). Elphick and Malherbe (1989: 11) point out that the directors considered the Khoikhoi a free people who were 'to be treated with respect and consideration'. These seemingly altruistic ideals were contradicted when the later instruction ordered Van Riebeeck to find out where the best lands and pastures were located and to map them 'as a proof that such arable ground and fields have been taken possession of by you for the Company' (Moodie 1960: 9). From the moralist high ground of those who saw themselves as chosen by God to lead the heathen of southern Africa to salvation, the directors urged their commander to treat the herders with respect and consideration, but none the less to plunder their pastures. The instructions thus simultaneously affirmed and subverted the VOC notion of the Khoikhoi as 'a free people' even before the settlement was established. It is difficult to imagine anything more injurious or disrespectful to a herder community than taking unauthorised possession of their best lands and pastures.

Treating the Khoikhoi with respect while taking their land is only one example of the subversive irony in VOC texts which the Company itself never confronted. Irony also lies in their dependence for success on the abhorrent, excluded *Other*. It lies in the anger expressed in Van Riebeeck's journal when the Khoikhoi moved their herds away from Table Bay and refused to barter, although it was the Company that had driven the herders away by appropriating their grazing. Irony lies in the manner in which Khoikhoi were taken to task and punished for stealing stock, while the Company went scot free for stealing lands and pastures. And it lies insidiously in the way that those outsiders excluded from the founding document in the VOC discourse of domination, the Oath of Allegiance, are none the less a pervasive presence in VOC texts.

The VOC attempted to cover up duplicity in various ways. The noble task of Christianising the heathen and the policy of non-violence towards the Khoikhoi hide the violence of colonial occupation. Textualising the land, submitting it to the science of cartography, justifies its taking. Ostensive meanings in VOC texts always need to be treated with circumspection, and I want to focus here on the meaning of the word 'injury', as I believe the Dutch text suppresses its polysemy, making it refer only to physical injury. This left officials free to deploy any other forms of injury they deemed necessary for suppressing the Khoikhoi.

In order to understand the full gamut of injury inflicted on Khoikhoi communities by Dutch colonialism, we need to know something about Khoikhoi society. Whereas Parkington (1984) has focused on hunter-gathering sites, Smith (1992) has conducted extensive excavations at Kasteelberg, the major herder site in the Western Cape, where there is also evidence for hunting.

Situated on a granite outcrop on the Vredenburg Peninsula, this site has yielded the earliest dates thus far for herding in the area, namely 1860 BP and 1790 BP in levels with sheep bones and pottery. In one of the three sections of the site, KBC, a later Stone Age occupation with wild fauna dated to 2160 BP underlies levels with sheep and pottery dated to 1270 BP and is separated from the latter by a sterile horizon (Smith 1992). The earliest date for cattle, of 1300 BP, comes from the bottom of an area below the hill designated KBB. Since no cattle were found with the early sheep and pottery at KBA, Smith feels there are good grounds for assuming that cattle were introduced later than sheep, which means, as he expresses it, 'that the Khoikhoi were shepherds before they were cattle herders' (Smith 1992: 24). Dates from the Later Stone Age site areas also seem to indicate that disruption of hunter-gatherer economies was underway before the introduction of cattle.

At Witklip, a small shelter close to Kasteelberg, a lower-level sequence is dated from 3000 to 1400 BP, while middle levels with pottery date between 1400 and 800 BP and upper levels between 500 and 300 BP. Smith believes this indicates a hunting economy existing contemporaneously with pastoralists at Kasteelberg (Smith 1992). His interpretation of the evidence reads as follows: 'Incoming herders moved into territory already occupied by aboriginal hunting people around 1,900 BP, and probably displaced them from some of the areas they had previously occupied' (Smith 1992: 204). Shepherds and hunters probably coexisted, but the later introduction of cattle brought a greater degree of disruption to the latter. This is because small stock can thrive in drier areas unsuitable for cattle. With the introduction of cattle, herders would have required riverine areas with a regular water supply and better grazing, thus more forcefully preventing hunter-gatherers and wild animals from optimal use of these resources.

It appears that the majority of archaeologists who have worked on hunting and herding sites in the Western Cape, Parkington (1984), Smith, Sadr, Gribble and Yates (1991) and Smith (1992), agree that what the Dutch colonists encountered when they began to settle at the Cape in 1652 was small numbers of hunters continuing to eke out an existence which included thieving; and well-established herder communities which had successfully been building up flocks of sheep for about 1500, and herds of cattle for about 500 years. Like Parkington, Smith and his co-workers reject Elphick's (1977) cyclical model which sees one indigenous group, the Khoisan, living at the Cape prior to the arrival of the Dutch. Elphick proposes that indigenous people practised pastoralism during fortuitous times, but easily reverted to hunting and foraging when overcome by stock loss. When circumstances improved, they returned to herding. This model is based on historical documents and does not take archaeological evidence into account. Schrire and Deacon (1989), however, claim to have found archaeological evidence for the model in their analysis of stone tools from a single site, Oudepost I, on the Langebaan Lagoon. They argue that the difference in cultural patterning found by Parkington (1984) could be the result of herder/foraging rather than culturally and economically separate hunters with some herder influence. Schrire and Deacon conclude that 'it is the context of the artefacts rather than the form or typology that will inform on who made them' (Schrire and Deacon 1989: 12), and the context at the Company outpost of Oudepost I was one of Khoikhoi/colonial contact. Smith *et al.* (1991) reject this interpretation, chiefly because it does not take into account a period of twelve years during which the post was abandoned by colonists. Instead they suggest that the indigenous material could have been deposited by visiting hunters while colonists were absent. This rules out a Khoikhoi/colonial context.

For Smith and his collaborators interpretation of evidence from a number of sites demonstrates that hunters and herders maintained separate cultural and economic identities with hunters 'on the fringes of pastoral society in a lower class or subservient status' (Smith *et al.* 1991: 90). Current work on Kasteelberg sites by Sadr *et al.* (2003) has not as yet produced sufficient evidence to warrant a revision of this view (Smith, pers. comment). The debate continues.

Whereas it has been possible to identify the presence of a separate Khoikhoi society archaeologically, it is more difficult to glean information about the nature of such a society. A paper on cattle keeping among second-millenium agropastoralists in southern Africa (Hall 1986), however, raises issues which could be relevant to Khoikhoi pastoral society. Extending the work of structuralists (Huffman 1981; Kuper 1980) by using Giddens' structuration theory as a framework, Hall stresses the inadequacy of faunal analysis alone for informing us of the social values with which cattle keeping is invested. Kuper and Huffman have shown that there is more to cattle keeping than mere subsistence. Besides possession of cattle itself, for example, the very processes of the acquisition and alienation of the animals are invested with value. The processes themselves play a structuring role in agropastoralist societies, mainly in the creation and maintaining of hierarchies. Following Giddens, Hall sees the behaviour involved in cattle herding as recursive, 'that is, recreating patterns of behaviour, intentionally or unintentionally, by the very action of living them out in the present' (Hall 1986: 84). Part of this behaviour involved establishing networks of reciprocity among groups. Such networks, in which cattle stood at the centre, served as insurance for farmers against future adversity.

It is perhaps unlikely that the 'Bantu cattle pattern' of the structuralists (Hall 1986: 84) was as fully established among Cape herders of the seventeenth century as it was among early agropastoralists, but it could have been developing towards something very similar. Hall's paper shows that the role played by cattle was not static, but changed through time.

Smith believes that cattle did indeed play a social role among Cape herders, at least in signifying wealth and leadership. Cattle may also have been involved in marriage transactions. What is more, the fact that the Khoikhoi soon became reluctant to barter too many head of cattle for worthless consumables (copper, beads, tobacco) suggests that the type of insurance for the future described above may already have taken root at the Cape by the seventeenth century (Smith 1992). If this is so, cattle would have had values and meanings for the Khoikhoi ranging beyond the merely economic.

Interesting ethnographic information suggesting what seventeenth-century Khoikhoi social life may have been like has come to light from anthropological studies of modern remnants of a Khoikhoi group which was forced to move northwards beyond the boundaries of the old Cape Colony into the desert regions of the Richtersveld and the present Namibia. These are the Namaqua or Nama people who were able to continue with a herding existence as major disruption did not occur until they lost most of their cattle and much of their grazing in the nineteenth century.

The language many of the older Nama people still speak is believed to be a modern dialect of the original Khoikhoi language and a few of the traditions have also survived – mostly in the memories of older people, but occasionally, as with the Nama dwellings, also on the ground (Smith 1992). Smith reports on anthropological work by Hoernlé during the early years of this century among surviving Nama speakers of the Richtersveld and Namibia. He sees this work as 'the restricted data base from which Khoi social structure is reconstructed' (Smith 1992: 200).

Because of their pattern of transhumance the Khoikhoi had few material possessions. Only goods which could easily be transported on the backs of oxen were used regularly. These included reed mats, baskets, pottery, and personal items such as clothing, ostrich egg shell beads, weapons, and so on. According to Smith, Hoernlé describes a Khoikhoi camp as a circular layout of *matjeshuise* (reed mat huts) surrounded by a thorn fence for protection. Only immature animals were penned. Unpenned adults occupied the central space in the circle. Huts were used for sleeping, while cooking was done in a *skerm* (windbreak) next to the huts. The basic camp composition appears to have been the clan, that is, an extended family of men and their wives and children, as well as any clients that might have attached themselves to them. The huts were arranged strictly according to seniority of the clan males. A hierarchical system was thus visible in the Khoikhoi camp. Smith (1992), whose archival work is wide ranging and thorough, says that there is remarkable consistency in the historical accounts of Khoikhoi settlements. The number of huts varied, some villages having seventy or more.

One cannot write about Khoikhoi domestic architecture without acknowledging the work of James Walton (1995) on the *matjeshuise* of Namaqualand. According to Walton, the Nama continue to maintain many features of Nama life and 'this is particularly noticeable in their *matjeshuise* which they still build and which are identical with the traditional homes of the Khoikhoi' (Walton 1995: 13) (Figs. 5.2 and 5.3). In a valuable piece of ethnographic writing Walton goes on to describe precisely how these houses are constructed, from the pegging off of the required round or oblong shape, to the making of the reed mat covers. His chapter on the Nama ends with a description of how age-old traditions are being swallowed up by modernity, for now huts are sometimes covered with plastic, sacking or commercial matting instead of handmade reed mats. In a seminal paper on the architecture

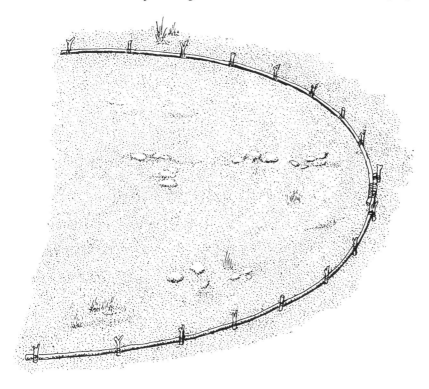

Fig. 5.2 Pegging off the framework for a Nama hut.

Fig. 5.3 A completed *matjeshuis*.

of mobile communities in southern Africa, Parkington and Mills (1989) explain how Khoikhoi settlement patterning and the use of space was also invested with social meaning. They see Khoikhoi settlements as material manifestations of social relations and closely connected to Khoikhoi personal identity. Just as livestock meant more than mere sustenance to the Khoikhoi, their huts meant more than mere shelter against the elements.

Besides focusing on Khoikhoi spatial organisation, the chapter highlights different concepts of dwelling between Cape hunter-gatherers and herders. This points towards considerable differences in beliefs and ideology, and strengthens the arguments of those who believe that easy switching back and forth between the two modes of dwelling probably only occurred in extreme cases. Whereas the Khoikhoi put a considerable amount of time, energy and care into the manufacture of their reed huts and used them over and over as they were transported when they trekked after grazing, hunter-gatherers slept in caves or rock shelters, or in hastily constructed temporary windbreaks of brush and rushes which were simply abandoned when they moved on. Historical documents testify to the use of such abandoned shelters by early European travellers at the Cape.

In contrast to the random and isolated windbreaks of the San, Parkington and Mills see Khoikhoi villages as constituted on the basis of asymmetric relations and encoded rules about how society ought to be and how people of varying status ought to conduct themselves in everyday Khoikhoi life. Settlement design was thus one way of reinforcing and preserving Khoikhoi values and power relations. Because of the constant production and reproduction of a traditional ideology, the authors believe that San or Soaqua rarely became Khoikhoi, and Khoikhoi did not simply become San by losing stock. Such a view is only possible when subsistence is seen as everything and little value is placed on signification and symbolism (Parkington and Mills 1989). The way in which people dwell, that is, live in their houses and inhabit their space, has everything to do with what a person is. Forcefully changing a person's manner of dwelling can seriously damage that person's sense of identity.

The transformation of Khoikhoi society

The transformation of Khoikhoi society centres around various forms of injury inflicted on the people. Physical injury occurred, for the most part, during two wars which began when Dutch frustration with thieving, refusal to barter and reluctance to labour for the Company boiled over. Injury owing to personal Dutch/Khoikhoi vendettas was relatively rare during the VOC period. But physical injury almost pales into insignificance when we consider the more subtle social, ideological and symbolic injury inflicted on Khoikhoi communities and we begin to realise the inadequacy of the simplistic instruction not to injure their persons or their cattle. Clearly, too, injunctions to treat them with respect and consideration were seldom, if ever, acted out in practice. To the colonists at the Cape, the Khoikhoi remained the despised unoathed, the outsiders, the inferior Other.

While loss of stock through barter and appropriation, and loss of pastures through ploughing of the land for expanding colonial agriculture, as well as the Company's increasing need for grazing for its own growing herds, had important economic ramifications for the Khoikhoi, it is not possible to discuss these losses in terms of economics only. We have seen how livestock, perhaps cattle especially, had meanings for the Khoikhoi over and above the purely economic. Discussing what he refers to as 'pastoral psychology', Smith sees it as embedded, among other things, in the very different attitudes to animals between hunters and herders. Informed both by ethnography and by rock paintings, Lewis-Williams (1981) has explained how wild bovids, especially the eland, played a role in the structuring of San identity. Assuming that something akin to the Bantu cattle pattern was developing at the Cape, we can be sure that domestic animals would have played a role in the structuring of Khoikhoi identity. This means that the different attitudes to animals would have been even greater between Khoikhoi and colonists than between Khoikhoi and San. What the Dutch received when Khoikhoi were persuaded to part with their livestock was meat. What the Khoikhoi gave was more precious than meat, and included not only wealth, prestige and security for the future, but something of their human identity as well.

Not all researchers fully take into account the significance of the loss of identity when explaining the rapid disintegration of Khoikhoi society after colonisation. Elphick and Malherbe, for instance, seek reasons for decline in internal weaknesses in Khoikhoi society itself, mainly in 'their penchant for prolonged vendettas and stop-start wars'. These authors see the European presence as merely aggravating 'a normal phase in this recurring cycle of Khoikhoi history' (Elphick and Malherbe 1989: 19). They are only prepared to concede that the Company's demands on Khoikhoi livestock prolonged and intensified the decline and prevented what might have been 'normal' recovery.

Rejecting internal weaknesses as a possible cause – and pointing out that the herders had been operating successfully for about 1600 years – Smith (1992) ascribes the decline solely to European intervention, not least important of which was the VOC's ban on raiding between Khoikhoi groups. Smith has researched pastoral groups throughout Africa and speaks with authority when he stresses the importance of raiding, proclaiming it to be an integral part of pastoralist society and political structure. He maintains that it is misleading to explain Khoikhoi raids in terms of vendettas and stop–start wars. Finding documentary evidence for raiding at the Cape, he claims that the fortunes of the stronger clans were dependent on maintaining their ability to raid. The VOC interfered indirectly by acting as protectors to the weaker clans, or by arbitrating between groups. Smith sees such interference as having had a damaging effect on Khoikhoi concepts of the self. We may therefore conclude that raiding marks another point at which economic and social factors converge.

As Parkington (1984) has suggested, the Khoikhoi were, in a sense, suffering a fate similar to that inflicted centuries before on the aboriginal hunter-gatherers. While some groups, for example the Nama, trekked away, others became labourers for the Company or on free burgher farms. Here, like the hunter-gatherers of yore, they became loosely affiliated to colonial society at a level on the social ladder lower even than that of the slaves (Crais 1994).

The illiterate Khoikhoi leaders left no journals. We have no day-to-day accounts of pastoral life under colonial rule. To try to understand the disruption of Khoikhoi society we have to make use as judiciously as we can of what Thomas (1996: 63) has called our 'archaeological imagination'. What, for example, did it mean for a Khoikhoi person to enter into a boss/labourer relationship on a free burgher farm?

In the first place it probably meant survival, but there was a price to pay in terms of lost identity. Bonds with the extended family of the clan system – a system which daily kept people secure in the knowledge of who they were and where they ought to be within it – would have been severed. Living in isolation would have been strange to the Khoikhoi person. Even though farm labourers were at first allowed to live in their own huts (Elphick and Malherbe 1989), the behaviour-structuring process of the Khoikhoi camp, like that of the clan system, would have been lost. Isolated huts, removed from their context within the village, would have lost much of their signifying power. Removed from its social setting, a single hut might have played a negative role by marking the labourer's menial position and reinforcing otherness. Then, too, the practical value of the *matjeshuis* was connected to the mobility of the transhumance pattern. When stasis replaced mobility there was, perhaps, little advantage to living in a reed mat hut. The few head of stock some labourers were allowed to keep probably brought consolation, but stock possession, too, would have lost much of its meaning when deprived of its ability to structure relations within clan or community. In addition, there would have been no further purpose for information networks carefully built up over time. As Thomas (1996) has eloquently explained, having a stable identity means living in a relationship with the people and the things around you, being in attunement with the rhythms of everyday experience, and engaging in your world in a meaningful way. When a world is disrupted, personal identity suffers – and the world of the Khoikhoi labourer would have been radically disrupted.

Understandably, then, Khoikhoi society grew more and more divided through the eighteenth century. On the one hand there were those who tried to continue with the traditional way of life by moving away, out of the reach of VOC tentacles. Then there were those who became conditioned to farm labour and developed a new loyalty to their employers. It became impossible for a leader to come to the fore – a form of politics which had in any case always been foreign to the Khoikhoi way of life – around whom the remnants of the pastoralist population could rally in order to organise a meaningful and united resistance. The increasing employment of both Khoikhoi and San as farm labourers was aggravated during the 1780s by a system of indenture according to which so-called 'slaaf Hottentotte' (slave Hottentots) were hired for their lifetime. As the name implies, the lot of these people was no better than that of slaves (Crais 1994). Crais believes that a sub-culture developed among the unfree during the late eighteenth century, but it was not until the nineteenth century that we see the emergence of a consciousness which linked widely dispersed people and led to the gathering together and recording of memories of better days. Outright questioning of 'the economic exploitation and patriarchal pronouncements of the master-class' (Crais 1994: 276–7) could only occur much later.

The materiality of Khoikhoi existence, the physicality of rituals, cattle keeping, packing up and moving at regular intervals, and dwelling in accordance with an established signifying system changed radically as more and more people were made to live by Dutch rules and regulations. People in whose lives literacy had never been a factor were drawn ever more closely into the textuality of Dutch colonial existence: the landscape where they had once roamed freely with their livestock had fallen prey to the VOC's obsession with measuring, surveying and mapping, whether of urban plots, town layouts, farms or the colonial boundary itself (Brink 1992, 1997). Although often unfenced on the ground, farms were bounded on paper by carefully written descriptions and precisely drawn diagrams. Injustices such as stock theft were resolvable no longer by in-your-face revenge attacks or raids, but through drawn out and often unintelligible rhetoric in courts of law. Labour was organised by indenture, the hated *inboekstelsel* (booking-in system) (Crais 1994), and mere words uttered by the boss could mean cooption into military service to fight the Company's battles against their own people.

All of this aggravated the loss of personal as well as social identity. Following Thomas (1996) once more, identity means knowing your past, knowing who you are in the present, and being able to project your innermost possibilities into the future. Members of the Cape pastoralist communities must have been very uncertain of their position in the present, and the future must have looked bleak in 1774 when a General Commando was called out by the now distant VOC government to punish the Khoikhoi because too many complaints of raids and attacks on homesteads were being received from Bushmanland, as the Karoo region was then called. Given the authority to recover stolen livestock, but also 'where required to wage war against all of the region's Khoisan', the slaughter was immense (Elphick and Malherbe 1989: 27). By this decree the ban on physical injury to the Khoikhoi and their cattle was formally shelved forever, while the plundering of indigenous territory continued unabated.

Eighteenth-century mission work (by German Moravians, not by the Dutch) offers an indication of how Khoikhoi attachment to their own social values had weakened over a period of about fifty years. When missionary Georg Schmidt first founded a mission station at Baviaanskloof (later Genadendal) in 1737 to work among the Khoikhoi there were so few genuine converts that he was forced to close it in 1744. But when three Moravians reopened the mission in 1793, many Khoikhoi were eager to accept the Christian way of life (Elphick and Malherbe 1989).

When the British first occupied the Cape in 1795, instead of a tiny halfway station they found a fully fledged colony measuring roughly 110,000 square miles (Giliomee 1979) with a north-eastern frontier, where the disruption of Khoikhoi society was virtually complete. It was with the socially more organised, militarily stronger and generally more warlike agropastoralists of the Eastern Cape that the British were mainly destined to contend.

Acknowledgements

I thank Mrs A. Simmonds for kindly granting me permission to reproduce two of James Walton's illustrations, Antonietta Jerardino for drawing the map, and Mrs Hanna Botha of the J. W. Gericke Library, Stellenbosch, for giving me access to Walton's original work.

6 | Contact archaeology and the landscapes of pastoralism in the north-west of Australia

RODNEY HARRISON

Introduction

Archaeological research on contact sites in the south-east Kimberley region of Western Australia provides a database with which to examine social change as well as changes in material culture that occurred as a result of contact between indigenous and settler Australians on pastoral stations in the recent past. One such station is Old Lamboo, located south of the town of Halls Creek. The history and archaeology of the station highlights some of the ways in which Aboriginal people in the east Kimberley developed new social identities for themselves, which were separate from both the colonising group as well as the parent society itself. In doing so, they created new meanings for existing items of material culture as well as for 'exotic' items from the settler groups that were incorporated into the existing material culture. As a result of such contact, both indigenous and settler Australians on pastoral stations developed new, shared ways of understanding landscape that were the product of the unique historical circumstances of contact in the north-west of Australia.

The study area: south-east Kimberley

The setting

The Kimberley region is located in the far north of Western Australia (see Fig. 6.1), and has a semi-arid to arid monsoonal climate (Beard 1979: 17). The effect of monsoons on rainfall is extreme, resulting in hot, wet summers and cooler, dry winters. The Kimberley receives over 90 per cent of its rainfall between the months of November and April (Bureau of Meteorology 1996: 16). Halls Creek, the largest town in the south-east Kimberley, receives on average 521mm of rain per year (Bureau of Meteorology 1996). These two seasons, the 'wet' and the 'dry', and their associated extremes, form one of the most important rhythms of life for all living creatures in the region.

The topography of the area is diverse, and ranges from the sand plains of the Great Sandy and Tanami Deserts in the extreme south, to the broad

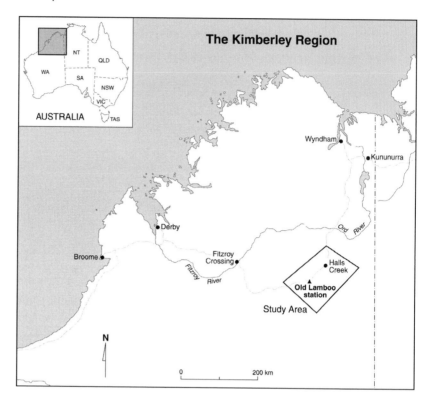

Fig. 6.1 Map of Kimberley region showing major towns and river systems and location of the study area.

dissected Kimberley Plateau and rugged, rocky uplands of the King Leopold Ranges. The vegetation of the south-east Kimberley is characterised by spinifex grasslands with woodland and shrubland cover (Beard 1979: 41–2). The location and reliability of freshwater sources changes seasonally, and most rivers and creeks flow only as a result of wet season rains. The most reliable permanent water sources are the Ord and Fitzroy rivers (see Fig. 6.1). The Margaret, Mary and Black Elvire rivers are the main river systems in the study area.

Very little is known about the pre-contact history of the southeast Kimberley. Excavations at the site of Carpenter's Gap in the west Kimberley have revealed basal radiocarbon determinations of 39 220+/−870 years before present (O'Connor 1995, McConnell and O'Connor 1997), suggesting that Aboriginal people have been present in the greater Kimberley region for over 39 000 years. Dortch (1977) undertook salvage excavations at a number of rockshelters in the Ord River Valley in the east Kimberley during the 1970s. Type sequences in the Ord River Valley are generally considered to show changes in stone tool assemblages at around 3500 years before the present, with the beginning of biface point (commonly known in Australia as 'Kimberley' points because of their limited distribution in the north of Australia) manufacture (Dortch 1977). This may be considered part of a set of Australia-wide changes in stone toolkits during the mid to late Holocene period (Bowdler and O'Connor 1991). The study area covers the traditional lands of Jaru, Kija and Gooniyandi language speakers, whose fluid estate boundaries met around the modern town of Halls Creek. My own excavations at rockshelters located in the area to the south of Halls Creek town have shown evidence of mid to late Holocene period occupation (Harrison and Frink 2000).

Indigenous–settler relations in the east Kimberley

The contact history of the east Kimberley is complex, but can be divided into a number of phases. In the earliest period, settlers attempted to pacify and disperse Aboriginal people using force. Aboriginal people often call this period 'killing times' (Kimberley Language Resource Centre 1996; see also Cribbin 1984 for Central Australia). After these initial contacts, Aboriginal people were slowly drawn into increased contact with Europeans through the establishment of ration stations. At around this time and shortly after, many Aboriginal people began to take up work in the pastoral industry. This was to cease in the 1960s after the closure of the government ration stations and the establishment of an award rate for workers in the pastoral industry.

Earliest contacts

The Kimberley region represented one of the last frontiers for European exploration, colonisation and settlement of Australia. As recently as 1870, there had been no successful British settlement in the far north-west of Australia. Although there were some initial contacts along the coast, the inland exploration and settlement of the Kimberley was a phenomenon of the mid to late nineteenth century. There had been several early abortive attempts at establishing British settlements in northern Australia. Port Essington in the Northern Territory was settled from 1838 until its abandonment in 1849 (Allen 1969, 1980), while Camden Harbour in the west Kimberley lasted only from 1864 until 1865 (Forrest 1996: 13ff). The failure of these settlements was largely a result of isolation from the major cities located in the south and east of the continent, and the general unsuitability of soils on the northern Australian coasts for agriculture. These forces remain as limiting factors to the settlement of the area even today (Mackenzie 1980: 43).

The Kimberley region was named in 1880 after the Earl of Kimberley, who was then Secretary of State for the Colonies (Beard 1979: 2). It is customarily divided into east and west. The east Kimberley experienced pre-settlement intrusion and contact with Europeans much later than the west Kimberley (Clement 1988). While the earliest contact between Aboriginal people and Europeans on the Kimberley's west coast dates to the Dutch explorations of the seventeenth century, there were no contacts with Europeans in the east Kimberley until well into the nineteenth century. By the 1890s the dominant forms of pastoralism had also divided the Kimberley, with beef in the east and sheep in the west (MacDonald Holmes 1963: 171).

Following the expeditions of Alexander Forrest in 1879, which named the Margaret and Ord rivers, southern and eastern pastoralists and prospectors were drawn in numbers to the Kimberley as a result of Forrest's exaggerated praise of the area as grazing land. A number of leases were taken up during or shortly after 1881, predominantly (though not exclusively) by large corporate interests (Buchanan 1934: 98). The first east Kimberley homestead to be founded and stocked was the Ord River Station in 1884 (Clement and Bridge 1991: xi). These events represent the earliest significant inland presence of Europeans in the east Kimberley.

The numbers of settlers increased even more significantly with an influx of European and Chinese prospectors after 1885, when Hall and Slatterley discovered gold at Halls Creek. In fact 1885 was a watershed in the history of the east Kimberley – the year that the Emanuels began to stock country on the Fitzroy River with sheep, and to establish several pastoral stations, and the year that the Duracks arrived further to the north with herds of cattle from their overland trip from Queensland. A port was established at Wyndham to service the new town of Halls Creek, and later the pastoral stations of the west and east Kimberley. By September 1886 there were reputedly some 2000 prospectors in the Halls Creek area (Clement and Bridge 1991: xiii), and at least 6500 prospectors and pastoralists travelled to the Kimberleys during the period of the Halls Creek goldrush (Durack 1933). At the height of the Halls Creek goldrush, there may have been almost as many Europeans as Aboriginal people in the east Kimberley (Shaw 1992: 14). A small fringe camp grew up around the town of Halls Creek. By the 1890s much of the alluvial gold had been worked out, and most of the itinerant prospectors had moved on to the far more profitable goldfields around Coolgardie and Kalgoorlie further south in Western Australia.

The first pastoralists in the east Kimberley brought their own labour force with them. The Duracks, for example, were assisted in droving their cattle across from west Queensland and through the Northern Territory by several Aboriginal people from Queensland (Rowse 1987: 82) in addition to a group of European family members and associates (Durack 1959). These men formed the first and most well trusted Aboriginal labour force on the Durack's east Kimberley pastoral properties. In 1901 there were fourteen Aboriginal 'insiders' working on the Duracks' Argyle Station (Rowse 1987: 82–3). Rowse characterises these Aboriginal people as 'trusted lieutenants' (Rowse 1987: 83), and it is important to realise that pastoralists in these early years drew a very strong distinction between their own Aboriginal labour force and local Aboriginal people. It was not until several decades after the first European settlement of the east Kimberley that the fear of local Aboriginal people which characterised this period had dissipated enough for pastoralists to begin to engage any but exceptional local Aboriginal people as station workers. For example, some local Aboriginal people were 'acquired' in these early years when orphaned by massacres, and 'brought up' in the subculture of station life. This time lag was also encouraged to some extent by the availability of a non-indigenous labour force after the slump in the Halls Creek goldrush, when prospectors found work within the burgeoning pastoral industry.

Killing times

There are a number of published oral accounts of massacres from this early period, many of them allegedly reprisals for cattle spearing or retribution for the killing of Europeans which were led or instigated by early pastoralists and officially sanctioned by the police force (e.g. see Lanigan 1996; Nunkiarry 1996a, 1996b). There are also a number of accounts that implicate prospectors in massacres (Green 1995). Initially Aboriginal groups responded to these attacks with militancy, and a number of Aboriginal resistance leaders appeared. In the west Kimberley in the late 1880s and 1890s, the exploits of the Aboriginal resistance fighter 'Pigeon' were widely reported in the media. He avoided concerted attempts by several police patrols to apprehend him, surprising, raiding and wounding several Europeans and their Aboriginal assistants over a period of five years (Green 1995: 33–52). The hunt for Pigeon and his associates was bloody and violent, and possibly hundreds of Aboriginal people were killed in the areas around Derby, Fitzroy Crossing and the Margaret River. As recently as 1926 in the Forrest River area near Wyndham, a group of police and assistants shot indiscriminately at

Fig. 6.2 Ration day, Moola Bulla pastoral station, pre-1954.

Aboriginal people whom they met during the search for Lumbulumbia, an Aboriginal man who had speared a white pastoralist called Hay in retaliation for Hay's molesting his wife (Green 1995).

Welfare

Following this period of initial and brutal contact, a series of Royal Commissions investigating atrocities committed against Aboriginal people in the east Kimberley by European settlers were held. At first Commissioner Roth made serious allegations about police methods of arresting and holding Aboriginal people in chains, and claimed that Aboriginal people were being arrested and falsely accused of spearing cattle (Roth 1905). In 1909, the Chief Protector of Aborigines Mr Gale noted in his annual report that cattle killing was the most serious problem in native affairs of the day (quoted in Green 1995: 72). In the absence of positive responses to calls for pastoralists to kill enough beef to feed Aboriginal people surrounding their stations to try to alleviate this problem, the government-run Aboriginal cattle and ration station at Moola Bulla was opened in 1910. This was shortly followed by a sister enterprise at Violet Valley in 1911. Initially the stations butchered cattle and distributed tobacco, tea, flour and blankets for rations, in return for 'as much work as possible' on Moola Bulla Station (Moola Bulla Native Station File 652/993, quoted in Rumley and Toussaint 1990: 84). Up to 300 people were reported camping at the station in 1911 (see Fig. 6.2).

Station times

By 1920 much of the east Kimberley had been taken up for pastoral lease. A major shift in attitudes of white pastoralists towards local Aboriginal people occurred during the first half of the twentieth century as their potential as a labour force for pastoral work became apparent. Aboriginal people began to be actively sought out by pastoralists and rationed in return for taking part in station duties. The shift in pacification of Aboriginal people through forced 'dispersal' to rationing is one of the most important changes in the history of indigenous–settler relations in the north of Australia. These changes did not develop in the east Kimberley alone, but in response to the experiences and attitudes of pastoralists throughout the north of Australia (Rowse 1987: 84–6). The shift was not so much an event as a process; the Duracks had begun to 'let in' Aboriginal people as early as the turn of the century (Rowse 1987), while massacres of local Aboriginal people for cattle spearing were still occurring in the 1920s. A number of changes contributed to this process, particularly the 'quietening down' of local Aboriginal resisters by violence, and the geographical expansion and increased intensity of grazing in the pastoral industry which led to escalating contacts between settler pastoralists and indigenous people. The example of successful, local Aboriginal involvement in cattle work on Moola Bulla and Violet Valley stations was also a catalyst. The need for indigenous labour was accelerated by the departure of many European stockmen during the Second World War (Shaw 1986: 9).

At this time 'high-status' jobs such as driving bullocks into the port at Wyndham that had previously only been performed by white station workers were transferred to Aboriginal people.

Before the last war they had here in 1941 if you had a boy or a half-caste in your plant they wouldn't give you bullocks to take into Wyndham . . . You could work for the boss drover but you weren't allowed to drive the bullocks . . . But since the Second World War broke out and everybody galloped away we poor buggers took the bullocks down then when they bombed Wyndham. (Laurie 1992: 99)

Thus 'coming in' was an erratic process, which occurred at different times over varying periods, and to different degrees for Aboriginal people in this area. Although some people had began camping on the margins of the earliest pastoral stations by the turn of the century, some Aboriginal people resisted European settlements until the 1950s or 1960s, particularly Wangkajunga, Kukatja and Walmajarri people living in the extreme south of the region (Kimberley Language Resource Centre 1996). Indeed, several Aboriginal people from Halls Creek told me that they recalled their own first experience of contact with Europeans as children in the 1930s.

Coinciding with the change in attitude of white pastoralists was the desire among many Aboriginal people in the east Kimberley to 'come in' and seek work and rations on pastoral stations. Contact is the natural outcome of meeting of groups of people who inhabit the same time and place. However the reasons why Aboriginal people chose to make continued contact with European station owners and allowed this contact to develop into a sustained relationship of interaction is not immediately apparent and deserves some consideration (after Kelly 1997: 352). Aboriginal people were actively involved in a continuous recontextualisation of both European and indigenous 'things' as part of the contact process (Byrne 1996: 83ff; see also Thomas 1991), which provide ways of understanding the motivation for and process of coming in to pastoral stations.

Aboriginal oral accounts, both published and recorded by the author, suggest a number of reasons for 'coming in' to pastoral stations in the southeast Kimberley, including a preference for European foodstuffs, a taste for stimulants such as tea and tobacco, and the need for security. European foodstuffs provided an easy and quick alternative to gathering and hunting bush foods.

The old people would try bits of it, tasting it slowly.
Was it good?
Yeah, it was good, really good food. They said 'We'll try a little bit, we'll try that gardiya tucker, it might be good'. After that they would always sit with the gardiya and have a good feed. (Duncan 1996: 63)

The desire for stimulants such as tea and tobacco seems to have played an important role (see Baker 1999 for an in-depth discussion of the process of 'coming in' in northern Australia).

In those days we used to work just for shoes and trousers, blanket and calico – no money at all – hat and boots and two sticks of tobacco. We used to get those twists of tobacco. We used to chew a lot of them. (Deakin 1992: 129)

Another important reason was fear of European retribution via killing parties. Station workers were generally well looked after by 'the boss', and camping close to the station ensured protection from other Europeans. The life of the station generally gave Aboriginal people a sense of security that it was no longer possible to have living in the bush after the killings of the first few decades of contact in the east Kimberley. The desire for security is often cited by both indigenous (eg. Laurie 1992: 97) and settler Australians (Schubert 1992: 11–12) in the east Kimberley as a reason for 'coming in'.

We left our home in the south and grew up at Lamboo then. We never saw our home again . . . The old people said, 'You can't go back south to live'. There were white men with guns, early days white men going around then. (Brumby 1996: 67)

Other reasons cited include the desire to be with kin who had already moved on to stations and that people were 'rounded up' by Europeans and forcibly brought in. While there is no single answer as to why Aboriginal people in the east Kimberley chose to start living and working on pastoral stations, the interaction of Aboriginal people with European pastoralists must be understood as situated within a network of cultural strategies that are dictated by personal as well as group needs and desires.

Award wages and the end of station work

Moola Bulla Station was sold off to private interests in 1955 and hundreds of Aboriginal people were moved off it (Kimberley Language Resource Centre 1996: 120–1). Some went to the United Aborigines Mission in Fitzroy Crossing, others to the town of Halls Creek, or to seek work at other pastoral stations in the area. It was not until after the Second World War that Aboriginal people began to be paid monetary wages. By the 1960s there were calls for equal wages for Aboriginal and white pastoral station workers, triggered by a number of developments including the 1967 National Referendum that officially included Aboriginal people in the census. The consequence of the new pastoral industry award for Aboriginal workers of 1968 was that many Aboriginal people were forced off stations and into the fringes of towns, as pastoralists were unable, or unwilling, to pay the new award wages to their Aboriginal workers and families. In Halls Creek, the indigenous population of the town rose from 200 to 600 people in a matter of months and the town required emergency airlifts of flour to cope with the sudden increase in population (*The West Australian Newspaper*, 27/2/69).

Cattle work and sense of worth

The critical role of Aboriginal people in the pastoral industry of central and northern Australia has been discussed at length by a number of authors (e.g. Baker 1999; Lukin Watson 1998; McGrath 1987; Rowse 1987, 1998), and is a recurrent theme in the life histories of Aboriginal people in the east

Fig. 6.3 Aboriginal stockmen, Moola Bulla pastoral station.

Fig. 6.4 Station work, Moola Bulla pastoral station *c.* 1910–18.

Kimberley (Kimberley Language Resource Centre 1996; Ross and Bray 1989: 38–46; Shaw 1986, 1992; Sullivan 1983). Work on cattle stations came to be crucially important to the construction of a personal identity and sense of self-worth for many Aboriginal people in the east Kimberley. Life histories of Aboriginal people from the east Kimberley stress the importance of cattle work and the rhythms of the pastoral industry 'calendar' to their way of life (Figs. 6.3 and 6.4).

The story what we did on the cattle stations, mustering and branding and all that [is] better than that wicked turnout, all those murdering and fighting stories . . . Cattle work was the best. (Sullivan 1983: 128)

This theme is also well illustrated in the life history of Bill Laurie, as recorded by Bruce Shaw.

What I liked most was chasing cattle and branding up and everything like that. I didn't like anything else, only to work on the station . . . That was our life. (Laurie 1992: 95)

Cattle station imagery is incredibly important in the east Kimberley today. Many older men will describe stages of their own lives as well as the lives of other men in terms of cattle work.

I was a little feller then, not riding horses . . . this feller taught me how to ride a horse. (*J.J. describing his relationship with friend and elder P.I., discussion with the author in Halls Creek, 1997*)

Cattle station work was also very important to women, taking the form of either stockwork or, as in many cases, domestic duties.

Working. I was working la station, kitchen job. [When] stock camp start, I go out la bush. I used to ride horses . . . Hard work, bin working longa outside. Riding horse. Later on, bin start up the motor car, truck. (Ida Milbaria in Ross and Bray 1989: 40)

Rowse has discussed the role of the patronage of the pastoralist in assigning rank to cattle station workers (Rowse 1987; see also Bruce Shaw's introduction to Sullivan 1983: 10–27). A scale of prestige operated on pastoral stations that was expressed not only in the ways in which workers were treated, but also in the distribution of food and other resources, how individuals were paid for their labours, and the physical distance at which the individual was commonly allowed to approach the homestead (Rowse 1987: 89–90). Membership of groups of station workers was so important that Aboriginal people in the east Kimberley today commonly refer to themselves in terms of station orientation, rather than language group, kin or tribal orientation, e.g. 'that Lamboo mob' (see also Sullivan 1996: 13).

Jaru and Kija narratives about contact-insiders and outsiders

Jaru and Kija stories about station work in the east Kimberley have a number of common features that reflect the importance of station work in the

Table 6.1 Structured oppositions in Jaru and Kija contact stories

Station	Bush
settled	wild
inside	outside
physically bounded by European boundaries	free to go where they like
working	walkabout
actions governed by European 'rules'	unpredictable, actions governed by different sets of rules

development of a new cultural and social identity that was in many ways distinct both from the parent group as well as from the settler society. Kija and Jaru oral narratives emphasise structural oppositions between 'settled' people who live on stations, and those whom people refer to as more 'wild' people who were yet to 'come in' to stations or towns. An example can be found in the text of a contact story by Bennie Duncan, a Kija man who now lives in Halls Creek.

Anyway, this later lot of white people were a bit better. They tried to settle the people. They were getting better, and settling down. The gardiya gave them blankets and clothes and showed them how to wear hats and clothing. My father was middle aged by then. . . .

And everyone learned how to work. The gardiya would say to them 'OK, you do this, you do that easy job. You people understand now, you know how to work'. Some people would get water, and others would get wood to stack it up, others would light the fire and put the billy on. The lot.

Sometimes wild bush people came across the working mob. The working mob would call out to them, 'Bring them in, bring them in and teach them about the gardiya side, its good, really good. This white man has good tucker to eat and clothes to wear.' (Duncan 1996: 62–4)

In this story, as in other published accounts as well as those collected by the author, language emphasises the differences between station and bush life. These binary oppositions are a fundamental part of the structure of Kija and Jaru contact stories, and of notions of the experience and process of contact. Drawing on a range of Kija and Jaru contact stories, these oppositions can be summarised as in Table 6.1.

Other oral histories that I have collected discuss the differential access to different kinds of resources that station and bush people experienced. Although station people had access to all kinds of prized European items, such as glass, metal, blankets, flour, tea, sugar and tobacco, they were tied to the station by their work obligations. This meant that they could not get particular woods that were required for making spears, woomeras, shields and coolamons, nor could they often access ochres that were important for particular ceremonial activities. Many people first came in to stations because of the availability of rations; however, station people soon grew tired of tea and flour and longed for the bush food that they had been used to gathering. There is also an association in these stories between bush people and the wild and at times unpredictable natural world.

Old Lamboo Station: a case study

Old Lamboo Station was chosen as a field site at which to examine the documentary and oral accounts of relationships between settler pastoralists and Aboriginal people in more detail, and to explore how these relationships are reflected in the archaeological record. Through looking at the archaeological evidence for fringe camping I hoped to examine some of the ways in which Aboriginal people expressed cultural identity as pastoral station 'insiders' or 'outsiders'. As a collaborative community-based archaeological project (after Greer 1995 and Greer *et al.* 2002), a dialogue developed between myself and a group of Aboriginal people for whom Lamboo is an important symbol of their past, and this had an impact on determining the methodology for the project (see also Harrison 2000). The occupation and use of the station covers the critical periods in indigenous–settler relations identified in the historical accounts, and oral accounts of station life were available from this group of Aboriginal people who had lived and grown up on the station during the 1930s to 1960s. The examination of archaeological evidence for 'contact' in this context included mapping indigenous and settler pastoralist sites, and in particular recording the material evidence of Aboriginal people associated with the pastoral station.

Frederick Charles Booty, an Oxford graduate and nephew of Osmond, owner of Ord River Station (Durack 1959: 386), first took up the station lease in 1901, and several leases in the immediate vicinity were later amalgamated to form the current station boundary. The first station homestead was constructed between 1903 and 1910, at which time sheds, a well, stone-based water tank and trough, and several fences were built (see Fig. 6.5).

Booty is implicated in a number of local massacre stories, but he seems to have availed himself of Aboriginal labour soon after building the station. In a twist on the pioneering theme of European histories of pastoralism in

Fig. 6.5 Old Lamboo original station homestead *c*. 1950.

the north-west, George Nunkiarry relates simply, 'Booty shot a lot of people there, and then he went west and built the station at Lamboo' (Nunkiarry 1996a: 42). Booty recounts that 'Kimberley in the early eighties and nineties was a wild country and contained wild men' (Buchanan 1933: 198). The logic of these actions was almost taken for granted, and Jaru and Kija people often use euphemisms for killings by early pastoralists and miners such as 'quietening down' or 'settling down'. One such massacre has imprinted itself permanently on the landscape near Old Lamboo Station by lending its name to a tributary of the Margaret River at Hangmans Creek (see Nunkiarry 1996b).

The station was taken over by Ben Taylor in the late 1940s, after which the current station buildings were constructed. The homestead was abandoned in the 1960s because of problems with flooding and the quality of the water supply, after which Taylor moved the homestead further north. Charles Booty was a local Justice of the Peace, and apparently treated Aboriginal station workers and fringe campers well. Previous residents of the Aboriginal fringe encampments remember both Taylor and Booty fondly, despite Booty's appearance in several early massacre stories.

It is not known exactly when Aboriginal people first started camping on the fringes of the station homestead, but artefacts made from glass that date to around the turn of the century in these camps suggests that it was shortly after Booty first took up the lease. The area was probably used intermittently before this time as a semi-permanent water source and as a hunting and

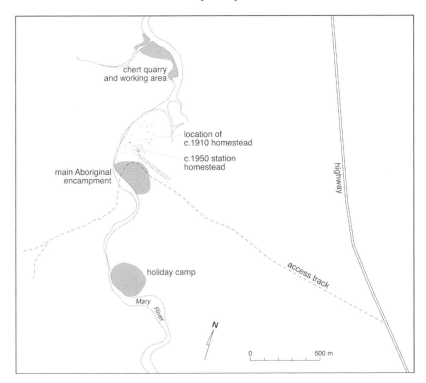

Fig. 6.6 Old Lamboo Station site plan.

fishing ground. There are few pre-station period stone artefacts in this area, which may be distinguished from those of the station period by the level of oxidisation, patination and water wear on the surface of the most abundant stone type, a white chert. Oral histories that I have collected suggest that the fringe encampments were home to a seasonally shifting population of at times up to seventy or more people. Booty and Taylor employed many of these people as stock-workers and domestic assistants. Today the camps consist of a discontinuous scatter of stone and European bottle glass artefacts, utilised metal pieces and well-defined hearths that spreads over an area of approximately 500 × 500 m on the banks of the Mary River (see Figs. 6.6 and 6.7).

Spatial patterning in the archaeological remains at Lamboo

The station contains a complex of sites associated with life on the pastoral station. Stockyards, wells, troughs and the remnants of the two station homesteads are the structural remains of the working activities of both indigenous station workers and settler pastoralists on Old Lamboo. The

Fig. 6.7 Old Lamboo Station looking towards the second station homestead from the original station homestead, 1998.

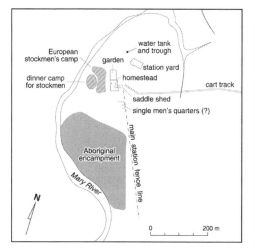
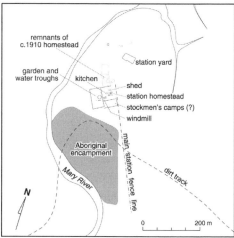

Fig. 6.8 Old Lamboo Station: left, *c.* 1918; right, *c.* 1950.

material remains of Aboriginal station workers and fringe campers consist of fringe camps adjacent to the station, a large 'holiday camp' used according to oral accounts during the wet season holiday time as a camping and corroboree ground, a men's law site, and a large station stone quarry. These sites are shown on Figs. 6.8, 6.9 and 6.10.

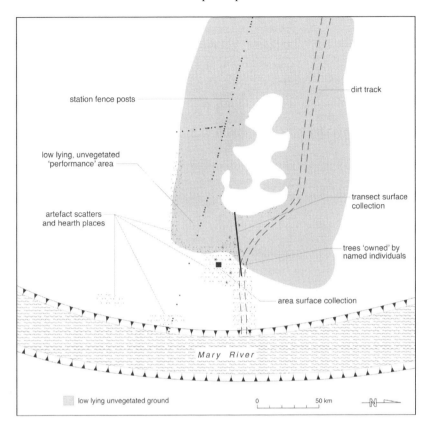

Fig. 6.9 Old Lamboo holiday campsite plan.

Oral histories were recorded from informants who had lived and grown up on the station from the 1930s to 1960s, predominantly Jaru language speakers who now live in Halls Creek. Oral histories helped identify many other areas of significance to informants such as birthplaces, the campsites of named individuals, burials, areas where bush food was regularly collected, and ceremony and meeting areas. This research was carried out in the context of a wider survey of archaeological sites in the surrounding area. Sites and named places were recorded and mapped on base maps of the area. Surface collections and excavations were carried out at several of these sites to answer specific questions about cultural and social change as a result of contact with Europeans.

Spatial patterning in the distribution of sites at Old Lamboo Station

Figure 6.6 shows the spatial relationship between the main Aboriginal encampment, the structural remains of the two station homesteads, the

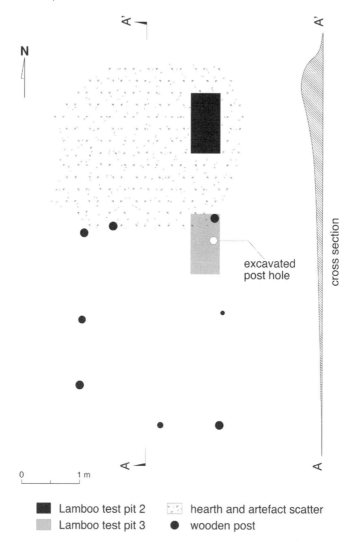

excavated
post hole

cross section

N

0   1 m

■ Lamboo test pit 2   ░ hearth and artefact scatter
▒ Lamboo test pit 3   ● wooden post

Fig. 6.10 Plan of surface collection and excavation of Aboriginal domestic structure, Old Lamboo Station.

station chert quarry and the holiday camp. One interesting feature is that the station homestead and Aboriginal fringe encampments grow closer together over time. This is illustrated in the comparison of sketch plans of Old Lamboo Station during *c*. 1918 and *c*. 1950 based on data obtained through field survey, aerial photographs and documentary and oral accounts of the station (Fig. 6.8). It is likely that the Aboriginal encampment grew up in its marked location in response to the location of Booty's original station homestead, suggesting that Aboriginal fringe campers initially favoured a large distance between indigenous and settler domestic spaces. Over time, it appears that these spaces increasingly merged. These changes in the relationship between European and indigenous domestic areas reflect some of the more general changes within the pastoral industry discussed in the historical account of indigenous–settler relations. Documentary histories suggest that at the time of the construction of the first station homestead, there was still a great deal of animosity between Aboriginal people and European station owners. By 1950, there had been a sharp turnaround in the relationships between Aboriginal people and European station owners, who actively sought the services of local Aboriginal people and their families for station duties. At this time many Aboriginal people were also choosing to take up this form of employment in preference to bush camping. The changes in the location of domestic spaces would have occurred gradually and reflect more general changes in the increasing 'entanglement' of indigenous and settler Australians on the pastoral frontier over the period represented.

Oral accounts that I collected about Aboriginal life on Lamboo Station discussed the use of the area marked on Fig. 6.6 as a 'holiday camp', used during the wet season by Aboriginal station workers (see Fig. 6.9 for a more detailed plan). Ceremonial activities and large meetings are reported to have taken place at this site. Ethnographies carried out in the 1930s (Kaberry 1939) suggested that Aboriginal people in the east Kimberley traditionally held ceremonies and meetings during the beginning of the dry season, when travel was not impeded by rain and flooding, and when food was plentiful and waterholes and rivers held large quantities of water. During the wet season, Aboriginal people dispersed in smaller groups. This pattern was not compatible with the rhythm of the pastoral station, which required the bulk of the work to be carried out in the dry season. However, Aboriginal station workers were regularly 'laid off' for several months during the wet season, generally in October or November until March, when there was little work carried out on the station. During this time, Aboriginal people would 'go walkabout', visiting family and friends and undertaking ceremonial activities and group meetings (Durack and Durack 1935: 65ff; Head and Fullagar 1997: 420–2; Laurie 1992). This led to a shift in the nature and timing of ceremonial activities and meetings throughout the east Kimberley in the twentieth century.

Given that people are reported often to have travelled long distances during holiday times, it seems strange that the holiday camp is located so close to Old Lamboo Station. Several factors may help to explain this. The wet season would have been a time of decreased mobility for Aboriginal people, because of the heavy rainfall and frequent flooding that occurs at this time of year (Head and Fullagar 1997). This may have led to a preference for camping at specific locales for longer periods. However this particular location is very open and would not have provided any shelter from wet season rains. Oral histories suggest that this was a ceremonial meeting place, where large inter-language group meetings were held. Rationing may also have been of importance. Oral accounts collected from Lamboo Station workers suggest that rations were still provided during the wet season, which may have tied people to the main station homestead. Jack Ryder recounts:

When corroboree bin getting on, old man Old Booty, he bin always look happy, 'Ah, there's all everything bin go right', and he bin always talkin that way 'Ah, when that lot old people gotta go back, langa Moola Bulla? I'll killem bullock, and they can go back gotta beef'. They can go back gotta beef and everything, they get ration, might be tea, sugar, flour, everything, tobacco, jam, treacle, all kinds, they goin back with ration them old people. That old man Booty bin always agree langa them, because they bin bringem something, Law, langa blackfella way. (Jack Ryder, interviewed by RH and JB, 1998 KLRC Tape 1184)

This may well have been a strategy employed by Booty to ensure the return of station workers after holiday time. Finally, it is possible that the Aboriginal people did not feel secure travelling great distances from the station because of memories of the violence of Europeans towards Aboriginal people in the immediate past.

Artefactual remains

The Aboriginal workers' encampment at Old Lamboo is defined by a series of clearly visible hearths, characterised by dense mounded concentrations of charcoal and associated knapped stone and glass artefacts. A total of fifty-three distinct groups of such hearths were recorded (in some cases a large hearth was surrounded by smaller ones, suggesting the use by family or kin groups of smaller hearths around a central nucleus). Knapped stone artefacts are not limited just to this encampment area, but are found in a background scatter that extends across the clearing in which the home station site lies. The density of flaked stone and glass artefacts across the site is very high by comparison to late Holocene period open sites recorded nearby. At Old Lamboo, artefact densities of higher than 100 flaked stone artefacts per square metre were recorded. Artefact densities were recorded

Fig. 6.11 Old camp residents, possibly Moola Bulla pastoral station, *c.* 1919.

for surface scatters of stone artefacts at ten comparable late Holocene surface
sites located with a 25 km radius of the station by counting the numbers of
artefacts present in a 2 × 2 m grid square. Artefact densities at other sites
were all fewer than twenty (most fewer than five) stone artefacts per sq. m.
This suggests that the camping activities at Lamboo were more intensive
than at comparable late Holocene period sites, which are thought to have
accumulated over a much longer time scale.

    Structural features from Aboriginal dwellings have been preserved within
the Aboriginal encampment at Old Lamboo. A set of posts and associated
domestic debris was subject to detailed mapping, surface collection and
excavation (see Fig. 6.10). This structure consisted of several wooden posts
with a large mound of charcoal, stone artefacts, glass and metal fragments
at one end. Postholes suggest the structure had dimensions of 6 × 2.5 m,
which appears to be similar to structures shown in historic photographs
(see Fig. 6.11). Excavations were shallow because of the lack of artefactual
material below 15 cm in depth. Further postholes were uncovered during
the excavations, which revealed a construction of substantial timber posts
excavated deep into the ground and cut with a metal axe. Although there
were only shallow archaeological deposits in this area, other excavations
uncovered several stratified hearths indicating long-term repeated use of a
single structure or campsite.

    This points to the construction of substantial dwellings by Old Lamboo
fringe campers, who appear to have used the same dwelling and campsite in

the station encampment repeatedly. No such structural features were noted at any other open sites nearby or at the (contemporary) holiday camp, despite the more adverse conditions that would have been experienced camping there during the wet season. Indeed, oral histories recorded amongst former station residents suggest that camping on the holiday camp was often out in the open underneath a tree, sometimes with a simple piece of canvas strung up as a shelter. I also collected oral accounts in which informants stated that people on the station were living close together, and that people preferred not to camp so closely when they had the choice. The high density of artefacts across the Lamboo fringe camps reflects the 'semi-sedentary' living refuse of a large group of people living in close quarters. This is considered to be a radical departure from the usual domestic spatial organisation employed by Jaru people, even in historic times while bush camping, which would have been more spatially dispersed.

Stone raw materials

The dominant stone material used in the manufacture of stone artefacts at Lamboo is a white chert (*guruwal*), sourced from a quarry (*dalga*) approximately 2 km to the south-east of the station camps (see Fig. 6.12). Oral histories that I collected about the quarry suggest that during station times one or more powerful men, who needed to be consulted and 'paid' for the use of the stone, controlled access to it. This quarry is said to have formed an important point on trading routes during station times. Prestige items such as hairbelts and pearlshell pendants, as well as bamboo for making spears, lightwood dancing shields (*igabayi*) and ready-made hardwood spears, were said to be traded in from the west, while red, yellow and white ochre, hardwood shields (*mirda*) and boomerangs were traded from the east. Items traded for stone were distributed among the family of the quarry owners and other people living in the station camps. Even station people required permission from the owner of the quarry to use the stone. It is interesting to note that Booty used stone from this quarry to build the foundations of part of his house, water-tanks and troughs, and that stone was then quarried from the foundations of these buildings to manufacture stone artefacts. One oral account suggested that even Booty had to pay the old men who owned the quarry for using the stone to build his houses. This payment is believed to have taken the form of extra rations.

In approaching the archaeological work to be undertaken at Lamboo, I was interested in whether it would be possible to pick up on patterning in the distribution of raw materials across the camps which might suggest

Fig. 6.12 Quarried chert (*guruwal*), Old Lamboo Station quarry, 1998.

differential access to particular raw materials, such as the white chert from the station quarry, more exotic stone raw materials, and prized European goods such as glass and metal. I chose to lay out several large transects across the site, collecting in 1 × 1 m squares across the transects, in addition to grid area surface collection and excavation. These act as a cross section of the distribution of artefacts across the site (see Fig. 6.13).

The patterning of artefacts in these transect surface collections suggests that while the white chert is the dominant raw material in the fringe camps, an abrupt change occurs in its frequency in the northern transect (Transect 2). Outside of the main camp area, there is a shift towards a greater number of exotic fine-grained raw materials such as other cherts, and an increase in worked dolerites and flaked quartz (see Fig. 6.14). This drop in frequency of the white chert is associated with an old pastoral station fence line and occurs in the area identified as one of the places that 'outsiders' had been camping when they came to trade with station people. Inside the station fence line the scatter of artefacts is relatively continuous and dense, while outside of the fence line only isolated scatters of artefacts occur. Although detailed analysis of this material is ongoing, this allows a novel comparison of the material culture of different yet contemporary Aboriginal social groups in the recent past.

Figure 6.8 shows that the main station fence bounded the Aboriginal encampment at Old Lamboo Station. This physical boundary reflects the

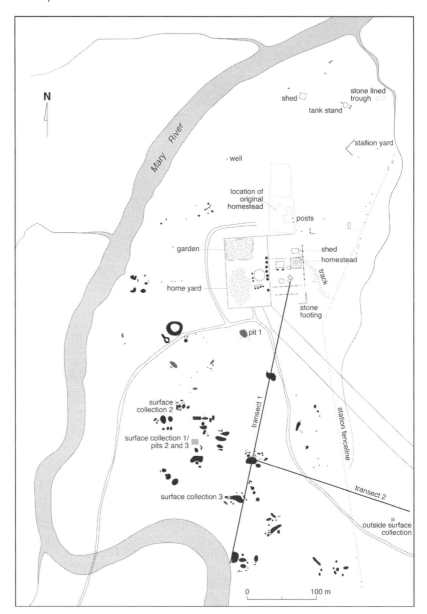

Fig. 6.13 Plan of Old Lamboo Station showing location of surface collections and excavations discussed in the text.

social boundaries implied by notions of 'insiders' and 'outsiders' discussed in the previous section. The station boundaries and fences are a major component of the cultural cartography of indigenous station workers. They are not just European fences but a part of the shared cultural landscape of indigenous and settler Australian pastoralists. Aboriginal people define and

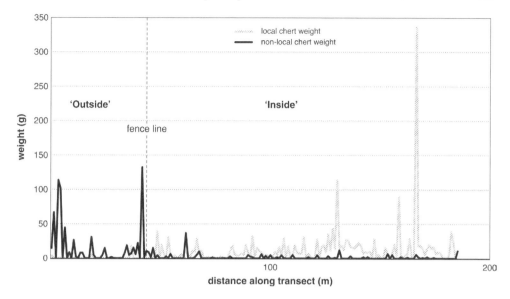

Fig. 6.14 Graph showing weight of all stone artefacts along Transect 2 running through main station fence line.

maintain a sense of identity as pastoral station 'insiders' through their working activities within these fences, which reinforce and reproduce the cultural difference between station workers and outsiders. That the archaeological record should reproduce this pattern so strongly, though, is problematic. From other oral accounts of station life, it appears that the relationship between insiders and outsiders was fluid, and that station workers would sometimes 'go bush' for long periods of time (e.g. see Laurie 1992). The holiday period also saw the distinction between bush and station dwellers blur. This change was symbolically expressed by leaving behind the station uniform of cowboy boots and hat and putting on loincloth (*naga*) or older 'bush' clothes.

During holidays we stopped working with the cattle, and we had to take all our new boots and clothes and hat back to the store and leave them there until we came back to work. When we came back we got the same set of clothes. They gave us a bag of flour for our holiday rations. (Huddleston 1996: 88)

Station campers would often have kin who were still living in the bush, who would occasionally visit and camp with station campers. Finally, oral accounts suggest that bush dwellers often acted as middlemen and -women in trading transactions between pastoral station camps. Very little evidence of the use of European foodstuffs and of artefacts made of introduced materials was found in surface collections on the Old Lamboo holiday camp.

Table 6.2 Differences in 'inside' and 'outside' station fence stone assemblages, Old Lamboo Station

Inside station fence	Outside station fence
assemblage dominated by white station chert	range of lithologies, very little white station chert
more finished tools	few retouched pieces
many biface points	few points
modified European raw materials, e.g. flaked glass, ground horseshoe points	few modified European items
posts from domestic dwellings, dense artefact scatters, closely spaced hearths	sparse artefact scatters only

This may suggest a cultural strategy to maintain the knowledge and skills of bush crafts by returning to hunting and gathering bush foods at this time. Further analysis of artefacts recovered from excavations and surface collections may assist in teasing apart the threads of this fluidity between insiders and outsiders in the oral accounts and station archaeology.

The exotic raw materials that make up the bulk of the stone scatter to the north of the old fence line are the same exotic raw materials that appear in the station camps as favoured raw materials for the production of biface points. There also seem to be differences in the kinds of artefacts that are present in the station camps and in these camps outside the main station fence line. This difference is primarily in the range of artefacts present. On the station camps, points make up the bulk of the finished tools (and represent a great portion of all of the stone artefacts present), whereas on the other side of the fence there are fewer retouched pieces. Artefacts such as stone axes are rare in the station camps but occur more frequently outside the fence boundary. It is possible to represent these differences in a table (see Table 6.2).

In Transect 1 (within the station camps), white chert is more abundant closer to the homestead buildings, as are modified non-traditional items, such as metal shovel-headed spears and flaked glass (see Fig. 6.15). This suggests that the distance at which Aboriginal people could approach (and camp near) the homestead may have been dictated by a complex set of social rules and status indicators. Those camping physically closest to the station homestead may have been favoured station workers, who would have better access to European raw materials because of their increased contacts with settlers through their working relationship. This also reinforces the oral histories that suggest that the 'boss' or traditional owner

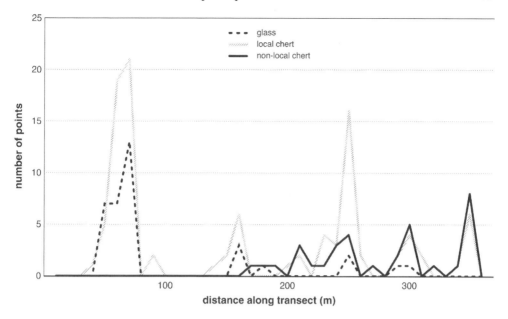

Fig. 6.15 Graph showing number of points and point fragments made on different raw materials along Transect 1 running from station homestead to river.

of the quarry was also usually the head stockman on the station, and points to the role of the station manager in attributing status and prestige to favoured workers that extended beyond the range of Aboriginal–European relations, and into the realm of social interactions between Aboriginal people as well.

Large numbers of bifacially worked Kimberley points are present within the Aboriginal encampment at Old Lamboo Station (see Fig. 6.16). The high numbers of worked stone bifaces and bottle glass spear points is difficult to account for using functional explanations. Station workers would have rarely had time to use points as spearheads for hunting, because much of their time on the station would have been taken up with station work. Oral accounts recorded during this project suggested that station workers rarely went hunting during the dry season, and that it was only during the holiday time in the wet that men would often hunt. Male station workers (points were only made and used by initiated men according to oral and documentary accounts – see Harrison 2002a; Kaberry 1939: 14, 163; Love 1936: 75) would also have spent much time away from the main camp mustering. I have argued elsewhere that Kimberley points were produced in such high numbers during the contact period because they acted as cultural signifiers among people who had been forcibly dislocated from their country

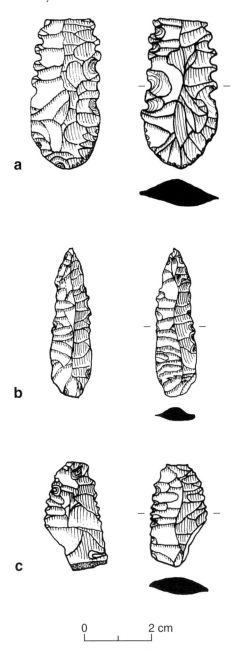

0   2 cm

Fig. 6.16 Kimberley points, Old Lamboo
Station: (a) and (b) bifacially pressure flaked
chert points; (c) bifacially pressure flaked point
made on European bottle glass.

(Harrison 2002a). Points were also a potent symbol of masculinity, and men are recorded as competing to make the most aesthetically pleasing points (Love 1936: 75). This competition may have intensified as a result of the large numbers of people living in continued close contact on the pastoral station. Points were only made by men from particular language groups, so they also acted as symbols of group membership and belonging. Kimberley points are found made on a variety of different exotic raw materials, despite the abundance of the 'mundane' white chert from the station quarry. Oral accounts of point manufacture on Lamboo Station suggest that the colour or totemic association of these exotic stone materials made them more desirable for point manufacture.

Points are one of a series of items from existing Aboriginal material cultures that are actively recontextualised by Aboriginal station workers. In addition to stone points, worn iron horseshoes were bent, battered and ground into iron points that are reported to have been used in ceremonial fighting (Fig. 6.17; see Harrison 2002b for further details). Grinding stones that had been used for grinding grass seeds within the living memory of ex-station residents became millstones for grinding metal, and concrete blocks were reused in the Aboriginal encampment as grindstones. New European raw materials became part of traditional trading patterns, and new materials and transportation methods (horses, trucks and cars) and routes (roads) allowed for increases in trade over longer distances by Aboriginal station workers and non-station workers (Akerman 1979). This had widespread repercussions for the spread of sociocultural practices and material goods among Aboriginal groups in the historic period. For example, there is documentary and oral evidence that some Aboriginal groups began to receive Kimberley points by trade for the first time during the historic period (e.g. Davidson 1934: 153; McNiven and David 1989). The material culture of Aboriginal encampments on pastoral stations reflects the continuation of existing material culture along with creative innovation.

Shared histories

The issue of relationships with land has become of critical importance to post-Mabo Australia. Settler pastoralists have been quick to respond by expressing their own special attachment to land. Leslie Schubert, ex-manager of Louisa Downs Station in the south-east Kimberley, has this to say about leaving the station:

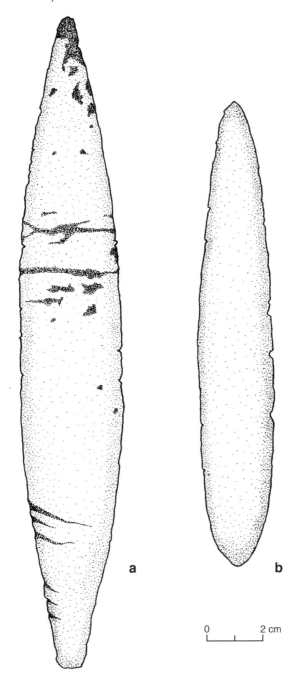

Fig. 6.17 Ground metal points, Old Lamboo Station:
(a) iron point made from old flour tin; (b) iron point
made from straightened and ground horseshoe.

I must confess that it is the only place I felt a longing to return to, after leaving. There seemed to be something missing out of my life for some time afterwards. This gave me a faint insight into the terrible feelings of abandonment and insecurity the Aboriginal [sic] feels when denied access to his homeland. (Schubert 1992: 11)

Nick Gill (1997) has undertaken one of the most detailed studies of the construction of social identity by pastoralists in Australia. His work centres on the pastoralists of central Australia and their responses to environmentalist and indigenous claims to land through asserting territoriality (Gill 1997: 50). The constructions of social identity that Gill documents among Central Australian pastoralists have close parallels to those of the indigenous station workers under discussion. Authority over pastoral land in the face of environmental discussion is claimed by pastoralists who stress that the character of their work embeds them in nature in a far more personal way than others, such as environmentalists and planners (Gill 1997: 55). Through working 'in' and 'on' the land, pastoralists gain knowledge, both ecological and spatial, about the areas in which they work. The tasks that are regularly undertaken on the pastoral station require frequent movement around the station, involving intimate physical contact with the land over different seasons of the year (Gill 1997: 58). The relationship between pastoralists and their pastoral lands is played out intimately in the cause and effect of pastoral management, which the pastoralists apply to their lands. Gill also discusses ways in which Central Australian pastoralists have developed cultures of exclusion and inclusion based around those that live and work on the land and those who do not (Gill 1997: 62).

This worldview stands in opposition to that evident from the literature produced earlier in the pastoral period. The pioneering myth (Lukin-Watson 1998), established and perpetuated by descendants of early white settlers such as the Duracks, emphasises the actions of pioneering white colonists who toil against the harsh and unknowable outback, eventually to subdue the Kimberley countryside. The landscape is described as an unpeopled parkland that waits to have its true potential realised (in this case as cattle fodder). If Aboriginal people are mentioned at all, it is as an obstacle in the path of the spread of settlement and pastoral expansion. Mary Durack summarises the arrival of the first Durack expedition to the Ord River in the east Kimberley in these terms:

Arrival in a harsh land . . . hard travelling and hostile natives. Deep rivers and open plains. (Durack 1959: 211)

This change in the way in which understandings of place are expressed by settler pastoralists finds strong parallels in the indigenous oral literature on work and attachment to place. Like Aboriginal station workers, settler pastoralists stress the relationships with land that are developed in the act of working in and on the land. Aboriginal station workers gain prestige and stress social cohesion through the work of the pastoral station. People's rhythms of life are patterned on the seasonal and pastoral round. Compare Gill's discussion above with Jack Huddleston's story about life as an Aboriginal stockman on Flora Valley Station:

> That work taught me a lot about my country. I can't leave here now . . . I've got my own food and my free will. (Huddleston 1996: 89)

Such similarities should not come as a surprise, because the current system of pastoralism in the Northern Territory and the Kimberley is based on the shared histories (after Murray 1996a) of both indigenous and settler Australians. There are a number of important areas in which Aboriginal and settler pastoral station communities experienced entanglement through the unique historical circumstances of the development of the pastoral industry in Australia's north-west. The social interactions between Europeans and Aboriginal people were incorporated into changed notions of social responsibilities. For example, rationing appears to have been widely understood by indigenous participants as reciprocity (McGrath 1987; see critical discussion in Rowse 1998: 25–46). There is also good documentary evidence that Europeans played a role in the timing and encouragement of the continuation of ceremonies and meetings. Mary and Elizabeth Durack relate that they received invitations to attend and participate in particular corroborees from Aboriginal station workers on Argyle Station (Durack and Durack 1935: 43ff), and Lamboo Station workers made it clear that Booty did not interfere with corroborees at the holiday camp and allowed station workers time off work for important ceremonies.

In the realm of material culture, in many instances it becomes impossible to talk about 'Aboriginal' and 'European' things on these pastoral stations because of the thorough entanglement of material objects and places through the specific historical circumstances of living and working together, and the constant recontextualisation of indigenous and European objects and concepts. For example, many white pastoralists developed large collections of indigenous artefacts. Aboriginal people appropriated and 'Aboriginalised' such European activities as tea drinking with its paraphernalia of billy cans and occasional tea cups, which represent frequent finds in Aboriginal encampments on pastoral stations (Fig. 6.18). Tea has a Jaru name (*nalija*)

Fig. 6.18 Hearth at Old Lamboo Station showing corroded billy can and cache of stone points, 1998.

and is still considered to be a very important part of the diet of Old Lamboo Station residents. Such items are so thoroughly 'entangled' in both indigenous and settler pastoral station cultures that it would be impossible and foolhardy to attempt to classify them as belonging to one or other culture. The entanglement of landscape is expressed through the white pastoralists' appropriation of indigenous place names (*Lamboo* is a Jaru word meaning paperbark), and the way in which the pastoral station 'maps on' to places that were traditionally resource rich and used by Aboriginal people such as waterholes and river margins.

   That indigenous and settler Australians in Australia's north-west should express similar sentiments in terms of their attachment to land, then, is not difficult to understand. Aboriginal and white station workers 'created' the pastoral landscape of station homesteads, fences, stockyards and cattle runs through their shared experience of working in and on the land. Nothing is created new; the pastoral landscape was the product of a shared reimagining based on the cultural building blocks and social trajectories of both indigenous and settler culture. This is not to say that these cultures were the same, or that Europeans had become Aborigines and Aboriginal people Europeans. Richard Baker (1999: 22) has eloquently expressed this entanglement of indigenous and settler understandings of landscape as two intersecting circles that overlap in the centre but have areas that are separate from each other. Aboriginal people chose to express their attachment to place using a medium that was socially and culturally acceptable to the colonists – in this case, through the work and life of the pastoral station. Indigenous viewpoints must also be considered 'traditional' in the sense that these changes are mediated through the structure of indigenous tradition and law systems. It is possible to see many of the changes as strategies for the maintenance of a range of social behaviours and aspects of material culture in the post-contact world.

Conclusion

The archaeology of Old Lamboo Station reflects many of the themes identified in historical accounts of indigenous–settler contact in the south-east Kimberley. However it also provides an opportunity to examine the ways in which Aboriginal people expressed their social identities, which were separate from European settlers as well as from those Aboriginal people who did not 'come in' to pastoral stations, through the analyses of spatial relationships and material culture in the archaeological record. For the Aboriginal people who lived and worked on Old Lamboo Station, this is an important part of their life story, and the dialogue between oral history and archaeology in this case study has been critical in making the archaeological record meaningful. Aboriginal people were active in recontextualising both indigenous and European 'things' as part of the process of 'coming in' to pastoral stations. The entanglement of indigenous and settler Australians on the pastoral frontier led to the development of new, shared ways of understanding and relating to landscape through station work, which are products of the unique historical circumstances of contact in the north-west of Australia.

Acknowledgements

The fieldwork for this research was funded by the Australian Institute of Aboriginal and Torres Strait Islander Studies and the Centre for Archaeology at the University of Western Australia. I have been generously assisted in the field by the Kimberley Land Council, Kimberley Language Resource Centre, Mirima Language Centre and Halls Creek Art Centre, particularly by Kate Golson, Clare Johnson, Joe Blythe, Anna Mardling and Mary Anne Taylor. Thanks to the Lamboo Mob and Mardiwah Loop, Nyunjuwirri and Yadgee communities, particularly Jack Ingan, Stan Brumby, Jack and Doris Ryder, Pattercake Imbelong, Barbara Imbelong, Charlie and Winnie Yeeda, Jerry Woodhouse, Josey Farrer, Doris Fletcher and my fearless field team Kathryn Przywolnik, Danny Tan, Genevieve Clune, Stewart Morton and Ashley Johnson. Jane Balme and Kathryn Przywolnik read and commented on an earlier version of this chapter.

7 | Tenacity of the traditional: the first hundred years of Maori–European settler contact on the Hauraki Plains, Aotearoa/New Zealand

STUART H. BEDFORD

Archaeology in Aotearoa/New Zealand has a lengthy history spanning some 150 years (Davidson 1984). Its predominant focus during most of that time has been concerned with the archaeology of precontact (1769) Maori. Since the 1970s, concomitant with a worldwide phenomenon, there has been a greatly increased interest in historic archaeology (Smith 1990). What has been glaringly absent, however, in this increased interest is the archaeology of Maori sites which postdate 1769. The explanations for this absence and neglect are somewhat varied and often complex (see Bedford 1996) but a number of persistent interrelated influences can be pinpointed. These include the idea that postcontact Maori were seen as being somehow contaminated by European influence and contact and consequently the archaeology was not seen as authentic. Related to this theme were nineteenth-century assumptions regarding the fragile nature of indigenous societies and their innate vulnerability particularly when exposed to European expansion. It had been accepted that Maori society and material culture would be swiftly and radically transformed and would therefore contribute little archaeologically in the search for the 'exotic' and the unfamiliar.

The above scenario began to change in the 1980s and build further momentum in the 1990s when a series of archaeological research projects began to focus on postcontact period Maori sites. This coincided with an increased interest in the field of culture contact studies and postcontact Maori history across a number of disciplines which can be partly explained by the growing political awareness of Maori ethnicity nationally and within universities across the country from the early 1980s (Webster 1993: 18).

This chapter outlines archaeological research which has been carried out on the Hauraki Plains (Bedford 1994; Bedford and Allen 1992, 1993; Phillips 1986, 1988, 1994, 2000; Prickett 1990, 1992) where a variety of Maori sites dating to both the pre- and postcontact periods have been investigated. The research has both provided a more balanced narrative of the first one hundred years of Maori–European settler interaction in the region and contributed to an enhanced understanding of the precontact archaeological record of the area.

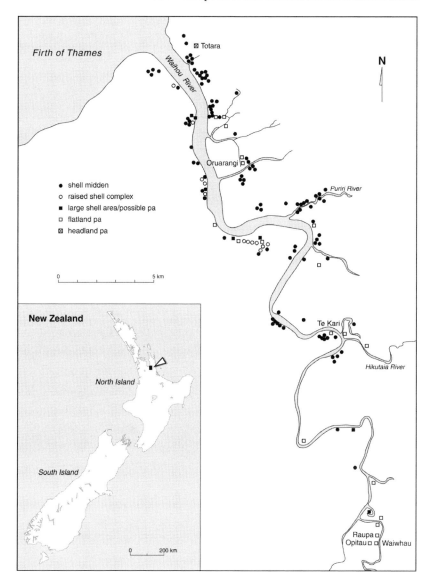

Fig. 7.1 The Hauraki Plains, located south of Auckland.

The Hauraki Plains, located south of Auckland (Fig. 7.1), was once partly made up of a vast (25 by 40 km) swamp of bulrush (*Typha angustifolia*), flax and kahikatea (white pine, *Dacrycarpus dacrydioides*), rich in natural resources. The river levees and meanders within the swamp are generally slightly raised areas which are mostly better drained than other areas of the swamp. It is in these areas of raised ground, focused close to the Waihou River and its tributaries, that a very rich archaeological landscape is concentrated

(Fig. 7.1). The majority of archaeological site types located thus far on the Hauraki Plains are raised shell complexes of varying size representing *kainga* (undefended settlements), with a smaller number of large raised shell areas and *pa* (fortified settlements) of varying sizes (Best 1979; Crosby and Loughlin 1991).

It seems likely that the *pa* and raised shell complexes were occupied contemporaneously, the *pa* being central to group identity and a focus at times of political stress, and the raised shell complexes and large shell areas represent habitations associated with cultivation and the utilisation of swamp and forest resources. The decrease in concentration of sites upstream can be attributed to a number of factors, including siltation, flood mitigation work and the decrease in the use of shell in the construction of occupational surfaces (Crosby and Loughlin 1991). The decrease in the use of shell is also apparent as you move eastward from the Waihou on to higher ground and may also account for fewer sites being recorded in that area. The river systems provided both an abundance in resources but also convenient transport routes throughout the area, a series of highways in an otherwise intractable landscape.

During the nineteenth century, European exploitation of the Hauraki Plains was largely restricted to the extractive industries of timber and flax which for the most part required Maori approval and/or involvement. But from the beginning and throughout much of the twentieth century, the area has been subjected to intensive clearance and drainage work to facilitate European farming activities. In the 1980s a renewed and more grandiose flood control scheme was the catalyst for a number of archaeological salvage projects. These were initially focused on the *pa* sites of Raupa, Waiwhau and Opitau (Phillips 1986, 1994; Phillips and Green 1991; Prickett 1990, 1992). Of central interest to these projects was the fact that these sites spanned the pre- and post-European contact periods. At a later date a number of the smaller raised shell areas or *kainga* were also excavated. These again spanned both the pre- and postcontact periods and in one case dated to the 1860s (Bedford and Allen 1992, 1993). All of these projects utilised a wide spectrum of investigative media, including historical records, oral traditions and archaeological excavation.

This more recent research was initially overshadowed somewhat by the lengthy and controversial history of archaeological research that had centred on the artefact-rich swamp *pa* known as Oruarangi (Best 1980; Furey 1996), a site which has an almost mythical status in New Zealand archaeology. The *pa* which was probably visited by Cook in 1769 (Beaglehole 1955) and was recognised as the most important settlement in the area in 1801

(Anonymous 1801) had been abandoned by 1820. The large site (23,000 m^2) comprised primarily of some 20,000 m^3 of shell fill (Best and Allen 1991) has produced the largest and most wide-ranging collection of artefacts from any site in New Zealand, albeit largely unprovenanced, having been recovered from fossicking expeditions (Furey 1996). The artefact collection from Oruarangi was incorporated into early theoretical frameworks relating to culture change. Golson (1959), in an article that was to have lasting influence on New Zealand archaeology, set out to define the Archaic (early) and Classic (late) phases of Maori material culture and Oruarangi was identified as the Classic type site. This assertion was later refuted by Groube, who argued that Golson's characterisation of Classic Maori material culture could not be relied upon (1964: 32), emphasising instead the theme of tremendous, even revolutionary change after European contact. It is this latter issue, one that remained largely unresolved until the more recent research on the Hauraki Plains, which returns us to the main theme of this chapter. What can the archaeology of Maori sites postdating European contact and settlement tell us about this vitally important period of entangled interaction?

Maori demonstrated a complex reaction to contact with Europeans: different experiences occurred in different parts of the country, at different times with different groups of Europeans. But for much of the first hundred years following Cook's appearance on the horizon (1769) Maori were very much the senior partner in their relationship with the fledgling settler society. Aspects of this scenario are hinted at in the archaeological record from the Hauraki Plains, where the indications are that traditional Maori activities and implements continued in use well into the nineteenth century. What is first noted from the sites which were occupied until *c.* 1820 (some fifty years after initial contact and limited settlement) and later is the small number of European items. This may be partly explained by lack of access, the poor survival of many trade items and also that the items were initially highly prized. Despite these factors, the number of items of traditional Maori material culture points to the small effect European contact had on the people of the Hauraki Plains. As Prickett states in the case of Raupa, a *pa* that was occupied until 1820: 'Archaeological evidence [at Raupa] suggests that stone adzes were still used for wood working, obsidian and chert knives for cutting and scraping tasks, and bone fishhooks, bird spears and needles still occupied their place in everyday life (Prickett 1992: 94). European materials on Hauraki sites occupied up to the 1820s (Oruarangi, Raupa and Waiwhau) included glass beads (Oruarangi, Raupa), metal adzes (Oruarangi, Te Kari), gun flints (Oruarangi, Te Kari), ceramic

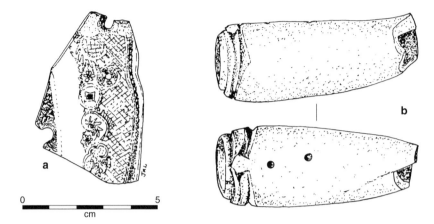

Fig. 7.2 (a) Modified ceramic plate; (b) modified clay pipe recovered from
Oruarangi *pa*.

material modified into pendants (Fig. 7.2a) (Oruarangi, Te Kari), bottle
glass (Raupa), pig bone (found at all sites but in limited quantity), pigs tusks
made into pendants (Te Kari) and clay pipes some of which were modified
(Fig. 7.2b) (Oruarangi, Raupa). However, the artefactual assemblages from
all of these sites were very much dominated by traditional items of Maori
material culture, a conclusion which contradicts Groube's assertion (1964)
in relation to change being revolutionary. Settlement pattern, site construction and layout also remained unchanged.

The composition of the European material from the *pa* site of Opitau, on
the Hauraki Plains, dates from the 1830s and here there is a greater frequency
and variety of items. Slate and slate pencils appear and are most likely to be
related to missionary activity in the area. Clay pipes, ceramics (not modified
as pendants), bottle glass, nails, gun flint, beads and a number of pig bones
were also present. Despite these items being recovered, the archaeological
record (Phillips 1994) and the sketch of Opitau in 1848 (Fig. 7.3) would
suggest that many aspects of life were still very similar to precontact patterns,
notwithstanding a degree of involvement with the production of food for
market exchange (Bedford 1994: 53–4).

The excavation of a late nineteenth-century Maori house site on the
Puriri River recovered again a wider array and greater quantity of European
items, including ceramics, bottle glass, miscellaneous metal items and pig,
chicken and turkey bones. Items not recorded at the earlier sites included
kitchen utensils, furniture and building hardware. Slate pencils and slate
were also present. There were no items recovered that could be identified or
termed traditional, but some continuity of lifestyle could be identified. These

Fig. 7.3 Opita on the Thames, 29 March 1848, by J. J. Merrett.

included methods of cooking, separate living and cooking areas, shellfish as a food source and shells being used as a free-draining fill to build up the living area, and continued fowling and fishing (Bedford 1994: 198). Settlement pattern remained fluid throughout the nineteenth century, paralleling the early observations of Cook and others collected during the eighteenth century.

The patterns that have emerged from the research on the Hauraki Plains have close parallels with the somewhat limited number of other postcontact Maori sites which have been excavated in other parts of New Zealand. The archaeological record suggests that traditional Maori activities and domestic implements continued in use well into the nineteenth century. Both the persistence of traditional aspects of Maori material culture and adaptation to newly introduced items are clearly demonstrated. Certain European items are regularly recorded as being present. It appears that European items that were easily absorbed into Maori material culture were initially the most popular, and there is evidence that other items were adapted for alternative purposes. There are numerous accounts in the historical records of European items being incorporated into the existing Maori worldview, particularly materials of a practical nature. Items such as beads, adzes and blankets were immediately adopted as they filled the same role as traditional materials,

Table 7.1 Return for period 1 January to 31 March 1853 of numbers of canoes that arrived in Auckland; including crews, quantity and type of produce as nearly could be ascertained (AJHR 1865) (*Hauraki tribes)

Name of tribe	Ngatimaru*	Ngatipaoa	Ngatiwhatua	Ngatitamatera*	Ngatiwhanaunga*	Ngatiwhakane	Ngatimahuta	Ngatital	Ngatibine	Ngapuhi	Total for quarter ending 31/3/1853
No. of canoes	196	202	93	20	8	7	2	2	2	1	553
Crews:											
Males	633	626	326	73	40	39	1	8	7	5	1758
Females	246	294	161	33	14	18	2	3	1	1	773
Total	879	920	487	106	54	57	3	11	8	6	2531
Where landed:											
Commercial Bay	45	73	81	8		2	2		2	1	214
Mechanic's Bay	151	126	10	12	8	3		2			312
Freeman's Bay		3	2			2					7
Kits of potatoes	720	794	790	106	22	24	2	10	10	6	2484
Kits of onions	327	276	91	58	14	7			4		777
Kits of maize	11	10	7								28

									Total
Kits of kumaras	13	8		2		2			25
Kits of cabbage	2	37	251	4		2		3	299
Kits of peaches	737	631	133	66	50		30	6	1653
Bundles of grass	3	691			10	3			707
Tons of wood	173	206	4	17	7	9	1/2		417
Tons of fish	11.25	7.25	19	0.25		0.5			38.25
Pigs	120	147	28	21	5	6	1	4	332
Goats	2	2					1		5
Ducks	27	21	8	8	1	2	2		69
Fowls	79	135	47	13		6			280
Cwts of flour	1								1
Turkeys						4			4
Kits of pumpkins		8	10						18
Kits of watermelons	10			16					26
Kits of grapes	100	14		18					132
Kits of apples		6			10				16
Kits of quinces			3						3
Kits of shellfish		6							6
Bundles of straw	6	30			10				46

Notes: Estimated value £1246. Average kit weight: potatoes 75 lb, onions 50 lb, flax 50 lb.
Compiled by James Naughton, Inspector of Police. The return does not include the produce brought overland or in coasting vessels.

but not all items were used for the purposes for which they had been originally designed. For example, Colenso (1881: 65) noted that clay pipes were
used for smoking tobacco but also for decoration in the ears, that red ties
were accepted because they could be unravelled and woven into the borders
of mats and that red sealing wax was used to decorate white sharks' teeth
that decorated the ear. Colenso also commented on 'hooks being made from
iron nails' and how they were fashioned on traditional styles of fishhook and
not the European forms (Colenso in Best 1977: 44). Best (1974: 97–9) commented that miscellaneous metal was at times fashioned into *patu* (hand
clubs) and traditional grinding stones or *hoanga* were used to sharpen steel
axes. As noted above, among the artefacts recovered from Oruarangi were
pieces of a ceramic plate fashioned into a pendant and a clay pipe decorated
and transformed into a *nguru* (flute).

By the 1850s Maori on the Hauraki Plains had become increasingly
involved in commercial activities, with an enormous quantity of trade being
conducted with Auckland and elsewhere (Table 7.1). Intensive commercial
gardening, timber extraction, flax, flourmills, involvement in the labour
market and trading trips to Auckland began to dominate the seasonal cycle.
However, in the latter part of the nineteenth century several significant events
occurred which were to cause major long-term disruption to this cycle. The
first was the discovery of gold, which brought greatly increased numbers
of Europeans into the area. This in turn was closely followed by the sale
of land once the Native Land Court[1] had been established in 1865. These
events also coincided with a period of marked Maori depopulation (Pool
1991) and involvement in the Land Wars of the 1860s (Belich 1986). None
the less, despite seemingly overwhelming odds, Hauraki Maori continued
vigorously to contest ownership of resources. Regular meetings were held
to discuss the issue of goldmining.

A large gathering in 1857 emphatically decided against Europeans mining
in the area, with many speakers presenting emotional pleas in favour of
retaining the land. One of the speakers was Aperahama Te Reiroa.

Friends, think of the land which descended to us from our ancestors. They died and
left us with their words which were these – 'Farewell; hold fast to the land, however
small it may be'. And now as gold has been discovered in our land, let us firmly
retain it, as we have the power over our own lands, lest the management of them
be taken by the Europeans. Who made them chiefs over us? No we will ourselves be
chiefs. (AJHR 1863)

However, with increasing pressure and the well-established Native Land
Court, land sales began in earnest. The Crown also managed, over a period

Fig. 7.4 Meeting *c.* 1852 between Lieutenant-Governor Wynyard and local Maori regarding the discovery of gold in the Coromandel region. Lithograph by Charles Heaphy, from the *Illustrated London News*, 1853.

of some years, to negotiate mining leases in the area which had a tendency to lapse into long-term ownership. There were many areas which were not initially sought after by Europeans, particularly the more swampy areas near the Waihou River. Maori landholders also attempted to maintain connection with the land and to prevent disturbance of significant places by surveying out small reserves from the lands sold. Surveyed *urupa* (burial grounds) and rights of way can be identified all along the Waihou River and its tributaries. Maori, increasingly involved with the money market economy, were correspondingly affected by downturns and land was sold in the depressions of the 1880s and 1930s. The majority of the land blocks adjacent to the Waihou River and many of its tributaries seem generally to have been sold either in the later nineteenth century or the 1920s and 1930s.

Despite the fact that these events brought major change to the social, political and geographical landscape of the area they must be seen in the context of the long-term history of the region. As Aotearoa/New Zealand approaches 250 years of Maori–settler cohabitation we are constantly reminded of the vibrant ongoing process of cultural interaction and the resilience of the indigenous population. At the time this chapter was being written the Hauraki tribes were in the process of preparing their case for the Waitangi Tribunal,[2] where past grievances relating to loss of land and resources are considered along with an assessment of appropriate compensation. Any illusions that the 'fatal impact' scenario of European colonisation had been played out during the nineteenth and twentieth centuries have long been glaringly discredited.

These most recent events are a timely warning for archaeologists, and highlight the need for added caution when interpreting Maori sites postdating 1769. The archaeology of Maori sites dating to this period is in its infancy and has, up to this time, relied heavily (as do aspects of this chapter) on notions of culture change being evidenced through the presence or absence of European/Maori artefactual remains. This is clearly a somewhat precarious and inadequate approach (Lightfoot 1995: 206–7). The fact that Maori may have absorbed or adopted European materials or aspects of culture by no means necessitates that this is unambiguous evidence of any form of social dislocation or cultural dissatisfaction (Howe 1973: 46). By the same token neither does it necessarily need to lead to disorganisation or social collapse. Finally the recognition of such ambiguity does not lessen the validity of, or the requirement for, archaeological research. To establish greater understanding and more inclusive perspectives on the past it is crucial that archaeologists engage in the developing discourse on cultural interaction. In the words of a pioneer in the field, 'to know where all of us have truly been cannot be a bad thing to know' (Deetz 1988: 232).

Notes

1. A court established by the government to identify Maori owners and issue European-style titles to land previously held according to Maori custom. The establishment of the land title system had the effect of both legitimising and greatly facilitating the purchase of land.
2. Established in 1975 to hear Maori tribal grievances. In 1985 it was given greatly increased power to hear retrospective grievances to 1840, the year of the signing of the Treaty of Waitangi between the Crown and Maori.

PART II

Issues and methods

8 | Fur trade archaeology in western Canada: who is digging up the forts?

OLGA KLIMKO

Introduction

Over the past century the fur trade era has become a part of Canadian mythology replete with visions of beavers, hardy traders battling rapids in canoes or traversing portages (Figs. 8.1 and 8.2), major trading company posts in the wilderness, and trading ceremonies with aboriginal groups – all described within a prevailing atmosphere of romanticism and adventure. For testament, one needs but turn to such popular book titles as *The Company of Adventurers* (1985) and *Caesars of the Wilderness* (1987) by Peter C. Newman or *Battle for the West: Fur Traders and the Birth of Western Canada* by Daniel Francis (1982).

The fur trade – this early exploratory and pioneering European venture into a frontier wilderness – also has a captive academic audience including historians, both social and economic, cultural geographers, anthropologists and archaeologists. From an archaeological perspective the western land-based fur trade provides a unique opportunity to observe and interpret cross-cultural exchange and interaction in an early contact setting. Archaeological artefacts and features represent one text having the potential to add another 'voice' for fur trade studies. In western Canada (as defined in Fig. 8.3 for purposes of this paper) over 300 excavations were carried out in the second half of the twentieth century. This large number of trading posts represents various phases of the fur trade and includes small 'pedlar' or independent posts, primarily of the late eighteenth century, posts of the major companies, the Hudson's Bay Company (HBC) and the North West Company (NWC), during the competitive era of the 1780s–1821, and large administrative centres, such as York Factory, Fort Garry and Fort Edmonton, before and after the amalgamation of the HBC and NWC in 1821. Unfortunately, the major focus of this research has rested on ethnocentric Euro-Canadian issues with little regard towards aboriginal peoples – participants to varying degrees in this venture.

Much money, time and labour have been invested in these archaeological ventures, yet the level of archaeological knowledge produced has been severely criticised both within and outside (for example, fur trade historians)

Fig. 8.1 'Shooting the rapids'. Oil painting by Frances Anne Hopkins.

Fig. 8.2 Carrying a 30 foot birch bark canoe used to haul HBC freight.

the discipline as being redundant or irrelevant as a consequence of inherent academic weaknesses. Criticisms include the lack of defined research goals, low-level theoretical orientation, the inability to support scientific analyses, poor artefact analyses and emphases on structural description. If accepted at face value with no consideration of contextual factors, these

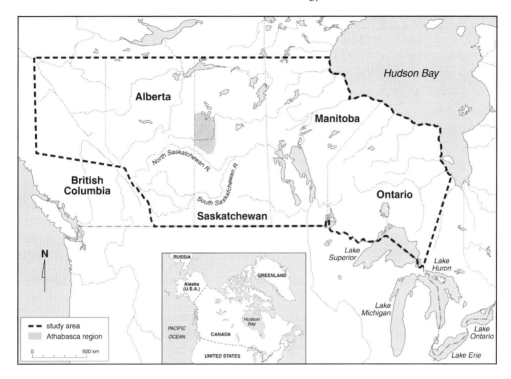

Fig. 8.3 The study area in western Canada.

are sad statements in light of the energies and funds expended in this pursuit.

The ethnocentric Euro-Canadian bias and the academically weak nature of fur trade archaeology are interrelated and did not evolve in a vacuum. Theories, relationships with cognate disciplines, institutional structures, and organising concepts and categories greatly influenced the course of fur trade archaeological research. In addition to seeing it as an intellectual, economic, historic or scientific pursuit, many practitioners also view archaeology as a social and political practice. Trigger (1980, 1984, 1986), for example, has argued that close relationships exist between the nature of archaeological research and the social milieu in which it is practised, and that what people believe about the present conditions their understanding of the past. On the topic of politics and archaeology, Shanks and Tilley (1987: 187–90) raise issues dealing with relationships, particularly those between academia and the wider social context; major institutions (such as museums) and the public and archaeology; and archaeological research and minority interests. Gero has observed that archaeology is 'fundamentally and uniquely an institution of state-level society. It is only the state that can support, and that requires the services of, elite specialists to produce and control the past' (1985: 342). In a dialogue between archaeologists and historians from the First and Third Worlds, the power of the state was also recognised as a major factor in the manipulation, creation and control of histories and the past (see Schmidt and Patterson 1995: 4).

This chapter focuses on the political and academic forces, past and present, to examine their influence on the pace, design and outcome of fur trade archaeological studies. By establishing the context within which fur trade archaeological studies flourished, determining factors should become evident. According to Schuyler (1976: 29) the context within which scholarly research is conducted, rather than the specific methodology employed, eventually determines the quality and type of end product. Preucel (1995: 163) specifically identifies the need for archaeologists to 'confront the intersections of power and knowledge by examining the institutions, funding agencies, and professional vehicles for knowledge production and dissemination'. To this end the study will employ a historical analysis of trends revealed by examining the timing of archaeological studies, the institutions involved, the intent and results of studies, the distribution or use of studies, and the prevailing theoretical climate.

Fur trade

This chapter began with an adventurous public portrayal of the fur trade. However, this reflects only one image. Depending upon the researcher, date of research and area of interest, the topical focus shifts and reveals not a single fur trade experience, but a number of different experiences influenced by such factors as conditions in Europe, competition among companies, geography, biotic zone, climate and different aboriginal cultures. While the fur trade can be viewed as exploration, empire building or a capitalist venture to procure furs for the European market, it also fostered social and economic forces that played an important role in the development of western Canada. Some of the central themes are touched upon below, while more detailed information may be found in Innis (1956), Morton (1973), Ray (1974), Rich (1958) and Williams (1970).

The potential wealth of the northern fur trade was known by the late seventeenth century through the exploits of the French explorers Groseilliers and Radison, who offered this information to the English after being spurned in New and Old France. As a result the English launched a successful trading expedition into Hudson Bay in 1668, and in 1670 established the Hudson's Bay Company (HBC) by right of Charter (Williams 1970: 5–7). The HBC preferred to maintain a few posts along the shores of the Bay to keep costs to a minimum. The HBC was to maintain this policy for 100 years, and aboriginal groups were forced to travel to the Bay to do business with them. The French challenged the HBC's purported monopoly to trade within the Bay, and from 1682 to 1713 provided stiff competition which resulted in coastal trade posts often changing hands and trade becoming erratic (Russell 1982: 98). With the signing of the Treaty of Utrecht in 1713, the HBC gained control of the Bay and continued their isolationist policy.

While the HBC concentrated its early interests on the coastal trade within the Bay, the French from Quebec had established a network of interior posts as far west as Lake Superior by the 1690s. Later French expeditions, such as La Verendrye's search for a route to the western sea in the mid-1700s, served to intercept trade destined for the British posts on the Bay (Morton 1973). By 1754 the HBC began sending personnel into the interior to encourage aboriginal groups to trade at the Bay and to report upon their inland competition. The surrender of Montreal to the British in 1759 did little to curb French competition. Many acted as independent traders, referred to as pedlars, and they continued trading inland. Their presence eventually forced the HBC to build an inland post that marked the beginnings of HBC inland expansion.

As the HBC was expanding inland along the Saskatchewan River, the trader Peter Pond entered the Athabasca District, revealing the potential wealth of the area (Williams 1970: 32). This led to the creation of the North West Company (NWC) – an event which would greatly effect western trade. A period of intense competition and bitter rivalry (at times resulting in violence) broke out between the HBC and the NWC (Morton 1973). The number of posts rapidly increased, with the NWC scattering small short-term mobile settlements throughout the country. Many of these new posts were established for the primary purpose of obtaining provisions to sustain brigades destined for the fur-rich Athabasca country. The HBC's response to this challenge was an intensive campaign centred on the building of inland posts adjacent to or further ahead of the NWC (Morton 1973).

By 1821, after suffering the effects of prolonged, intense competition, the HBC and NWC amalgamated into a single operation under the HBC (Rich 1958). This event heralded a new era in the fur trade affecting not only the trade but also its social nature. Charged with reorganising the new company, Governor George Simpson reduced the number of posts and personnel, centralised administrative power, initiated animal conservation practices, encouraged the replacement of canoes with York boats to transport goods, provided fewer gratuities to aboriginal groups, and forbade the use of alcohol in trading with aboriginal people (Morton 1973; Williams 1970). Although not universally popular, these new policies brought economic stability which was to last until the 1860s. After that time, the decline of bison herds and the arrival of permanent white settlement associated with agriculture relegated the fur trade to a minor role in all but the northern regions. These events served to initiate the growth of a new cultural fabric involving European and aboriginal peoples. In the west, European explorers and fur traders encountered aboriginal groups possessing a wide variety of social and economic formations, from groups exhibiting occupational differentiation and food production systems in settlements, to nomadic bison hunters of the plains or small, mobile groups of the forest who hunted more solitary prey.

Aboriginal groups did not constitute discrete social entities isolated within a particular geographical region. Alliances and warfare, as well as social gatherings, brought people together often, and sometimes in extremely large aggregations. Fur traders viewed such gatherings with much consternation. Activities such as bison pounding or warfare diverted the energies of aboriginal groups away from the more 'important' task of trapping furs. Worse, from the traders' perspective, battles could lead to the death of aboriginal people who owed debts to the fur traders. At times, hostilities between aboriginal groups spilled over into the fur trade itself. For example, the Gros Ventres, who initially lacked firearms, viewed fur traders as allies of their enemies, the Cree, who did have them. As a result the Gros Ventres attacked Manchester House on the North Branch of the Saskatchewan River, and the HBC and NWC South Branch Houses, resulting in the area being abandoned by the fur traders until the early 1800s (Morton 1973: 457).

Friendly relationships also developed between traders and aboriginal peoples. Many European men married aboriginal women for reasons as diverse as forging political alliances, securing trading opportunities or indeed personal fulfilment (see Brown 1980). The progeny of such marriages – the French and English *métis* – would greatly influence western Canadian history. Furthermore fur traders often depended on the knowledge of aboriginal peoples for survival and learned many aboriginal skills, such as making pemmican (dried meat), or fishing with nets (Arthurs 1980). In the early days of the fur trade aboriginal groups controlled the trade and their own culture (Fisher 1977; Lytwyn 1991) and the traders' influence in aboriginal life was minor and directed to encouraging aboriginal people to focus their attention on the acquisition of furs. Conditions and cultural dynamics, however, changed with the ever-increasing encroachment of Europeans and a growing reliance on European goods.

Fur trade archaeology

Timing and institutions

Fur trade archaeology in western Canada was influenced indirectly by the early efforts of the Historic Sites and Monument Boards (HSMB) in the 1920s and directly by the individual enthusiasm of famed western Canadian historian Arthur S. Morton. In their consideration of regional themes the HSMB identified 'discovery and exploration' as representative of western Canada and, as such, set the tone for commemorative sites and future research. Morton, on the other hand, believed in the importance of geography and the discovery of tangible historic evidence (Klimko 1994: 70) and also viewed fur trade posts as representing 'British' qualities of understanding, tolerance and mutual appreciation among races. He saw the conservation and restoration of these posts as 'preserving the symbols of honour and fair play upon which the West had been built' (Champ 1991: 4; Klimko 1998: 203). To this end, geography and the discovery of tangible historic evidence were extremely important, and from the 1920s to the 1940s Morton devoted much personal energy trying to locate fur trade posts and also to encouraging students and colleagues in this venture.

Apart from the early forays of Morton and to a lesser extent other individual enthusiasts, it was not until the early 1960s that systematic, professional fur trade archaeology began in earnest in western Canada. A number of groups, agencies and institutions have been engaged in fur trade archaeology since that time, the major participants including universities, museums, provincial and federal government agencies and consultants. Their level of involvement, however, has varied through time, and these shifts have had a profound effect on the pace, design and outcome of the studies.

In the 1960s the majority of fieldwork projects ($n = 44$, or 66 per cent) in fur trade archaeology were equally divided between museums and universities. These institutions continued to exert an equal influence into the 1970s, but shared the arena with provincial and federal agencies whose accelerated involvement soon matched them (Fig. 8.4). These four groups conducted a total of 100 projects or 87 per cent of the work, which resulted in a marked increase in the overall number of projects ($n = 115$) carried out and the number ($n = 95$) of posts investigated.

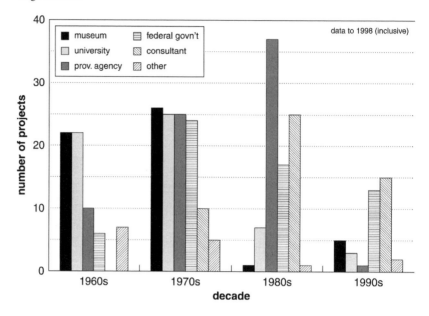

Fig. 8.4 Number of projects carried out by various institutions per decade.

The situation changed markedly in the 1980s. Museum and university involvement in fur trade archaeological field projects dropped sharply from fifty-one projects conducted in the 1970s to only eight projects in the 1980s (Fig. 8.4). Provincial participation, on the other hand, continued to increase, as did the role of private archaeological consultants. Federal government activity decreased slightly, but along with private consultants and provincial agencies, these three groups carried out 79, or 90 per cent, of fur trade archaeological field projects. Despite this activity, the 1980s witnessed an overall decline in the number of projects conducted and posts investigated (Fig. 8.5). In the 1990s there has been a noticeable decline in fur trade archaeological projects (Fig. 8.4). Provincial government involvement in field studies became almost nonexistent, with the federal government and private consultants conducting the bulk ($n = 28$) of the fieldwork (Fig. 8.4).

Types of studies and results

Since the 1960s twenty-seven institutions/groups have carried out 309 projects at 153 posts. While these numbers sound impressive, the analysis does not provide information on the type of studies conducted and why they were undertaken, as well as the resultant information and its dissemination. These factors play a significant role in the state of knowledge

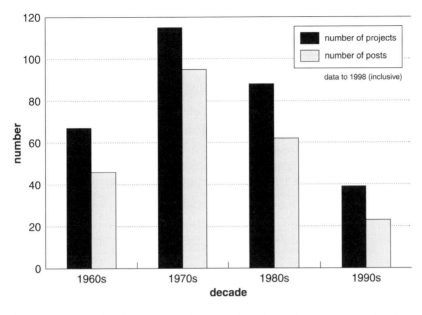

Fig. 8.5 Number of projects conducted and number of posts investigated per decade.

produced and its use. Practitioners of fur trade archaeology in the 1960s faced a situation characterised by a rich archaeological resource base with great public appeal and interest, as well as much historical information. What they lacked, however was basic comparative data and the material culture studies needed to build a foundation for broad-ranging research concerns. A number of individuals, most trained in prehistoric archaeology in the United States and recruited to work on Canadian fur trade sites, tackled these problems, and as a result major excavations took place at sixteen posts throughout the west. The background training of the archaeologists, as well as the needs of provincial or federal Historic Sites Advisory Boards and of public programmes related to the development and interpretation of designated historic sites, led to an excavation focus on architectural and artefactual information (Klimko 1994). Reports tended to be highly descriptive accounts of fieldwork, architectural features and site layout, with limited artefact analysis. Most were, and remain, unpublished.

Also lacking was a comprehensive knowledge of the resource base, and to this end numerous surveys were conducted in the 1960s to locate posts. Documentation of survey results was sporadic, and most often general in nature, and results are mostly unpublished. Developmental priorities and the search for comparative data continued to direct archaeological research into the early 1970s, thereby perpetuating the focus on historic and architectural information for reconstruction and display. However, some important changes were taking place. Researchers from the United States no longer predominated, there was more university involvement through field schools or contracts, and there was a move away from a strictly historical orientation towards an anthropological perspective (Klimko 1994). The latter change became evident towards the end of the 1970s, with the presence of a cohort of younger archaeologists who came into their own in the 1980s and 1990s. The end of the decade also marked the emergence of private consultants in the field of fur trade studies. While the level of fur trade archaeology increased during the 1970s, reporting and dissemination of information lagged far behind. As in the previous decade, reports often were general in nature, varied greatly in coverage and analysis, and appeared long after the completion of the field project. Report content focused on basic research methods, location and identification of sites, and the description of features and artefacts.

In the 1980s the new generation of archaeologists was acutely aware of the lack of problem-oriented research in fur trade archaeology and was eager to test new approaches to it. For example, interests included artefact pattern recognition, subsistence economies, diet, status, ethnicity, social composition, acculturation, land use and symbolism of both European and aboriginal peoples involved in the fur trade. Despite the academic respectability of producing problem-oriented research and publications, this group faced a number of problems that made it difficult to achieve their goals. A major reason was the continued focus of fieldwork on minimal data acquisition, a situation that resulted from the 'mission-oriented' studies carried out by cultural resource management initiatives that steadily grew during the 1980s. These resource management projects reflected managerial priorities concerned with site documentation and identification, determination of site integrity and vulnerability to destruction (Hamilton 1990: 194; Klimko 1994: 163). Such studies were tightly focused to satisfy legislation in the most cost-effective manner, and rarely permitted time and finances for a fuller investigation beyond data gathering and preliminary analysis (Fladmark 1980: 15; Hamilton 1990: 195; Klimko 1994: 163).

Private consultants and government agencies conducted most of the research in the 1980s (Fig. 8.4), a trend which continued into the 1990s. Also, the federal agency responsible for much fur trade archaeology shifted its focus from site development to site management. This shift, along with the increase of cultural resource management projects in the 1980s and 1990s, is reflected in the types of reports produced and their dissemination. Despite the efforts of researchers to progress beyond basic site description, reporting and publication changed little from that of the 1970s. Despite changes in institutional participation and priorities or researchers' academic objectives over the decades, one aspect of fur trade archaeology has remained constant. Whether an intended objective or not, archaeological excavations in themselves often come to represent a major event prompting public visitation where there is ready access.

Prevailing theoretical climate

This general situation has attracted criticism, the most prevalent being the lack of problem statements and the sense that not much knowledge has resulted from the great deal of work that had been done (Adams 1981; Pyszczyk 1987). A number of explanations for this have already been advanced, including field practices and background training, legislative concerns, government directives and development priorities. However, fur trade archaeology did not grow haphazardly, despite such appearances, but flourished within a prevailing archaeological climate that influenced practice and interpretation in the entire discipline, including historical archaeology.

Despite its infancy, historical archaeology was also greatly influenced by the fundamental changes that swept North American archaeology. Although archaeological work on historic sites occurred prior to the 1960s it was not identified as a field until the founding of the Society for Historical Archaeology in 1967. The early practitioners were few, and with most trained in history and the humanities (Cleland 1993: 13) debate centred around whether the new field should be history or anthropology, giving rise to a crisis of identity (see Harrington, Noel-Hume, Walker, Cotter, Fontana and Griffin, and Cleland in Schuyler 1978). While the historian archaeologists advocated a particularistic paradigm described as idiographic and inductive (the 'handmaiden to history' approach), the anthropological archaeologists, supporters of the 'New Archaeology', promoted the scientific method with an emphasis on discovering cultural patterns and processes (Cleland 1993: 13). Despite these alternative archaeological approaches, South (1993: 15) notes that most of the reports in the early 1970s were still 'narrative, site descriptive, methodological, or synthesizing in nature'.

Fur trade studies in the 1960s and 1970s paralleled the basic developments in historical archaeology at this time. Researchers focused their energies on discovering and identifying sites to establish regional histories and producing artefact typologies and chronologies, to provide a foundation for comparative studies. The overriding preoccupation rested with site layout, building construction, feature descriptions and artefact typology, manufacture and production. Also the federal government in the 1970s began training individuals in the identification and analysis of material culture.

Major developments in historical archaeology finally began to emerge in the late 1970s and, according to Deagan (1993: 20), can be attributed to three crucial works that appeared in 1977. South's *Method and Theory in Historical Archaeology* focused on quantification and pattern recognition, with an emphasis upon scientific and processual research; Deetz's *In Small Things Forgotten* promoted a humanistic and cognitive approach; and in Ferguson's edited volume, *Historical Archaeology and the Importance of Material Things*, discussion centred on different conceptual approaches available to study material culture. This recognition and early acceptance of a 'paradigmatic pluralism' (Fitting 1977: 67), along with an unwillingness to abandon the historical dimensions of the subject, helped historical archaeology escape the more dogmatic aspects of processualist archaeology which drove prehistoric archaeology in the 1960s and 1970s. However, it took until the mid-1980s for historical archaeology to break free of its 'famous person styles of research and its historical particularism' (Adams 1993: 29).

The expansion of research objectives in fur trade archaeology began to appear in the 1970s, and is most noticeable in the works that appeared after 1977. The most influential of the three was South's approach, which promoted a hypothetico-deductive method and the quantification of artefact assemblages. The popularity of this approach in western Canada, in one instance, coincided with the arrival of John Combes, an American historical archaeologist, as Chief of Archaeology at the Parks Canada office in Winnipeg. Combes had been directly involved with the South approach and this appointment provided a favourable environment for pursuing new research aims (Klimko 1994: 145). By the early 1980s, in a mere two decades, historical archaeology had made rapid theoretical progress from descriptive and chronological concerns, through cultural historical studies, to problems of culture process, cognition and archaeological principles (Deagan 1982: 153). This represents an ongoing trend which encourages myriad theoretical perspectives that include middle-range theory, symbolism, structuralism and postprocessual concerns, such as sociopolitical influences/implications, critical analysis and gender (see Beaudry 1988; Gould and Schiffer 1981; Gullason 1990; Leone and Potter 1988; Spencer-Wood 1987).

Fur trade archaeologists during the 1980s embraced advances in quantification (Prager 1980; Pyszczyk 1978), hypothesis formation (Klimko 1982) and pattern recognition (Christianson 1980; Forsman 1983; McLeod 1981; Petch 1983) which raised the application of scientific method to historical archaeology to its peak in the mid-1980s. A materialist position with emphasis on the role of the environment and culture pervaded most work, whether this was applied to an individual post or to thematic issues explored on a number of sites. Towards the end of the 1980s, a few researchers began reaching beyond processualism to symbolic (Burley and Dalla Bone 1988), cognitive (Pyszczyk 1987) and critical approaches (Pyszczyk 1989). Studies at other historic sites such as North West Mounted Police and *métis* and gold rush sites in western Canada contributed to the diversification of research perspectives witnessed in fur trade archaeological research.

In the 1990s research orientation became still more diverse. While scientific, problem-oriented research continued strongly, postprocessual, contextual approaches began to enjoy more attention. Examples include the analysis of the role of architecture, space and material culture in reinforcing social information within the fort community (Hamilton 1990); the identification of HBC's use of architecture at Lower Fort Garry to reinforce its dominant economic and social position within the community (Monks 1992); and concerns with gender and acculturation at Fort George (Gullason 1990). However, there is still a continued interest in traditional fur trade archaeology to supplement historical interpretation (Burley *et al.* 1996; Pyszczyk 1992) and an emphasis on resource overexploitation research (Burley and Hamilton 1990, 1991).

In sum, archaeological studies of the fur trade have tended to reflect prevailing theoretical developments in archaeology with respect to perspectives and methods. Changes in theoretical orientation began in earnest during the 1970s and continue today. While this broadening of research objectives is encouraging, the overriding concerns of many fur trade programmes still rest with historical questions geared to site discovery, identification and chronology – the same forces that initiated the early fur trade site surveys. This focus continues because the resource base is still virtually unknown, despite earlier work, and these basic historical questions still need to be answered before archaeologists can entertain more complex research concerns.

Discussion

Political and cultural influences

Western Canadian fur trade archaeological studies began with the historic site commemoration and development movement of the late 1950s and

1960s, a focus set by the Federal Historic Sites and Monuments Board in 1919. The Board viewed itself as part of an educated elite whose duty lay in imparting proper values of patriotism, duty, self-sacrifice and spiritual devotion to young and new Canadians and members of lower orders of society (Taylor 1990: 47). This group chose different themes for various regions of the country. For western Canada the central themes were exploration and the fur trade. These were seen as symbolising the opening of the West and defining its geopolitical boundaries (Payne 1991a; Taylor and Payne 1992). Fur trade forts figured prominently in this setting because they were physically imposing and attracted widespread public attention (Taylor 1990: 137).

By the 1960s and 1970s federal and provincial agencies had identified sites – usually large fur trade centres – for commemoration or reconstruction/restoration, and nationalist and tourist or economic (usually employment) concerns (Klimko 1994). This context proved to be qualitatively different and more delimiting than that pertaining to the practice of prehistoric archaeology. Early archaeologists working on fur trade sites found themselves incorporated into a well-established historical programme. Archaeology not only entered the scene as the 'hand-maiden to history', but also immediately took on a 'mission-oriented' approach to provide information required for restoration or reconstruction. As a result, studies carried out by archaeologists for heritage agencies placed emphasis on locational, architectural and technological concerns. This emphasis fostered descriptive reports on features and artefacts.

Reconstruction and restoration greatly contributed to the state of fur trade archaeology because of its requirement for authenticity. Archaeology, by presenting physical features and artefacts, demonstrated that the past really existed, and allowed for the experience of it via direct and real contact with it (Lipe 1984: 4). In addition to creating a Canadian cultural identity for the visiting public and reinforcing values, reconstructions also provided an economic vehicle that is in a mutually sustaining relationship with the tourism industry. This relationship means that archaeology and heritage management are also caught up in the concerns of the tourist market where interpretation is geared towards the largely white middle class and presents an inoffensive, sanitised and idealised version of the past (Bowes 1977: 20; Brown in Payne 1991b: 10; Coutts 1992: 287; Laenen 1989: 88). Instead of challenging visitors' perceptions or attempting to revise outdated, flawed or even racist interpretations, the Canadian myth of the hardy trader/explorer braving the wilderness and dealing with aboriginal people cast as 'noble savages' or friends of the fur trader is perpetuated (Brown in Payne 1991b: 10;

Coutts 1992: 287), as well as the view of the fur trade as a 'pre-industrial' state leading to civilisation (Klimko 1994: 182).

Archaeology played a role in this reconstruction/restoration fur trade scenario by providing authenticity in such tangibles as building locations and dimensions, but the interpretation often reflected contemporary views, both theoretical and functional. Most major restorations or reconstructions took place in the 1960s and 1970s, during an optimistic era when federal and provincial centennials were being celebrated (for example Canada's hundredth birthday in 1967). Since then no new sites, federal or provincial, have been developed and, as a result, most fail to reflect the 'new politics of fur trade historiography very well' (Payne 1991a) which include issues of gender relations, family patterns and most importantly the role of aboriginal people in this venture. However, redevelopment activities at some reconstructed sites such as Fort Carlton in Saskatchewan are rectifying this situation by focusing their efforts on aboriginal aspects of the fur trade (personal communication Ian Dyck, 1999).

Archaeologists trained in 'prehistoric' archaeology and armed with a culture historical focus were unprepared to deal with the large-scale posts chosen for commemoration and reconstruction by the various heritage agencies or groups. Archaeology proved to be an event in itself, providing the public with that tangible link to the past – their past. However, once the field season ended and had served its legitimating function, funds and time were rarely provided for laboratory work and publications. Development agencies requesting architectural information were not interested in integrative or regional studies. If the archaeologists wanted to pursue other avenues of research they could do so, but in their own time and at their own expense. In the 1970s historic fur trade archaeologists were willing and eager to employ a problem-oriented approach promoted by processual archaeology. Unfortunately, the lack of completed artefact analyses and site reports and the difficulty of obtaining manuscripts proved to be major obstacles. The net result of this situation was that fur trade archaeology jumped from cultural identification to cultural integration and missed the cultural descriptive stage – basically the culture history of material items within the context of the fur trade (Adams in Klimko 1994: 165).

The growth of cultural resource management since 1990 has continued to perpetuate low-level research as investigators fulfil minimum requirements. Despite the fact that large sums of money became available and the number of researchers increased, the managerial priorities of provincial government agencies charged with heritage management overrode any personal research objectives. 'Applied' archaeology done continually at the expense of 'academic' or 'pure' archaeological research leaves fur trade archaeology with some fundamental shortcomings. While many believe that universities should get back to doing 'pure' research, this is almost impossible with so few historical archaeologists working in university contexts, a situation not easily rectified in these times of economic constraint.

Although advances were made in the 1970s and 1980s, fur trade archaeology has never been able to break away completely from reconstruction, tourism or commemorative themes. Whereas fur trade archaeology in the past provided the details required to reconstruct or restore fur trade forts authentically for the visiting public, today archaeology itself often becomes the attraction, without reconstruction as the end goal. However, the final result is still the same, in that funds rarely exist for detailed analyses.

Aboriginal people and the fur trade

The early focus of sponsoring institutions on retrieval of architectural data for the purpose of reconstruction and interpretation circumvented any substantial desire for information about the participation of aboriginal people in the fur trade. If they were incorporated, aboriginal sites included either those somehow involved with the 'civilisation' process, such as the signing of treaties, or prehistoric sites such as Head-Smashed-In Buffalo Jump, which emphasised the association of aboriginal people with the wilderness, both of which needed to be tamed and civilised. An aboriginal participation in the fur trade was acknowledged, but only as a backdrop to substantiate their subservient role in the inevitable civilisation of the West. Indeed, the exploitation and manipulation of aboriginal people (as well as a discussion of frontier warfare) would not be deemed suitable themes for public presentation.

Archaeologists did not intentionally ignore the aboriginal elements of fur trade history, but they were required to work to meet the goals of the agencies that had employed them. For example, the restrictive mandate of federal programmes prohibited researchers from working beyond project boundaries (Herst 1994), with the consequence that rarely were aboriginal sites identified within the fort setting. Prevailing theoretical and philosophical issues also tempered research approaches. The archaeological work of the 1960s and 1970s has been criticised as being redundant or irrelevant, particularly in its inability to provide new or useful information for historians or interpreters, but what is overlooked is that it fulfilled its primary function of providing authenticity in the construction of the 'authoritative' fur trade story.

By the time major theoretical changes began to emerge in the late 1970s, the optimistic economic climate was being replaced by an atmosphere of uncertainty combined with economic hardship – a climate which prevailed throughout the 1980s and continues today. The optimistic broadening of research questions in the late 1970s, however, did not extend towards the role of aboriginal people in the fur trade. Questions dealing with the influence of the fur trade experience on aboriginal economy, technology and social organisation began to take root in the early 1980s, with continued growth throughout the decade. Studies began to address concerns such as aboriginal encampments adjacent to fur trade posts, as well as those beyond the immediate vicinity of the post, and gender relations. Such research objectives get us away from history set in terms of relations between European traders and aboriginal people (Brown 1990: 16). Although the potential of these aboriginal sites to reveal other events is promising, major problems, apart from funding, lie in getting these interests integrated into larger project goals and in finding and identifying such sites. Lack of stratigraphy, a problem often encountered in boreal forest areas, makes the separation of components difficult, while the short duration of aboriginal encampments leaves little evidence in the archaeological record (Klimko 1994: 187).

In Canada this trend towards aboriginal issues reflects the larger sociopolitical atmosphere presently pervading the country. Reactions against museum exhibitions to protest unresolved land claims, confrontation between aboriginal and non-aboriginal peoples, and increasing numbers of government and court decisions favouring aboriginal rights and title have brought aboriginal concerns into the public realm. If power in human relations is seen 'as the capacity to alter events', and if that capacity rests on 'the control of force, consciousness, tools, and the ability to create pleasure and a positive social sense of self' (Paynter and McGuire 1991: 13), then aboriginal groups have demonstrated their ability and willingness to alter events, and are a formidable force no longer to be ignored. Significantly, some of the archaeological fur trade projects carried out in the 1990s were initiated by aboriginal communities. All these activities are challenging the stereotypic image of aboriginal people as obedient children unable to change (Francis 1992: 220), or 'impediments to settlement' (Burley 1984: 13), or 'members of a disorganised, unsophisticated, scattered people occupying a virtually empty land' (Doxtator 1988: 26), or a group whose culture – technological and intellectual – was inferior and could not survive in competition with Euro-Canadian society. According to Doxtator (1988: 26), such images exist and persist because they function as readily understood symbols in the predominant culture and not because of their fallacy or accuracy. However, if knowledge and truth are always changing and always linked to power, as Tilley (1990a: 340) advocates, then the increasing aboriginal presence in the political arena should alter presently accepted 'truths', thereby forcing 'a viewing of past events from multiple directions simultaneously' (Wylie 1992: 593).

Conclusion

Favourable economic times, combined with a nationalistic programme to promote a 'Canadian' identity and potential tourism market, gave life, meaning and direction to early fur trade archaeology. That archaeology is a social product, often practised by white middle-class interests, has been asserted in this history of fur trade archaeology. Undeniably, the political and academic contexts in which archaeology is practised structure and influence the interpretation of the past (Fowler 1987: 240) – an issue of increasing concern amongst indigenous people world-wide (see Schmidt and Patterson 1996b). While aboriginal peoples were not totally left out of fur trade histories they were treated as 'them as seen by us' – a situation identified by Lorenzo (1981) in Mesoamerica. Fur trade researchers may have had their own ideas or objectives, but they followed the archaeological traditions in which they were trained, and for personal reasons, such as gainful employment, adhered to or followed government policy. At times the use of the past by the archaeologist may be the polar opposite to nationalist considerations.

Today the rise of aboriginal awareness, consciousness and education is demanding a re-evaluation of past interpretations. Fur trade archaeology can play an important role as a major source 'for understanding the cultures that "collided" at contact and the processes of cultural interaction and colonisation that then unfolded' (Wylie 1993: 9) in western Canada.

Acknowledgements

A number of individuals willingly shared information, thoughts and insights into the practice of archaeology and the fur trade and provided encouragement and support in the research of this topic over the years. In particular I would like to thank Heinz Pyszczyk, David Burley, Bruce Trigger, Alison Wylie, David Meyer and Gary Adams. I am deeply indebted to Ian Dyck and

Scott Hamilton who over the past decades have consistently supported my research and willingly shared their views through enjoyable and enlightening discussions, and also promptly reviewed an earlier draft of this chapter and provided their usual candid and thoughtful insights and comments. Shannon Wood kindly offered to computer draft the map for which I am grateful. As in all such histories and analyses, the observations and interpretations presented here are my own.

Contact archaeology and the writing
of Aboriginal history

CHRISTINE WILLIAMSON

Introduction

In recent years a significant gap has developed between the requirements
of the two main consumers of information about Aboriginal Australia.
Archaeologists have become increasingly concerned with pushing back the
chronological boundaries of human occupation on the continent and illus-
trating Pleistocene human behaviours. However, Aboriginal people have
tended to be more concerned with recent history, ancestors and ties to place
(particularly in light of the *Native Title Act* 1993). The differing agendas
and requirements of these two groups have highlighted the tension between
investigations of the recent and the more remote past – a tension exacerbated by the disciplinary divide that tends to see Aboriginal prehistory as
the domain of archaeologists and investigations of more recent time periods
as subjects for anthropologists and historians.

This division between history and prehistory, and therefore between
investigations of pre- and postcontact Aboriginal society, has not facili-
tated our understanding of the more recent Aboriginal past. Rather it has
led to a focus on the pivotal historical point of contact with Europeans, and
a failure to explore both the lead-up to, and the aftermath of, this process of
interaction. This has had the effect of dissociating recent Aboriginal experiences from those of the more remote past and weakening links between
the pre- and postcontact periods. It has also caused studies of Aboriginal
responses to contact with Europeans to be presented as isolated vignettes
that lack an overarching framework within which such experiences might
be investigated and understood.

In this chapter I argue that in order to explore the Aboriginal experience
of contact with Europeans, the pre- and postcontact worlds are most profitably investigated as a historical continuum and not as being divided by
the presence or absence of history or archaeology (or indeed as the exclu-
sive preserve of either discipline). The proposal that analyses of indigenous
responses to contact situations must cover a much longer time period than
the actual 'moment' of contact itself is not a new one (see, for example,

Bartel 1984: 12; Fowler 1991: 198; Lightfoot 1995: 200; Moore 1987: 86; Trigger 1983: 440). However, most studies that adopt such an approach use a brief synthesis, often derived solely from secondary archaeological and ethnohistorical sources, as a baseline description of 'traditional' Aboriginal society. Postcontact changes and continuities are then measured against this yardstick (see, for example, Broome 1994; Ryan 1975, 1996). Such general caricatures are often used by both archaeologists and historians to provide a backdrop to discussions on acculturation and the process of indigenous peoples 'losing' their culture and being drawn into a western lifestyle following contact (see, for example, Clark 1962). Few scholars have turned their attention to a consideration of how continuities and changes in indigenous cultures might be tracked from the precontact to the postcontact period, and what effects the use of both archaeological and historical data may have on the type(s) of history produced from such investigations.

This chapter continues an exploration of the issue of how archaeologists might define a field of discourse within which to investigate the indigenous experience of contact with Europeans. I do this for two reasons. The first is to engage with significant methodological issues related to the integration of historical and archaeological data and perspectives. The second is to contribute to the writing of a history of Aboriginal Australia. I argue that the divide created between studies of pre- and postcontact Aboriginal society reflects both the disciplinary split between archaeology and history, and a broader philosophical dichotomy between explanations invoking history/science, particularism/generalisation, event/process and agency/structure. These dualities have hampered investigations aimed at exploring changes and continuities in trajectories of Aboriginal behaviour following contact with Europeans. I suggest that the use of heuristic models derived from non-linear modelling may provide a more appropriate framework within which to incorporate both the historical and archaeological data sets relevant to the investigation of contact.

Past approaches to the writing of Aboriginal history in Australia

In a 1968 Boyer lecture, William Stanner made the claim that Aboriginal people were conspicuously absent from Australian historical works. This lack of discussion about Australia's indigenous population he called 'the great Australian silence' (Stanner 1969: 25). However, while Stanner was correct in identifying such a 'silence' in works of the twentieth century, considerations of the Aboriginal experience have not always been alien to Australian historical narratives. Most of the accounts on the newly founded Australian colonies produced during the early to mid-1800s included lengthy descriptions of the 'natives', their habits and their interactions with European colonisers. The authors of these works, moved by the then current philosophical sentiments regarding the 'nobility' of savage peoples and their lifestyles (and generally not personally confronted by the harsh reality of frontier life) often portrayed Aboriginal people in a sympathetic light as a naive people cruelly dispossessed by the lowest classes of English society. Prior Aboriginal claims to land were frequently recognised, as was the role of Europeans as invaders and murderers (see, for example, Rusden 1883). For many of these writers Tasmania served as a specific focus of research, owing to both the extreme violence of Aboriginal/European conflict and the subsequent removal of the entire Aboriginal population from the island and their (perceived) annihilation (see, for example, Burn 1973; Melville 1965 [1835]; West 1971 [1852]).

However, by the latter part of the nineteenth century the tenor of writings about Australian Aboriginal populations was changing. Darwinist theories were having an impact not only in biology but also in the area of social theory, and this, coupled with the increasing rate of industrialisation during the Victorian era, led to a philosophical movement that emphasised progress, advancement and social replacement. Whereas the authors of the earlier period had clearly acknowledged European culpability, these later works generally chose to place the blame for the Aboriginal decline on natural causes controlled by scientific principles outside the sphere of human influence (see, for example Bonwick 1870, 1884; Calder 1875; Roth 1899). No longer portrayed as the victims of a cruel and unjust invasion, Aboriginal people were now depicted as members of a Stone Age society whose regrettable decline was inevitable in the face of the unstoppable march of progress and the operation of natural (cultural) selection.

It was during this period that research interest in Aboriginal peoples began to shift from the sphere of history to that of the emerging field of anthropology. The idea of a hierarchy of human societies ranging from simple to complex was nothing new and had its roots in eighteenth-century orderings along the Great Chain of Being. However, when coupled with Victorian views on progress, social Darwinist ideas, the acceptance of an expanded and non-biblical chronology for human antiquity and the recovery of the archaeological remains of early human groups from across Europe, this hierarchical classification came to be seen as a chronological ordering, representing the progress of human groups through the ages. Aboriginal people, still using stone tools and living a hunter-gatherer lifestyle, were placed far down the scale, where they represented a stage that those groups ordered above them had passed through some time in their past. Huxley specifically focused anthropological and archaeological research interest on to Australian Aboriginal people when he compared them both physically, through a comparison of skulls, and technologically, by noting a similarity in stone artefacts, with the Neanderthals and other early human groups. In being cast as prehistoric analogues by Huxley and others, Aboriginal people came to be seen as the same as the prehistoric populations which had been (re)created in their image and became viewed as the remnants of a bygone era. Thus Edward Tylor wrote in the introduction to the first edition of Roth's *The Aborigines of Tasmania*:

if there have remained anywhere up to modern times men whose condition has changed little since the early Stone Age, the Tasmanians seem to have been such a people . . . the condition of man nearest to his lowest level of culture. (Roth 1899: v)

He added that:

these rude savages remain within the present century representatives of the immensely ancient palæolithic period . . . It is thus becoming clearer and clearer that the anthropology of this remote district can give us clues as to the earliest state of civilization . . . man of the Lower Stone Age ceases to be a creature of philosophic interest and becomes a known reality. (Roth 1899: vii)

Thus the Australian Aboriginal population was cast in the role of an unchanging and timeless people – a people without history, and consequently, with the formalisation of the disciplinary split between anthropology/archaeology and history at the end of the nineteenth century, Aboriginal people began to be 'eliminated from the historical conscious-ness' (Markus 1977: 170). Aboriginal people, unchanging throughout the ages and having left no written records, were seen as having no history and were therefore considered to be the subject material of anthropologists and archaeologists, whereas progressive, literate Europeans, who did leave written records, had a history and were best investigated by historians.

The structuralist/functionalist paradigm of early twentieth-century anthropology continued to stress the unchanging and static nature of Aboriginal society via a research agenda aimed at collecting as much infor-mation as possible about 'traditional' society before all the Aboriginal people died out or became acculturated. Archaeological studies during this time were also emphasising the conservative nature of Aboriginal societies. In his 1928 address at the opening of an anthropological conference R. W. Pulleine, echoing A. L. Kroeber's earlier statements of 1909 regarding North American Indian cultures, stated of Aboriginal studies that:

> in all our stations there is a uniformity of culture only modified by the availability of different raw materials for manufacture . . . it is also to be feared that excavation would be in vain, as everything points to the conclusion that they were an unchanging people, living in an unchanging environment. (in Mulvaney 1975: 12)

Therefore, during the late nineteenth and early twentieth centuries, Aboriginal people were effectively excluded from general Australian historical writings and relegated to essentialist, ahistorical subjects in anthropological and archaeological research (Attwood 1992: vii; Murray 1992a: 3). As a consequence the impact of contact with Europeans, and the subsequent changes evident in Aboriginal cultures, were not seen to be a part of the research programme of history, anthropology or the emerging field of archaeology.

Rowse (1988: 174) has argued that colonising cultures tend to construct idealised and ahistorical images of the societies that they subjugate. The study of 'traditional' society is seen as a valid scientific pursuit whereas postcontact changes are viewed as adulterations that serve to weaken and destroy the 'traditional' culture. Thus a paradox is created where, on the one hand, Aboriginal societies are presented as unable to adapt to changing circumstances, while any changes that do occur are viewed with dismay as evidence of a people in the process of losing their culture (see, for example, Berndt and Berndt 1988). In this manner the colonisers take control over the production of knowledge about indigenous cultures and reserve the right to distinguish what are the authentic and unauthentic elements of contemporary societies under study. The narrow focus upon 'traditional' and 'authentic' Aboriginal people has resulted in the anthropological and archaeological collaboration of the erasure of postcontact Aboriginal/European interactions from critical scrutiny (Cowlishaw 1992: 20). The view that Aboriginal groups are conservative, static and unchanging leads to the conclusion that any changes in Aboriginal societies were forced upon them from outside, placing Aboriginal people in the position of passive recipients of a contact experience that resulted in the degradation of the traditional system and gradual acculturation.

One of the first anthropologists to question the apparently unchanging nature of Aboriginal society, and to address specifically the question of the impact of colonialism upon Aboriginal groups, was A. P. Elkin. In 1951 he published 'Reaction and interactions: a food gathering people and European settlement in Australia', in which he attempted to develop a chronological model that classified the 'stages' through which Aboriginal societies passed following contact. In doing so he presented a far less static view of Aboriginal culture than had been developed previously within anthropology and reintroduced the notion of change and, by implication, history. While very broad and general, his discussions did provide some structure to attempts to investigate the contact experience and postcontact changes in Aboriginal societies and placed such issues on the anthropological agenda (albeit peripherally).

However, during the 1960s only a handful of researchers turned their attention towards the issue of Aboriginal/European contact which was still seen to be outside the mainstream interests of historians, anthropologists and archaeologists. The Australian Institute of Aboriginal Studies, established in 1961, has been seen often as representing the dawning of a new era of interest in Aboriginal studies. However, as Mulvaney (1986: 51) has noted, this group tended to perpetuate past attitudes. No Aboriginal people were present at the inaugural meeting, no papers dealing with postcontact Aboriginal society were presented and the general theme arising from the meeting was the continued need to collect as much information as possible before all 'traditional' Aboriginal groups died out.

The situation changed dramatically in the late 1960s and 1970s (see Mulvaney 1990a). In 1961 Mulvaney recovered the first Pleistocene date for the human occupation of Australia. Over the next decade the dating of more Aboriginal archaeological sites and the subsequent development of an archaeological chronology, along with myriad regional archaeological studies, began to demonstrate that prehistory had witnessed great variability in Aboriginal responses both across the continent and through time. Hence the situation in Aboriginal studies was one where archaeology was demonstrating that prehistoric Aboriginal culture had encompassed considerable diversity, while anthropology was emphasising the conservative nature of Aboriginal societies. This uncomfortable paradox, when combined with evidence that Aboriginal people were not going to 'die out', the clear failure of the Australian Government's policies of assimilation and the growing political voice of indigenous populations both within Australia and overseas, was the impetus for historians to begin to challenge traditional perceptions of Aboriginal people and their experiences of contact.

In the early 1970s Charles Rowley published his trilogy on the fate of Aboriginal populations following the arrival of Europeans, produced while he was Director of the Aborigines in Australian Society Project (Rowley 1970, 1971, 1972). The synthesis of such a vast amount of information has been branded as premature (Biskup 1982: 21); however, while the work was presented in narrative rather than analytical style, it none the less served to highlight future areas for study and placed the investigation of postcontact Aboriginal history firmly on the research agenda.

Rowley's works are vast and ambitious, and painstakingly meticulous in their attention to detail. However, many of the other works produced on Aboriginal/European contact during the 1970s were less scholarly, as a flood of books on the topic made their way on to the market. In attempting to ride the wave of popularism, highly emotive, simplistic and self-serving pieces focusing on frontier violence were produced which tended to cast Aboriginal people as warrior heroes engaged in a patriotic battle to defend their country. MacIntyre (1990: xiv) has written of this style of writing that 'if historians had previously emptied the Australian past of an active Aboriginal presence, they now drenched it in blood'. Such studies, labelled the 'national guilt brand' of history (Biskup 1982: 12), were seen as an attempt to address the injustices of Aboriginal/European contact and reach atonement in the present through highlighting the atrocities of the past. Within this agenda the writing of Aboriginal history became intimately intertwined with modern-day political aims and was seen as a potent tool in the reconciliation process. At its worst this style of writing ended up committing the sin of passing modern-day value judgements on past actions by ignoring the maxim that 'the past is another country', and ultimately served merely to update the noble savage myth. Thus Attwood (1989a: 136) has written that 'in dragging Aborigines out of the past to serve present purposes there has been a falsification of the past that denied them the historical specificity of their time and their "otherness", and which paradoxically repeated the oppression of colonialism'.

However, during this time other researchers were turning their attention to Aboriginal history and the description of Aboriginal/European interactions (see, for example Markus 1977; Mulvaney 1975; Reece 1974). Amongst them was Henry Reynolds, who published his first book, *Aborigines and Settlers*, in 1972. In this volume he presented the framework that was to overarch all his subsequent work, and that of most other historians investigating Aboriginal postcontact history. MacIntyre (1990: xiv) has argued that Reynolds is the historian who has done the most to alter our perceptions of the Aboriginal response to invasion and that his 'combination of commitment and scholarly imagination has opened a vast new area of historical inquiry'. While a watershed in terms of its demonstration that Aboriginal reactions to contact are amenable to investigation by standard historical means and the shifting of historical focus on to the issue of contact, Reynolds' work is ultimately unsubtle in both argument and substance.

Analysis is placed within a model of European dominance and Aboriginal resistance to that dominance – thus dividing Aboriginal people and Europeans into two diametrically opposed groups. However, as authors such as Trigger (1976: 23) and Sahlins (1993: 13) have pointed out, contact is not just about a meeting of opposites but also involves the mediation of relationships between a number of competing and cross-cutting interest groups. Many of Reynolds' investigations focus on the frontier where extreme examples of violence between the two 'sides' were most apparent. Aboriginal responses to invasion outside the geographical and temporal boundaries of the frontier, or those that do not fit within the category of 'resistance', remain unexplored and are generally not amenable to analysis. Such a focus upon conflict, to the exclusion of other interactions, has been criticised by Campbell (1997: 30).

In the 1970s and 1980s Reynolds' dominance/resistance model was the standard framework within which most research into Aboriginal/European relations was undertaken (see, for example, Loos 1982; Morris 1989; Ryan 1975). New bodies of information were provided; however, these were generally used to refine the master model rather than seriously to challenge it (Attwood 1989a: 137). Most authors were content to document the horrors of frontier conflict and did little to provide broader structures of meaning and analysis, or to facilitate investigations into contact dynamics. The continued emphasis on frontier violence further marginalised many Aboriginal people from the mainstream of Australian history by downplaying their experiences. More extreme examples even criticised those Aboriginal people who were thought to have been 'collaborators' rather than the expected resistance fighters (see, for example Rae-Ellis 1981).

During this time a few researchers were producing analyses that questioned the Reynolds model. In 1983, McGrath's doctoral dissertation on Aboriginal/European interactions on Northern Territory cattle stations was completed. This was followed in 1988 by Haebich's study on interactions in Western Australia, published in 1992. While still broadly framed within the dominance/resistance model, these smaller-scale regional studies pointed to Aboriginal responses other than resistance through violence, thus revealing some level of complexity to the issue of interactions. In highlighting the variability of Aboriginal responses they revealed that the Reynolds model, with its concentration on frontier violence, was not as all-encompassing as had been thought and was really only applicable to specific situations and time periods. However, these investigations also represented a shift in research emphasis towards particularistic studies, and a movement away from attempts to generate a synthesised understanding of contact as a phenomenon. This research trend towards particularism can be seen as a feature of the by then well-established rigidity of the disciplinary divide between archaeology (precontact) and history (postcontact). This division had the effect of limiting research upon postcontact Aboriginal groups to circumstantial narratives, as there was no basis upon which to make broader statements of process. Detailed comparisons with earlier time periods were not thought to be possible since information on the precontact situation was generally not to be found within historical documents.

In recognition of this, during the late 1970s and early 1980s, a number of investigations into Aboriginal history began to incorporate archaeological research and information from anthropology, linguistics, oral history, etc. in a manner not dissimilar to that developed by North American ethno-historians. However, this information was often used merely to provide a simplistic and stylised backdrop of precontact Aboriginal culture against which later frontier atrocities were carried out (see, for example, Broome 1982; Ryan 1975). Exceptions to this include Blainey's *Triumph of the Nomads* (1975) and Mulvaney's *The Prehistory of Australia* (1975). However, while both of these pieces of research incorporated archaeological and histori-cal data within an overall history of Aboriginal Australia, they did so in a descriptive manner and offered little in the way of frameworks within which such material might be investigated and long-term processes identified.

Australian archaeology is a relatively young field and most research to date has been focused upon the establishment of chronology and the iden-tification of regional variation through prehistory. Consequently, very little archaeological research within Australia has focused on Aboriginal societies in later historical time periods or the investigation of Aboriginal/European interactions. The first detailed investigation on this topic was Allen's PhD thesis (1969) on the European settlement at Port Essington. This elegant, and in many ways ground-breaking, piece of research still stands as the best example of contact archaeology in Australia. Since that time a num-ber of small-scale studies have been carried out, focusing on specific sites without any attempt being made to place the analyses within a larger frame-work of interpretation (see, for example, Coutts 1981; Coutts *et al.* 1977; Penny and Rhodes 1990; Rhodes 1986). Generally the reporting of sites belonging to the postcontact period is an unexpected outcome of research into prehistoric Aboriginal culture. One exception to this has been Birm-ingham's (1992) investigations at Wybalenna which adopted the Reynolds dominance/resistance model as the framework of analysis and focused upon the process of acculturation. However, almost all of the archaeo-logical research produced on contact in Australia has concentrated upon the investigation of contact within a European superstructure through focusing upon Aboriginal people located on missions or within other spheres of European influence.

The 1990s have seen increased interest in investigations of contact within both history and archaeology. Some researchers have turned to Foucault and Althusser in their attempts to analyse contact interactions as power relationships (see, for example, papers in Attwood 1992). Often these studies attempt to make the link between power relationships in the past and the construction of Aboriginal identity in the present. Murray (1993) has also framed his analysis of Aboriginal/European interactions within the ongoing present-day debates on the construction of identity (both Aboriginal and non-Aboriginal), the writing of Aboriginal history and the reconciliation process. However, most recent work has floundered for lack of a theoretical direction. Many researchers still place their research within a modified version of the dominance/resistance model (see, for example, Broome 1994), or turn their attention to the minutiae of contact through very specific case studies (see, for example, Bairstow 1993). Others provide detailed information about contact scenarios but are unable or unwilling to draw these together in order to provide a broader perspective (see, for example Mulvaney 1989).

Archaeology and history

Reviewing past approaches to the writing of Aboriginal history has revealed that, since the end of the nineteenth century, a split has developed between studies of pre- and postcontact Aboriginal societies. The time period before the arrival of Europeans and the creation of written documentary records is generally thought to be the domain of archaeologists and not a subject for historical research. However, Aboriginal societies in later time periods have received scant attention from historians because, as Reece (1979: 259) has stated, 'there is almost no documentary evidence of the Aboriginal experience of early contact and conflict, and where there is no documentation, historians are still fearful to tread'. The exploration of contact interactions has therefore tended to fall between the cracks of the two disciplines.

The paucity of documentation relating to indigenous cultures prior to, and even during, the contact period has often been cited as the main reason why it is not possible to write the history of such groups and why their study must remain the domain of anthropologists and archaeologists (Elton 1967; Urry 1979: 2). However, the view that history proper can only be written for literate 'progressive' societies reflects a nineteenth-century (and earlier) view of hunter-gatherer groups as unchanging, timeless and representative of a stage that more 'advanced' societies have passed through and progressed beyond. Such an approach is implicitly racist (Mulvaney 1990b: 157) and leads to the situation where indigenous peoples are continually presented in essentialist terms (see, for example, Murray 1992a, 1992b; Trigger 1985: 5). Condori has argued that 'prehistory is a Western concept according to which those societies which have not developed writing – or an equivalent system of graphic representation – *have no history*. This fits perfectly into the framework of evolutionist thought typical of Western culture' (1989: 51). Archaeologists have made frequent use of anthropological and historical sources detailing Aboriginal societies during the contact period. However, the use of such information on 'traditional' indigenous societies tends to be as a source of analogical inference. Rather than investigating these data sets for information about particular groups at particular points in time and the changes that they were undergoing, the documentary evidence is used to provide comparisons with prehistoric societies as defined by archaeological data. Considerations of dynamism or change in these historically documented Aboriginal societies are denied, as the material is presented in the timeless 'ethnographic present'. In utilising documentary sources in such a manner, archaeologists have unwittingly colluded not only in the denial of a historical trajectory to modern-day indigenous peoples, but also in the marginalisation of contact studies as a valid arena of research.

Murray (1992c) has argued that 'Aboriginal history has been the hidden history of Australia and . . . the primary task of the contact archaeologist and historian of Aboriginal Australia is to uncover it'. In order to investigate the Aboriginal experience of contact with Europeans and contribute to the writing of an Aboriginal history of Australia, archaeologists need to develop explanatory frameworks that will assist in the utilisation of data sources from both history and archaeology, as well as permit the crossing of the traditionally perceived precontact/postcontact divide.

One of the major challenges facing archaeologists investigating periods for which there are historical records is how to integrate information derived from both historical and archaeological sources. This involves a consideration of two related issues: (1) how to link the structure of the two data sets and the records produced from them, and (2) the manner in which the differing time periods, research areas, and theoretical and methodological approaches of the two disciplines might be incorporated. Frequently researchers deal with these two aspects as if they were the same problem and advocate an ethnohistorical approach that crosses the prehistory/history divide as a means of reaching a *rapprochement* between history and archaeology (see, for example, Head and Fullagar 1997). However, attempting to resolve the primarily epistemological questions of issue (2) in such a manner does not automatically lead to the resolution of the fundamentally ontological problems posed by issue (1).

It has been suggested that the writing of ethnohistory should be the place where archaeology and history reach methodological and theoretical reconciliation as it employs the theoretical framework of anthropology/archaeology with the research procedures of historiography (Cline 1972; Spores 1980: 474). Ethnohistory has been defined as 'anthropology with a time dimension or history informed by anthropological concepts' (Farriss 1986: 88), with its aim being to 'weld the methodologies of archaeology and historical research within the framework of anthropological theory to produce a view of the past not solely dependent upon the biases of either one' (Wilson and Rogers 1993: 7). Ethnohistorical research, pioneered by Lewis Henry Morgan, was primarily a North American development rising out of the direct historical approach. It became a research focus for anthropologists and archaeologists following the enactment of the *Indians Claims Commission Act* 1946 and the subsequent filing of over 400 land claims suits (Cline 1972: 11). Researchers were employed by Native American groups and the government to demonstrate or dispute indigenous peoples' claims of ties to particular tracts of land. This required the investigation of both historical documents and archaeological materials. Ethnohistorical research has also been a feature of Latin American studies; however, here its origins are somewhat different and derive from the presence of a vast body of documentation resulting from Spanish conquest as well as the indigenous epigraphic and pictographic records (Spores 1980: 577). It is only since about the 1970s that limited ethnohistorical research has been carried out in Australia.

Some researchers restrict the definition of ethnohistory to the use of documentary sources as an adjunct to anthropology (see, for example, Axtell 1992; Schuyler 1988). Others see it as an overarching term for the analysis of all the materials available for the study of non-literate societies, including data from linguistics, archaeology, palaeobiology, history, anthropology, etc. (see, for example, Cohen 1981; Merrell 1989). However, most researchers view ethnohistory as a methodology or set of techniques, rather than a discipline in its own right or a general term to describe indigenous history (Axtell 1978; Cline 1972; Spores 1980; Trigger 1985: 164; Wood 1990). Therefore, restricted to a methodology, ethnohistory has failed to live up to its original promise as the locus at which history and archaeology might come together through its inability to contribute to theory building and the resolution of some of the more intractable ontological issues involved in attempts to integrate historical and archaeological data sets.

As a result of this failure, the problem of how these two different records may be incorporated within an overarching theoretical framework for the investigation of contact remains unsolved. The lack of theoretical direction in historical archaeology in general, and contact studies in particular, has been lamented (see, for example, Cleland 1988; Deagan 1988: 8), with Bartel (1984: 9) bluntly stating that 'after a full century of examining colonialism and imperialism the archaeologist has yet to develop any comprehensive theory'. While it is easy to be seduced by the suggestion that a reflexive approach, in which the historical and archaeological data sets are played off against one another in a manner analogous to Binford's description of middle range theory, will result in a new synergy (see, for example, Leone 1988), recommendations as to how this might take place and what the result-ing product might look like have generally not been put forward. Typically a bowerbird type approach has been adopted, where bits and pieces are borrowed from other disciplines. However, Leonard (1993: 32) has argued that, 'without an overriding explanatory framework within which to oper-ate, this blending of perspectives leaves us in the situation where we can at best only supply ad hoc meaning to our considerations of the past'. What most frequently occurs is the relegation of archaeological information to the role of a data set subsidiary to the written documentary record which – viewed as the directly recorded thoughts of people – is prioritised as being the more accurate and detailed account. Archaeological data are therefore often used merely to illustrate the historical record with examples. As a result the conclusions of historical and contact archaeology are ultimately unsatisfying in that they serve merely to confirm what was already apparent in the documentary record.

Researchers have tended to focus upon forcing reconciliation between the archaeological and historical data sets rather than investigating and appre-ciating their different structural properties and looking for points where they do and do not intersect. However, as Ferguson (1977a: 7) has argued, 'the historical and archaeological records are different analogues of human behavior and should not necessarily be expected to coincide', with Graham (1991: 327) further stating that 'the data from ethnohistory and archaeol-ogy often lie in planes that do not intersect'. While several researchers have followed the work of historians such as Braudel (1989: 20) in arguing that history and prehistory are one and the same process, this does not necessarily translate into the archaeological and historical records being the same types of account of that process. Archaeological data consist primarily of items of material culture and other humanly produced residues that were created as a by-product of human activities, whereas the documentary database of history consists of deliberately recorded thoughts about and descriptions of human actions. As such, the broad structure of the two data sets is distinct and separate. Leone (1988: 33) has pointed out that, 'even within the one society, the artefacts and written records were used and produced by different people, for different purposes, at different times, and survived for different reasons'.

As well as these differences in the fundamental properties of the data sets of the two disciplines, there are structural differences in the two records produced from these data sets. These differences are frequently distilled into the notion that the view of archaeology is long-term and generalist whereas that of history is short-term and particularist (see, for example, Carmack 1972: 227; Elton 1967: 22). This perceived distinction between particularism and generalisation has a long history and has structured most of the discussions regarding the differences between archaeology and history (Leonard 1993: 33). While the work by historians such as Braudel and Febvre sought to elucidate long-term structural features through the investigation of documentary records, it is still often argued by archaeologists that only they can access information about long-term structures of human behaviour while historians are restricted to the investigation of short-term events and the actions of individuals. The ability of archaeology to inform about long-term behaviours that are thought not to be evident to historians is argued to be a reflection of the fact that archaeological materials recovered from sites tend to represent aggregates of behaviour or average tendencies over long time periods rather than the records of individual actors or events (see, for example, Bailey 1981a: 40; Foley 1981: 8).

However, this distinction between history as short-term and archaeology as long-term explanation is more conceptual than real, and has been exacerbated by the perpetuation of the processual characterisation of history as a particularising and non-scientific discipline. Since the 1960s there has been a conflict within archaeology between approaches attempting to illuminate human behaviour over the long term and generate 'laws' about human behaviour (the 'scientific' approach), and those aimed at 'humanising' the past and highlighting the role of individuals and human agency (the 'historical' approach). This tension within archaeology has led to the establishment of a philosophical dichotomy between explanations invoking history/science, particularism/generalism, event/process and agency/structure. The effect of setting up these oppositions has been to make the task of utilising both historical and archaeological data sets in the writing of Aboriginal history all the more difficult.

Processual archaeologists set as their agenda the elucidation of general laws or structures of human behaviour through the adoption of a scientific methodology. In making their argument that archaeological research needed to be conducted in a scientific manner, researchers adhering to the processual philosophy presented a simplistic caricature of historical research. Historical activities were described as being essentially descriptive, while the ultimate aims of archaeology were argued to be processual (Trigger 1978b: 22). Because of the focus on the search for cultural universals that cut across time and space, and the emphasis upon environmental factors, processual archaeology has been criticised as being ahistorical (Hodder *et al.* 1995: 3; Trigger 1983: 429) and incapable of dealing with individual actors and the less tangible aspects of human behaviour such as cognition and belief systems (Bell 1992: 158; Shanks and Tilley 1992: 123; Trigger 1991b: 553). In response, postprocessual archaeologists have sought to re-establish the links between archaeology and history and to reintroduce the individual into archaeological explanations. Such works tend to deny the existence of universal structure and argue that different cultures are quite distinct and need to be investigated within their own cultural context (Bell 1992: 144; Tilley 1990b). However, Hodder's critique of processual archaeology and his arguments that archaeology is a historical discipline are actually built upon Binford's initial characterisation of history as the descriptive study of events rather than the elucidation of process (Trigger 1978b: 5). Thus, in adopting such a view of history, postprocessual archaeology left itself open to being criticised for being unscientific, particularistic and ultimately unable to offer substantive explanations for cultural phenomena.

In recent times the distinction between history as short-term explanation and archaeology as long-term explanation has been the basis of much of the debate over the structure of the archaeological record. Following the works of the *Annalistes*, hierarchical schemes, aimed at explicating the links between the short-term 'events' visible to anthropologists and historians, and longer-term structures of the archaeological record, thought to reflect persistent patterns in human behaviour, have been proposed (see, for example, Bailey 1981a, 1981b, 1983; Bintliff 1991; Fletcher 1992). However, while the role of short-term events in the production of the archaeological record is acknowledged in these hierarchies, they are generally thought not to be identifiable through the analysis of archaeologically recovered data. Consequently the focus remains upon the explication of longer-term structures of behaviour and issues of scale. It is perhaps telling that, even for Braudel, the longer time scales at which human–environment interactions take place (*la longue durée*) are privileged as determinants over shorter-term events which are seem as epiphenomenal (Last 1995: 142). Consequently Braudel's historical actors are relatively powerless.

Clearly the data sets of archaeology and history are quite different, as are the structures of the records that are produced from them. However, as Morris (1997: 10–11) has stated, 'words and things are simply two different kinds of evidence. We need different techniques to think about each effectively, but they are all talking about the same thing.' Trigger has also argued: 'it is simply not true that historical disciplines have only descriptive objectives or are interested in determining matters of fact and discussing chronological relationships . . . current trends in history proper . . . reveal the irrelevance of the traditional dichotomy between history and science' (1978: 25–6). The perpetuation of the history/prehistory divide is due to the persistent perception of a disciplinary division based upon the view that archaeology is a generalist record of long-term human behaviour and history is a particularist record of short-term events. This view is simplistic and based upon false premises and a misconception, on the behalf of archaeologists, of what it is that historians do. In order to investigate the Aboriginal experience of contact through the use of both historical and archaeological data sets, there is a need to move beyond such arguments and to define what are the real differences between historical and archaeological explanations. Murray (1997: 455) has argued that the archaeological record differs from the historical record because of the minimum definable chronological unit, site formation processes and the notion of palimpsest. These parameters are not absolute and fixed, but will differ depending upon context. Therefore the fundamental differences between the archaeological and historical records have less to do with the scale or tempo of duration, and more to do with the scale of resolution.

There will always be a tension between our desire to understand contact and our ability to understand it, and it might be argued that the current conceptual instruments that we are using to investigate contact are actually making the job of understanding more difficult. I suggest that one way in which the archaeological and historical records might be integrated into the study of contact interactions and the writing of Aboriginal history is through the identification and tracking of trajectories of behaviour that treat prehistory and history as part of a continuum.

Archaeological trajectories

The idea of archaeological trajectories was introduced by Clarke (1978: 42), who argued that changes in the state of a sociocultural system result in transformations. When a series of these transformations follows a particular course, a trajectory is defined. Consequently, any system state can be described as either a time or a space transformation of another specific, and different, system state. The present state of any system is therefore a result of the impact of all its relevant past conditions (Clarke 1978: 57). In this manner the individual act, while not completely determined, is closely constrained (Clarke 1978: 96). While Clarke's argument was presented in the mechanistic and dehumanised terms of 1960s systems theory, the basic tenets have remained current in archaeological theory and even pervade some of the more recent literature on the use of non-linear modelling in archaeology.

Most archaeologists agree that human behaviour does have trajectories, or pathways. However, the degree to which these are constrained and our ability to 'discover' or 'predict' them is debated. Positions cover the spectrum from the highly regulated search for 'laws' of human behaviour of the processualists, to the extreme relativism of some postprocessualists. Taking something of a middle-ground approach, Trigger (1991b: 554) has stated that 'archaeologists now tend to believe that there is a greater variation in human behavior than processual archaeologists allowed for and that this behavior is shaped to a large degree by specific historical traditions, which have contingent and therefore largely unpredictable trajectories'. However, he went on to argue that, despite the great variability present in any human culture, its innovative capacity is limited and channelled by its existing set of values which act as constraints on the possible range of outcomes or responses (Trigger 1991b: 559). Therefore while the trajectory is unpredictable in its detail, it is possibly understandable in terms of its history.

A similar 'middle-ground' approach – comprising a blending of the postprocessual trend towards contextual historicism with the search for overarching structure which is generally seen as a feature of the processualist agenda – is adopted in this chapter. The need for such a meshing of materialist and idealist perspectives has been outlined by McGlade and Van der Leeuw (1997: 8). I argue that factors such as environment, past human history, and a society's set of values and technological capabilities, act as guiding parameters or structures for historical trajectories. However, this is not to take a normative view of culture or to say that social responses and historical trajectories are entirely predictable, which clearly they are not, but rather to suggest that such trajectories, and the human actions which lead to their development are, to some degree, constrained. In order to understand these constraints it is necessary to establish as clearly as possible a picture of what the parameters or range of possibilities of the society under investigation might be – hence the need for investigations into Aboriginal responses to contact with Europeans to begin in the precontact period. Trajectories need to be followed through time, and therefore the description of the history of a system becomes an essential part in understanding it (Van der Leeuw 1998: 40). It is possible that non-linear modelling of dynamical systems may be a useful heuristic tool in attempting to understand how such a notion of trajectories might operate. It may also assist in helping to model the relationship between short-term 'events' and the longer-term structures of human behaviour which are thought to be represented in the archaeological record.

Non-linear modelling

Since the 1990s non-linear modelling, or chaos theory, has made the transition from complicated and opaque mathematical theory to popular culture. In the process it has been applied to everything from stock market and weather pattern analysis, to an understanding of biological systems and populations growth, and even to studies of the human past. However, what role non-linear modelling may play in archaeological theory has been anything but clear. It is my purpose in this chapter not to debate whether or not chaos theory can, or should, be applied to archaeology (for such a discussion see Murray 1997), but rather to suggest that an understanding of non-linear dynamics may help to illuminate and model the process of human history through the notion of trajectories and their constraints. My use of non-linear modelling theory is therefore predominantly convergent rather than causal (Roth and Ryckman 1995: 32).

Shermer (1995: 72) has written that 'the apparently chaotic actions of the phenomena exhibit an interaction between the small, contingent events of a sequence and the large, necessitating laws of nature'. Thus, past processes can be divided into two qualitatively different categories: contingencies, which are 'a conjuncture of events occurring without perceptible design'; and necessities, defined as 'constraining circumstances compelling a certain course of action' (Shermer 1995: 70). Contingency, therefore, is the place where the effect of 'the event' is most acutely felt, while necessities reflect the more structural properties of the past. Since the past is composed of both contingencies and necessities it stands to reason that event and structure are both a part of the historical process. Superficially this definition of contingencies and necessities parallels Braudel's identification of three different 'levels' of historical time: *histoire éventuellement*, *moyenne durée* and *longue durée*. However, Braudel's levels, while incorporating divisions between event/process and agency/structure, essentially reflected the temporal scale over which, he argued, historical processes operate. Contingencies and necessities are more reflective of system state and the role of event and structure, irrespective of time scale.

The geometry of dynamical systems takes place in what is termed 'phase space' (Cohen and Stewart 1994: 200). Phase space is the region of the possible – it contains the past history of the system and all its potential futures. The juncture at which dynamical systems become chaotic or unpredictable (the loci of change) has been called the 'bifurcation point'. Dyke (1990: 370) neatly defines this as the 'point on the trajectory at which all hell breaks loose'. At a bifurcation point large changes may be produced in a system from seemingly small alterations in circumstances, and the role of contingencies becomes exaggerated. Thus necessities are the structuring properties that take a human system down a certain path until a bifurcation point is reached and the role of short-term 'events' becomes paramount.

The popular conception of chaos theory is that it forces us to throw the ability to anticipate what will happen in the future out of the window, because non-linear systems are unpredictable and subject to major fluctuations resulting from seemingly minor initial conditions (the 'butterfly effect'). As Coveney and Highfield (1990: 203) have written, 'chaotic evolution is apparently the antithesis of all that has been said up to now: it denies any long-term regularity or predictability in evolution through time'. Certainly it is true that simple causes can produce complex effects (Cohen and Stewart 1994: 2), and that the future of such systems is unpredictable in detail as a result of their sensitivity to initial conditions. However, chaotic behaviour is not random behaviour (Reisch 1991: 6), and as such it is still governed by laws. It has been argued that the lawless and random nature of chaotic systems is only apparent as order is hidden from view by the traditional means with which researchers tend to approach such systems (Shermer 1995: 72). Chapman (1997: 369) has stated that chaos behaviour is guided by parameters which can be seen as structures, and that 'this means that the dynamics, although unrepeating, and in a sense unpredictable (although not incalculable), are constrained'. Therefore, systems have histories.

It is argued that at bifurcation it becomes impossible to predict which pathway will be followed, based upon the past history of the system. Such an understanding is reliant upon all the possible futures or pathways being equally likely. However, as Stewart (1992: 103) has pointed out, while the list of absolutely everything that might happen in phase space is unimaginably long, the list of what is typical or likely is much shorter. In human systems (and, it might be argued, in many other dynamical systems as well), which trajectory will be followed will, to some degree, be a reflection of the interrelationship between the past history of the system, external constraints such as the environment and aspects of human culture. As Prigogine and Stengers (1984: 169) have pointed out, the behaviour of a system depends, in part, upon its history and the mixture of necessity and chance that constitutes the history of the system.

Shermer (1995: 72) has described chaos as 'a conjuncture of events compelled to a certain course of action by constraining prior conditions'. Human systems never completely break free of the past but always carry with them the 'shadow' of their history. However, while the seeds of the future were present in the past we cannot accurately predict which pathway was followed to reach the end point we are interested in investigating. We can, however, begin to narrow down the range of possibilities. Non-linear systems are in fact 'predictable' within certain tolerances. As McGlade (1995: 130) has stated, 'this framework generates a series of interrogative encounters by which we arrive, not at any single predictive model . . . but a series of evolutionary pathways to which the system is prone'.

Writing Aboriginal history

The investigation of Aboriginal–European contact and the writing of Aboriginal history have significant political implications. The denial of history to Aboriginal people has had the effect of severing links between pre- and post-contact societies, and even between those of contact times and the present. Murray (1992c: 18) has argued that part of the reluctance scholars have shown towards attempts to historicise Aboriginal people 'seems to stem from the false belief that historicising Aboriginal people weakens the link between the Aboriginal people of the present and those of the deeper pre-historic past'. However, it is also true that, 'while historicising Aboriginal Australia might make Aboriginality a less stable category, it most certainly argues that prehistoric Aboriginal societies were dynamic and flexible and well and truly capable of change' (Murray 1992b: 740). Therefore, the reinstatement of the notion of history to descriptions of the Aboriginal past will assist in the definition of links between present-day Aboriginal people and their ancestors by casting aside the notion of the 'traditional' Aboriginal person as essentialist icon and reintroducing the themes of cultural change and continuity, and hence dynamism.

The problem of linking historical and archaeological data sets and records and the resultant type of history that could be produced from such a fusion was alluded to by Reece (1979: 270) in his review of Blainey's *Triumph of the Nomads* (1975). In discussing Blainey's use of both archaeological and historical sources he noted that the disjointed evidence provided by prehistory did not enable Blainey to construct a historical narrative or discuss individuals, no matter how hard he tried. However, what Reece had failed to recognise was that Blainey's initial searching attempts had begun to reveal that the use of both historical and archaeological data required that a very different type of history be written.

An Aboriginal history written from both archaeological and historical sources, and spanning historic and prehistoric time periods, will differ greatly from a history based solely upon written documentary evidence. This difference will be a response both to the unique features of the historical and archaeological data sets and our approaches to them, and to the nature of Aboriginal society. As Murray (1992b: 732) has asked, 'what kind of history can be written for societies where there is no linear pathway of "progress" from simple to complex, and where the causes of change within the archaeological record are rarely simply specified and observed?'

In order to begin writing an Aboriginal history that stretches from the pre- to postcontact periods, and incorporates both archaeological and historical data, what is required is a radical rethinking of the way in which past behavioural systems are modelled. In this chapter I have suggested that inspiration for such models may be derived from an understanding of non-linear dynamics and how they may relate to human systems through the notion of constraints and parameters. Dyke (1990: 377) has suggested that when an understanding of non-linear modelling is applied to investigations of the past 'the linear billiard-ball conception of "causation" has to be re-examined and its hegemony as explanatory pattern of choice reassessed'. Similarly McGlade and Van der Leeuw (1997: 14) have stated that 'the first thing that a non-linear dynamical perspective does is it effectively destroys historical causality as a linear, progressive unfolding of events'. Therefore, it is not possible write a narrative style of history where societies progress in an orderly fashion from simple to complex, and historical causes and events follow one another like carriages of a train.

Murray (1992b: 730) has pointed out that 'differences of scale and ontology between the archaeological and anthropological [and historical] cannot be overcome by existing conceptual vocabularies'. Clearly what is required is the building of new archaeological theory and the development of a paradigm within which a new field of discourse might be defined. It has already been suggested that the investigation of contact must take place over a significantly long enough time period for the identification of trajectories, and hence cultural change and continuity, to take place. This approach necessitates the crossing of the traditionally perceived prehistory/history divide. One of the objectives of such research is to work towards the developments of a new framework of analysis, incorporating (although not necessarily meshing) historical and archaeological data within which the Aboriginal experience of contact might be investigated. The development of such a theoretical framework requires the acknowledgement that, while important, recourse to the physical referents of the archaeological record by no means exhausts all interpretive possibilities. In fact, taken on its own, the archaeological record, and our overly materialist approaches to it, may be limiting our ability to understand Aboriginal/European contact interactions. The sets of relationships that we wish to explore when attempting to understand contact require leaps of interpretation that cannot, in their totality, be tested against the archaeological data because they are primarily theoretical. As always with the development of new theory, we are required to work from the known to the unknown, as theory is always underdetermined by empirical data.

An Aboriginal history of Australia that incorporates both historical and archaeological data, and spans the pre- and postcontact periods, will exhibit discontinuities and not conform to a smooth narrative. However, the lack of a smooth fit between historical and archaeological data sets is not cause for dismay, and certainly not a reason to prioritise one type of explanation over the other, or even worse, to force the data into a narrative structure under the assumption that archaeology is history with 'holes' that can be glossed over through the use of historical data. As Trigger (1985: 203) has noted, 'the synthesis of archaeological and ethnohistorical information, as opposed to the simple use of one type to illustrate the other, requires a thorough knowledge of the potentials and limitations of both disciplines'.

The integration of pre-and postcontact Aboriginal experiences is a vital part of the agenda of research aimed at writing the Aboriginal history of Australia. However, the ultimate goal must be a more inclusive rewriting of the history of the continent. Aboriginal people have been excluded from mainstream Australian history or mentioned merely as a byline to discussions focusing upon the period following European settlement. Attwood has suggested that:

historians should seek to situate Aborigines within the broader circumstances of Australian history, investigating, for example, the ways in which historical experiences parallel those of other oppressed groups . . . unless ways to do this can be found, Aboriginal history, like the Aborigines themselves, will never be properly integrated with our past and our present. (1990: 135)

However, such an integration must do more than simply interweave the Aboriginal story into the pre-existing master narrative of Australian history. The traditional focus upon events and important figures needs to be realigned in order to incorporate the discontinuous and less narrative nature of the history of 40,000 years of Aboriginal occupation. There also needs to be a rethinking of the themes important to Australian history so that the Aboriginal past can be fully incorporated rather than just serving to highlight aspects of the European history of Australia such as colonialism, government policy and so on. One of the outcomes of the writing of such an inclusive history will be the recognition of the need for polyvocality in historical explanations and the realisation that there is truly no one history of Australia.

Conclusion

Traditionally Aboriginal societies have been perceived as static, unchanging and at equilibrium with their environment. However, since the 1980s archaeological investigations have demonstrated that change and variability have been features of the Aboriginal past for the last 40,000 years. However, such variability is usually explained deterministically in terms of human responses to large- and small-scale environmental fluctuations. Social change is therefore seen as being driven by forces operating wholly outside the human system. Rarely are prehistoric changes explained in terms of social choice. Explanations invoking 'science' and looking for regularities and laws in human behaviour as evolutionary responses to ecology are seen as being antithetical to more humanistic studies concerned with understanding particular societies within their own historical context. It has been noted that 'chaos pleases us . . . by introducing a sense of magic, a sense of many possibilities' (McClosky 1991: 22). However, it is also apparent that the use of an heuristic model based upon non-linear dynamics also pleases through its potential to interweave an understanding of the myriad small-scale events that make up human history with an understanding of the longer-term structures apparent in the archaeological record. It is possible that the use of a framework based upon non-linear modelling may enable us to 'humanise' the past and re-emphasise the notion of internally driven historical change while maintaining the possibility of there being a larger-scale structure to the dynamics of human behaviour over the long term.

The identification of 'laws' of human behaviour has fallen out of archaeological favour with the decline of processual archaeology. However, McGlade and Van der Leeuw (1997) have recently argued that the wholesale rejection of the notion of cross-cultural regularities may have been premature. In this chapter I have argued for an approach to the past that, while allowing for a historical investigation of short-term events, also acknowledges the presence of larger-scale structures that operate as the constraining parameters within which human actions take place. It has been suggested that such 'supra-individual structures' may be self-organising and operate at a level at which the individual is not aware (McGlade 1997: 299; McGlade and Van der Leeuw 1997: 10). It is possible that these larger-scale structures reflect fundamental motifs that structure human behaviour, and that these have a certain regularity irrespective of time or place.

10 | In the footsteps of George Dutton: developing a
contact archaeology of temperate Aboriginal
Australia

TIM MURRAY

> Is this how we hold onto the land they won't give us? Haunted land. To
> keep for our children – children whose names might be anything? . . .
> They will be the ones to understand. Violence goes with the country. If
> you want new land you have to take it. Yes. If you want to stay you do.
> And we will stay. What we've done in the country we've done.
>
> (Hall 1999: 63)

In this chapter I explore some of the more important issues raised by the need
for Australian archaeologists effectively to meet the interests of indigenous
communities, and of a broader Australian community which is seeking both
a deeper understanding of the human history of the continent, and a reconciliation with its indigenous peoples. Since the 1960s and the beginning
of a painful journey into the shared past of the country, Australian society
has been slowly, and with great difficulty, transformed by a new encounter
with Aboriginal Australia. A significant element of that transformation will
be a reconsideration of the role archaeology should play in constructing
new identities (national, ethnic, community), a reconsideration which will
demand a deep engagement with Aboriginal history, rather than simply the
melange of early radiometric dates and essentialist accounts of Aboriginality
that it currently obtains (see for example Attwood 1989b, 1992; Byrne 1996;
Murray 1992a, 1996b). My very brief and partial discussion of these issues
includes three small examples: the public acknowledgement and memorialisation of a nineteenth-century massacre of Aboriginal people at Myall
Creek, New South Wales; the consequences of a failed Native Title Claim
by the Yorta Yorta people; and the framework of a research project on the
history of large-scale pastoralism in the far west of New South Wales.

I will also briefly focus on the notion of 'conjectural histories', which I
have sketched on several occasions (see for example Murray 1996a, 2000a,
2002; Murray and Williamson 2003), and directly related to the need for us
to establish whether there is a role for archaeology in assisting indigenous
communities from settled temperate Australia to gain land justice through
the Native Title process.[1] Of course it is one thing to identify the need for new

histories that will trace the stories of people and landscapes in the period from 1788 to the present, and quite another to convincingly build them, but I will argue that there is every reason for optimism about the potential of such 'conjectural histories'.

The Australian situation in greater detail

For most Australian archaeologists the bulk of research into the archaeology of Aboriginal Australia has focused on the very earliest periods of colonisation and settlement, from about 45,000 bp to 25,000 bp. There are many reasons for this concentration, ranging from a perceived need to define the chronological 'corners of the room' to an explicit desire to plug Australian data into the models developed (predominantly by Europeans) of 'world prehistory', or of the evolution of fully modern human behaviour.[2]

Notwithstanding the fact that contemporary Aboriginal communities have benefited politically and culturally from the demonstration by archaeologists of the very long occupation of Australia by their ancestors, a demonstration which played a crucial part in transforming Australian public opinion about the need to seek reconciliation with the traditional owners of the country, it is now widely understood that many Aboriginal communities now find little meaning (if they ever really did) in the archaeology of high human antiquity. Of course there is a wide variety of opinion among indigenous communities about the value of pure research into the remote human history of Australia. However, since the 1980s the need for archaeologists to gain the informed consent of communities in order to conduct archaeological research (and the fact that the vast bulk of that research is undertaken in heritage or 'applied' settings) has fostered the evolution of collaborative research projects that serve a broader range of interests (both indigenous and archaeological) (see for example Davidson *et al.* 1995).

Two of the most important indigenous interests are in the revival and maintenance of traditional culture and community, and (directly connected to the first) the gaining of land rights, generally through the Native Title process. The provisions of Australian Government Native Title legislation (and the experience of subsequent case law) have made it clear that archaeological data from remote antiquity in Australia are not considered to be sensitive to tribal or clan affiliations, and as such, are thought to have a much reduced utility in establishing legal title to land, compared with information derived from ethnography and ethnohistories. Again, there are exceptions to this generalisation (see for example Weiner *et al.* 2002).

While recognising that generalisation is difficult among such diversity, it is common for indigenous communities (especially in temperate parts of the continent) to regard the period immediately before European colonisation, and the roughly 200 years of dispossession and occupation that followed, to be of the greatest political and cultural significance. Importantly it is also the period which has been, until the 1990s, rarely studied by archaeologists. A declining Aboriginal interest in the archaeology of high antiquity is beginning to provide a strong incentive for practitioners to broaden their area of interest.

Since 1990 the historical archaeology of Aboriginal Australia (or contact archaeology as it is more commonly known) has become a vital and significant field of endeavour. Building on earlier work by Allen (1969) and Birmingham (1992), a new generation of archaeologists (for example Byrne 1996, 1998, 2003; Byrne *et al.* 2001; Head and Fullagar 1997; Lydon 2000; Murray 1993, 1996b, 2000a, 2000b, 2002; Patterson 2000; and the papers collected as Harrison and Williamson 2002; Lilley 2000; Torrence and Clarke 2000) have broadened and deepened our understanding of what an archaeology of 'contact' and its aftermath can achieve, beyond an exploration of 'encounters' between invader and dispossessed (see, for example, Mulvaney 1989). Although there are real differences of approach and purpose among practitioners (for example, some believing that the historical archaeology of Aboriginal Australia is solely Aboriginal history) the resultant diversity provides a stimulating and rapidly evolving locus for making history.

The central issue here concerns the methodology of history-writing. Since 1990 Australian prehistoric archaeology has witnessed the final rejection of earlier views that Aboriginal history could only begin with the arrival of the Europeans. But what has replaced it? The most explicit candidate is that of 'intensification', which holds that Aboriginal society in the late Holocene was beginning to manifest signs of vertical social evolution, supposedly just like other societies around the world (see for example Lourandos 1985; Morwood 1987). On this (empirically and theoretically) questionable basis, intensificationists have maintained that since directional change has been established, progress can be argued to have occurred, and therefore history can be written.[3]

Its less explicit competitor in contemporary Australian prehistoric archaeology has been seen by some as the expression of a profound desire to dodge the issue altogether, because of its concern with chronology, seemingly above all else. This somewhat sweeping characterisation is said to be best demonstrated in the nature of the debate about the antiquity of human occupation of Australia. Here dates between 125,000 bp and 65,000 bp have been proposed, which (had they been accepted) could have added a minimum of another 20,000 years to the human history of the continent, which is generally thought to have begun about 45,000 bp. Significantly, apart from capturing considerable media attention, very little discussion has been devoted to what these extra millennia might mean (O'Connell and Allen 1998). Indeed one could be forgiven for assuming that Aboriginal people are thought to have been doing essentially Aboriginal things for even longer, raising the question of whether history (apart from environmental history) matters at all.

These divergent approaches (which spring from prehistoric archaeology) are in stark contrast to discussions flowing from contact archaeology carried out in Tasmania, Victoria, tropical north Queensland and the Northern Territory, where archaeologists have sought to reconstruct the trajectories of Aboriginal societies from 'prehistory' to history (see especially Williamson, this volume, and the papers in Harrison and Williamson 2002). Here the content and form of history matters very much indeed, and the spurious progressivism of intensification is replaced by the more difficult, but ultimately more satisfying, exploration of modes of history-writing which deal with horizontal (rather than vertical) social and cultural variability over long time periods.

Another significant issue has to do with the means by which archaeologists can identify the forces that have transformed indigenous societies in the past. The presence of additional data sets in the last 200 years gives archaeologists and historians a richer canvas to work with. But a better understanding of change and variability during the historic period (when allied to a more widespread understanding of the extent to which Aboriginal societies at contact had been radically altered by disease, population collapse and an increase in inter-group conflict) can (and should) also have the net effect of decreasing the plausibility of direct historical and general comparative analogies that have been the foundation of reconstructions of prehistoric Aboriginal societies, and reinforcing the need for history in 'prehistoric' times. Indeed it is probably time that Australian archaeologists reconsidered the very contentious issues encompassed by ongoing debates about the utility or otherwise of analogical inference (see for example Meehan and Jones 1988).

It is increasingly well understood that an indigenous interest in contact archaeology revolves around the need to comprehend the experience of dispossession and cultural survival. For Aboriginal people, exploring a historical archaeology of Aboriginal life over the past 200 years can enhance understanding about the histories of separation and sharing that are so much a feature of community life, while at the same time they provide a rich store of information from which such communities can renegotiate or reshape their identities within modern Australian society (see, for example, Weiner *et al.* 2002). Of course this is hardly a risk-free environment. Such histories (for example that of the Lairmarenga of south-west Tasmania, see Murray 2000a) can sometimes break archaeologists' rules of evidence in order to achieve their goals, and might therefore be considered to be of diminished plausibility outside those communities. Others, especially those which relate to the massacres which occurred on the pastoral frontier during the mid-nineteenth century, have become embroiled in serious disagreements among non-Aboriginal historians about the veracity of evidence, particularly of oral testimony or tradition (see for example Attwood and Foster 2003; Manne 2003; Windschuttle 2002).

Although such conflicts are important, they are far more significant in the Native Title arena. Here community histories can be tested as evidence in formal legal proceedings, and judgements are made as to their veracity. The experience of the Yorta Yorta people, which I will briefly discuss below, is an excellent example of why the content and shape of such histories particularly matters in those indigenous communities from temperate Australia that have been most transformed as a result of dispossession and colonisation.

The creation of new archaeological perspectives on the history of Aboriginal Australia will also need to take into account the impact of a widespread desire for reconciliation between black and white Australians. The building of a memorial at the site of one of the worst massacres in Australian history at Myall Creek exemplifies the creation and recognition of landscapes of reconciliation, where previously there had just been hurt and shame. Significantly, landscapes of reconciliation are the product of a series of revelations (profoundly shocking to many) of contact and its consequences. These revelations are more than just the massacre itself, but express the impact of such conflicts in the lives of people (both black and white) who were to live in the area for the next 170 years. Thus landscapes of reconciliation often flow from the difficult and confronting process of making the invisible (a product of ignorance, fear, or a desire to suppress or forget) visible, and of discovering how much of the history of such landscapes is shared among their populations (see also Byrne 2003; Harrison 2002c).

Landscapes of reconciliation: the Myall Creek massacre

One of the most striking aspects of contact history in Australia is the fact that identifiably Aboriginal responses to the reality of murder and dispossession were rarely heard until the early twentieth century. We have instead the poetic productions of the invaders, imagining what it must be like to be dispossessed and harried towards extinction, or the reports of governments and philanthropic societies condemning the bloodletting and injustice (see Reynolds 1998).

There is no better example of this genre than Eliza Hamilton Dunlop's *The Aboriginal Mother (from Myall's Creek)*, published in *The Australian* newspaper on 13 December 1838. Two stanzas suffice to make the point:

Oh, could'st thy little bosom,
    That mother's torture feel,
Or could'st thou know thy father lies
    Struck down by English steel;
Thy tender form would wither,
    Like *kniven* on the sand,
And the spirit of my precious tribe
    Would vanish from our land.
 For thy young life, my precious,

    I fly the field of blood,
Else had I, for my chieftain's sake,
    Defied them where they stood;
But basely bound my woman's arm,
    No weapon might it wield:
I could but cling round him I loved,
    To make my heart a shield.
                   (Webby 1980: 9)

Notwithstanding the practical effects of attitudes, policies and doctrines which led to the dispossession (and occasionally the slaughter) of Aboriginal people, this domination of the discourse of dispossession can at least be seen to be the most conclusive evidence of a more total domination, where non-indigenous Australians could be the victors and then tax themselves with their interpretation of the feelings of the vanquished as well. In recent decades Aboriginal novelists, poets, historians and songwriters (as well as their white counterparts) have filled this void much less sentimentally, and more successfully, to reveal hidden pasts in the ordinary rural landscapes where people go about their daily lives (see especially the work of Henry Reynolds 1984, 1990a, 1990b). Of course such voices do not always attract universal approbation in Australia, even in these more enlightened times (see for example Windschuttle 2002).

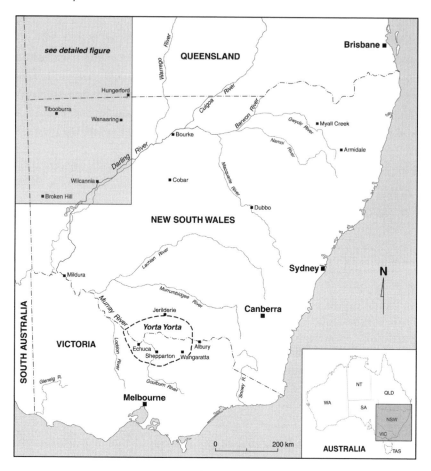

Fig. 10.1 South-east Australia showing the area of the Yorta Yorta claim, the site of Myall Creek and the far north-west of New South Wales.

The massacre at Myall Creek has been widely discussed and written about because, sensationally, white men were tried and hanged for killing Aboriginal people. Much more is known about the events because they were reported and became the subject of police inquiries and court action. The massacre and its aftermath aroused the citizens of New South Wales to such an extent that a rich harvest of letters, poems, reports and speeches have been left for the historian (Harrison 1978; Webby 1980).

On 9 June 1838 roughly twenty-eight Aboriginal people (men, women and children) were murdered at Myall Creek Station in the Gwydir Valley of northern New South Wales (see Fig. 10.1). The killers were a diverse party made up of assigned convicts, ticket-of-leave men (those who had served their sentences), and a free-born manager of another station, who were participating in an action that had become standard practice on the frontier (Denholm 1981; Townsend 1985). In these actions retribution for attacks on white people or on their property by Aboriginal people was exacted, frequently by stockmen and agricultural labourers, many of whom were themselves victims of a legal system which brutalised the poor and the powerless. Retribution sometimes took the form of rape and murder.

Such punitive actions were simply one stage in a cycle of violence which began when European occupation of the lands beyond the 'limits of location' began in the colony of New South Wales during the early 1820s. First contacts might be friendly, or unfriendly, depending on the attitudes of both parties. But as contact intensified, conflicts over women, Aboriginal hunting, and thefts from huts and settlements, also quickly escalate into violence. 'Trustworthy' blacks became treacherous; whites changed their policies from what they considered to be 'fair treatments' and 'conciliation', to a 'stern resolve' to uphold white law and protect white interests. This frequently drew equally violent responses from the blacks until massacres of the kind which occurred at Myall Creek took place. None the less it is worth remembering that they were also not the rule, and that the frontier experiences of blacks and whites did not inevitably link the reality of dispossession to that of open warfare (see for example Attwood and Foster 2003; Manne 2003; Windschuttle 2002).

We know a great deal about the events of Myall Creek, and the frontier culture which made the bushwhack or mounted action a regular part of frontier life, because William Hobbs, the station overseer, reported the deaths to his employer Henry Dangar and to Edward Denny Day, the Police Magistrate at the town of Muswellbrook – further to the south. Day subsequently informed the Colonial Secretary, who informed Governor Gipps. But what made Hobbs report to Day? Why was such a report not disregarded further up the line of authority? Why were the murderers brought to trial, and why were they executed? Here the complexity of the frontier experience assumes a special importance.

The party of forty Kwambial Aborigines had not been camped long at the station. Neither the stockmen nor the Aborigines had been violent, and no stock had been killed. Indeed one of the convicts (George Anderson) was sleeping with Impeta, a Kwambial girl, and the Kwambial men were frequently employed in helping out around the station. Anderson did not participate in the rapes and the massacre, but another convict, Charles Kilmeister, did. The action that was to claim the lives of the Kwambial did not originate at Myall Creek station, and the only reason why it finished there was because this group of Kwambial were the only group of Aboriginal people located by the party after a few days of searching.

It seems clear enough from Day's investigation and court testimony that all of the participants in the massacre knew that these people were not responsible for the cattle-spearing that had provoked the punitive raid (Atkinson 1985; Wilson 1985). It also seems clear, from the same sources, that the whites who had remained on Myall Creek Station (Anderson and Kilmeister) did not defend the Kwambial from attack, nor did they attempt to persuade the punitive party that they should seek the 'criminals' elsewhere. Indeed all understood that the act of roping the victims together so that they would be frightened (which was the explanation given to Anderson by the others) was simply a pretext. But what made Kilmeister go with the party and participate in the rapes and the massacre which took place in a set of stockyards only a couple of kilometres away from the hut where the Kwambial had sought the protection of their white friends?

Kilmeister's personal motivation is lost to us, but many (see, for example, Sturma 1985) have speculated that it was probably the expression of a generalised desire for murder and revenge, and the result of his fear of people whom he did not consider merited humane treatment because of their manifest lack of humanity. Perhaps this 'distancing' can explain the fact that twenty-eight defenceless people were killed in cold blood, the vast majority simply hacked to death where they stood. But it does not explain why Hobbs, who returned to the station several days later, should eventually respond as a human being, and seek justice for the murdered and abused. Perhaps Hobbs possessed the alternative view of Aboriginal people, that they were not brutes incapable of civilisation. What we do know is that Hobbs did not keep silent. He was to pay for his conscience: his boss Henry Dangar dispensed with his services later in the year and he was vilified by his colleagues in the district.

The story shifts to Sydney, where the eleven men charged with murder were tried in the Supreme Court on 15 November 1838. Why did Governor Gipps bring the case to trial? Harrison (1978) and Denholm (1981) among others have argued that there were larger forces involved. The British government (and its colonial administration) had for some time been concerned with lawlessness on the frontier – not the least being the fact that the frontier was to all intents and purposes outside the control of the government. Settlements 'beyond the limits of location' were technically illegal but squatting was expanding at a tremendous rate. The Myall Creek massacre was, therefore, a chance to reassert the rule of law and the authority of the government.

But Gipps chose a controversial case to demonstrate his power and fixity of purpose.

The trial of the eleven accused (they freely admitted to the murder) divided colonial society. The divisions fell neatly between those who thought the Aborigines to be human and those who did not. Each group had its newspapers (*The Australian* taking the first position, and the *Sydney Herald* the latter). Both sides poured out vast amounts of poetry, prose, discussion papers, letters and the like, which took pretty much every possible position.

If Gipps counted on legal sentiments about the inalienable rights of blacks under white law being upheld, then he must have been relieved and delighted by the summing up of the Chief Justice of New South Wales that it was 'clear that the most grievous offence has been committed: that the lives of nearly thirty of our fellow creatures have been sacrificed, and in order to fulfil my duty I must tell you that the life of a black is as precious and valuable in the eye of the law, as that of the highest noble in the land'. Imagine his chagrin, and the implied threat to his authority and to that of British law, when fifteen minutes later the jury returned a verdict of not guilty.

Gipps's action of holding the men in custody and retrying them using the same evidence was an attempt to exert the rule of law and to rescue his authority. It was also designed to enforce the principles of the civilised town on to the uncivilised frontier. In this sense the convicts and free agricultural workers employed by the pastoralists might be seen as being little different from Aboriginal people. In any event a second trial was held on 27 November, and this time seven men were found guilty of the charge of murder. On 7 December Governor Gipps accepted the verdict and sentenced the guilty to hanging. On 18 December justice was done amidst scenes of protest.

It took over 160 years for there to be any official commemoration of the massacre. These were the years of what the anthropologist Stanner has called 'the great Australian silence', where generations of Australians knew very little about the history of Aboriginal/white relations in their country and seemed to care even less (see for example Reynolds 1984). A first attempt to memorialise the events at Myall Creek was made in 1965, but was regarded by the local community – especially by the Apex club – as insulting and divisive. During the ceremony to open the memorial held on 10 June 2000, which was in part organised by the local Lions club, members of the community spoke at length about how the process of getting the memorial accepted and then built had healed very deep scars. Descendants of both the perpetrators and the victims publicly acknowledged (for the first time since 1838) what had happened. That acknowledgement was given further weight by a special motion of the NSW Parliament, and the creation of a website which tells the story of the massacre and the memorial.

Such goodwill obviously stands in stark contrast to the much tougher business of acknowledging rights to land, but it does represent a willingness to begin to explore the mutual or 'shared' histories and shared identities of Australia. How widespread this willingness is, or will become, is still uncertain. Equally uncertain is whether the discovery of hidden histories in such landscapes of reconciliation will assist the process of redressing the consequences of dispossession, in part through the granting of land rights to Aboriginal communities. None the less it does seem clear that an acknowledgement of mutuality provides the basis of a response to the Yorta Yorta decisions of the Federal and High Courts of Australia.

Landscapes of litigation and negotiation: the Yorta Yorta land claim

It is widely agreed that the Yorta Yorta case forms a kind of watershed in the evolution of Australian Native Title law (see for example Kerruish and Perrin 1999; Litchfield 2001). As such it brings my discussion of Aboriginal archaeology and history into somewhat sharper focus. It also helps us to reflect on the consequences of discontinuity in the last 200 years of Aboriginal history. In the Yorta Yorta case, the archaeology and anthropology of the area under claim played an insignificant role in comparison to a nineteenth-century account of the indigenous peoples of the area written by a white settler (Curr 1883, 1886–87). My fundamental purpose in this brief discussion is to highlight the consequences of the judicial interpretation of 'tradition' in indigenous communities as set down in the *Native Title Act* 1993 and in subsequent case law, especially in the three judgements (1998, 2001 and 2002) made concerning the Yorta Yorta claim (FCA 1606; FCA 45; HCA 58).

The concept of 'tradition' and 'traditional' is perhaps the most significant locus of connection between the interpretation of Native Title law, and the concerns of Aboriginal people about the consequences for them of the ways in which continuities and discontinuities in the occupation of traditional lands might be interpreted by the courts. Documenting occupation histories, changing patterns of land use, changes to ceremonial life, and the retention and/or transformation of custom and language are matters of very great consequence for Aboriginal communities engaged in the struggle for land rights under Native Title law. My secondary purpose here is to explore ways in which research into the historical archaeology of Aboriginal Australia can also help communities to create such documentation which underwrites the pursuit of their goal of cultural survival and enhancement.

The precise details of the Yorta Yorta Native Title Claim are quite straight-forward. Relating to more than 113,000 hectares of land and water in the vicinity of the Ovens, Goulbourn and Murray rivers in Victoria and New South Wales, the claim was referred to the Federal Court of Australia by the National Native Title Tribunal on 25 May 1995, when attempts to mediate the claim were unsuccessful. Justice Olney began hearing the claim on 8 October 1996. Given that the Murray River, the most economically significant water-way of inland Australia, flows through the claim area, the battle was always going to be a tough one (see Fig. 10.1). The claim was complex and subtle, and its long history has posed great challenges to lawyers, archaeologists, anthropologists, historians and, of course, the Aboriginal communities of the more densely settled south-east of the Australian continent.

The original judgement (and two subsequent appeals, first to the Federal Court and later to the High Court of Australia) went against the Yorta Yorta people. All three judgements turned on the question of whether traditional laws and customs, which lie at the heart of the concept of Native Title (see Riches 2003), had been maintained by the Yorta Yorta in the time since their first contact with Europeans in the 1830s. Justice Olney's original answer was that, notwithstanding the claim by the Yorta Yorta that their contemporary activities (in large part related to the management of heritage sites in the claim area) were based on traditional laws and customs, the traditional Yorta Yorta community ceased to exist around the turn of the nineteenth century. Although Aboriginal people were able to testify about traditional customs, the major authority cited by Justice Olney in his judgement was the work of Edward Curr, a pioneer white settler in the region.

Justice Olney's treatment of the evidential value of oral history in com-parison with documentary evidence was tested on appeal to the Full Federal Court of Australia, and subsequently to the High Court of Australia. In each case the Yorta Yorta based their argument on their belief that Justice Olney gave inappropriate weight to documentary historical evidence, and that this was both the cause and the effect of his judgement that contemporary Yorta Yorta society, although identifiably Aboriginal, was not 'traditional'. The appellants referred to this as 'a frozen in time' interpretation of 'tradi-tional', which failed to acknowledge that laws and customs could adapt to changed circumstances and still be 'traditional'. Importantly this meant that the revival of Aboriginal traditions, and the need for control over land title to enhance and make such revivals meaningful, were insufficient grounds to uphold a claim to Native Title.

Justice Olney was quite clear about how he interpreted discontinuity of occupation and of the passing on of traditional knowledge, and the legal value of attempts to revive culture as evidence of the maintenance of tradition in the Native Title context: 'Notwithstanding the genuine efforts of the claimant group to revive the lost culture of their ancestors, native title rights and interests once lost are not capable of revival' (FCA 1606: 121). He went further:

> Oven mounds, shell middens and scarred trees were described by a number of witnesses as sacred and deserving of protection . . . There is no doubt that mounds, middens and scarred trees which provide evidence of the indigenous occupation and use of the land are of considerable importance and indeed, many are protected under heritage legislation, but there is no evidence to suggest that they were of any significance to the original inhabitants other than for their utilitarian value, nor that any traditional law or custom required them to be preserved. (FCA 1606: 122)

He concluded that:

> The tide of history has undoubtedly washed away any traditional rights that the indigenous people may have previously exercised in relation to controlling access to their land within the claim area. (FCA 1606: 126)

In this view looking after heritage is not a traditional custom because Edward Curr never mentioned it:

> Preservation of Aboriginal heritage and conservation of the natural environment are worthy objectives, the achievement of which may lead to a more ready understanding and recognition of the importance of the culture of the indigenous people but in the context of a native title claim the absence of a continuous link back to the laws and customs of the original inhabitants deprives those activities of the character of traditional laws acknowledged and traditional customs observed in relation to land and waters which is a necessary element of both the statutory and common law concept of native title rights and interests. (FCA 1606: 128)

Justice Olney concluded:

> The facts of this case lead inevitably to the conclusion that before the end of the 19th century the ancestors through whom the claimants claim title had ceased to occupy their traditional lands in accordance with their traditional laws and customs. The tide of history has indeed washed away any real acknowledgment of their traditional laws and any real observance of their native customs. (FCA 1606: 129)

The Yorta Yorta lost their appeal to the Full Court of the Federal Court of Australia in 2001 (FCA 45). The majority (2–1), Justice Branson and Justice Katz, agreed with Justice Olney's finding that there was a period of time between 1788 and the date of the Yorta Yorta claim during which that community lost its traditionally Aboriginal character. In a dissenting judgement, Chief Justice Black concluded that Justice Olney was in error in that he applied too restrictive an approach to the concept of what is 'traditional' when he made his finding. The Chief Justice's discussion of the complex issues relating to the determination of when a community's Native Title rights expire because they are no longer a 'traditional' community raised many significant questions for Native Title law that were to be more fully considered in subsequent case law, not least of which was the Yorta Yorta appeal to the High Court of Australia (HCA 58).

Chief Justice Black's conclusion was subjected to rigorous analysis in the High Court Appeal, which was also lost by the Yorta Yorta. Although there were four separate judgements in the case, the great majority (5–2) disagreed with Chief Justice Black, arguing that Native Title claimants would have to concentrate on providing proof of their traditional laws and customs back to the time of dispossession. It was agreed that some allowance had to be made for adaptations or changes to those rights and customs – indeed for there being some discontinuity in their observance. None the less the majority held that it was still necessary to establish the continued existence of those laws and customs, which seems to require ongoing connection to traditional lands and the maintenance of language. The joint judgement by Chief Justice Gleeson and Justices Gummow and Hayne puts the matter clearly:

The relevant criterion to be applied in deciding the significance of change to, or adaptation of, traditional law and custom is readily stated (though its application to the particular facts may well be difficult). The key question is whether the law and custom can still be seen to be traditional law and traditional custom. Is the change or adaptation of such a kind that it can no longer be said that the rights or interests asserted are possessed under the traditional laws acknowledged and the traditional customs observed by the relevant peoples when that expression is understood in the sense earlier identified? (HCA 58)

What should the archaeological and historical response be to this inter-pretation of 'tradition'? A demonstration of the obvious, that the required link between occupation of land and the maintenance of tradition, makes it next to impossible for those Aboriginal communities most heavily affected by dispossession to gain Native Title through the courts. If the view that Native Title Claims can only succeed where continuity of occupation and the maintenance of traditional custom are *both* present accurately reflects the wording and intent of the legislation, then concerted legal and political action may well be required to develop a concept of 'tradition' that more accurately reflects the historical reality of communities such as the Yorta Yorta.

Surely the irony of using an agent of dispossession (Curr) as the authority on Yorta Yorta traditions should provide an incentive for archaeologists and historians to explore whether new sources of evidence can be established that might redress this imbalance. An additional incentive is the fact that the High Court's interpretation of provisions of the *Native Title Act* 1993 runs directly counter to many of the forces which have been harnessed by Aboriginal people in revitalising culture and transforming the terms of indigenous identity. In this sense the Act might be seen to be a hindrance to reconciliation. No matter what the Federal or High Courts have determined, cultural heritage sites (archaeological sites among them) now form the core and the visible expression of Yorta Yorta attachment to country, and of their spiritual and cultural connection to that country.

Given these observations, it seems obvious that one major focus of archaeological, historical and anthropological research should be on providing evidence and perspectives that will underwrite a more realistic approach to the notion of 'tradition', an approach which does not penalise indigenous groups from doing what their ancestors would have done – change and adapt to new circumstances. Compiling such evidence presents a considerable challenge, as it involves the successful integration of oral and documentary historical sources with archaeological evidence of Aboriginal community life over the last 200 years, to reveal the 'shared' histories that were briefly sketched in my discussion of the implications of the memorialisation of the Myall Creek massacre. Such histories are likely to be highly conjectural as they will require much argument and discussion to comprehend the significance and value of new sources of evidence and perspective.

The *Native Title Act* 1993 holds out the promise of another way for communities such as the Yorta Yorta, who are unlikely to be able to provide the proof of 'tradition' required by the Courts, but who wish to claim Native Title. The Act, as amended in 1998, has a structure to provide customised and voluntary agreements – Indigenous Land Use Agreements (ILUAs) – that make it possible to consider the rights and interests of indigenous people (and others) in land. The Native Title Tribunal has identified many of the contexts where ILUAs might advance indigenous interests in land – in particular issues of land management, the management of heritage places, and access to traditional lands (Edmunds and

Smith 2002: 70–102). Significantly, utilising ILUAs to provide a basis for a formal recognition of an indigenous interest in land in no way implies that the kinds of research required to achieve a more realistic understanding of the concept of 'tradition' in legislation, or in the Courts, should not also apply to the process of making and sustaining ILUAs. 'Conjectural' and 'shared' histories have an important role to play here as well (see also Harrison 2002c).

'Shared' histories and 'conjectural' histories

The existence of 'shared histories' and 'shared identities' does not mean that there can ever be, or should ever be, a single account of those histories or those identities. Indeed one of the most exciting aspects of history making in this field is the very diversity of interests and the strong sense that these interests are quite plastic. Acknowledging diversity, and recognising the fact that in some contexts, and for some audiences, constructing separate histories (separate in the sense of indigenous and non-indigenous, urban and rural, women and men, labour and capital, European and Asian) does not in any sense absolutely entail that this should apply in every case.

If Aboriginal history is the hidden history of Australia that is slowly being revealed and reaching out to people through the reconciliation process, it is also a history we have to imagine, to conjecture and to debate as new possibilities for understanding emerge from its practice. This is not a time for barriers and for the retention of models of Aboriginality that emphasise passivity and essentialism at the expense of action and transformation. The construction of 'conjectural histories' will help archaeologists and historians to unravel further the meanings and values of the historical archaeology of Aboriginal Australia, but it is worth remembering that this activity will take place in a highly political context. 'Conjectural' histories have real economic and political consequences, whether these are played out in the courts, in the making of ILUAs, or just in day-to-day interactions between blacks and whites.

The change in community attitudes that has been unfolding in Australia since the 1967 Citizenship Referendum (and which is enshrined in current and previous versions of the *Native Title Act*) was based on decades of Aboriginal political activism, and on the results of academic research into indigenous Australia (Attwood 2003; Attwood and Markus 1997). The primary sources of that research – universities, government departments, Royal Commissions and the like – spanned a host of disciplines, but it is commonly acknowledged that Aboriginal history, anthropology and prehistoric archaeology also played important roles. Significantly, given its late development in Australia, contact archaeology and the perspectives it brings to bear on the analysis of transforming indigenous societies made scant contribution to the thinking that underpins the *Native Title Act* 1993.

It is also now a very common observation that significant tensions (social, political, legal, cultural and historical) exist in our understanding of indigenous societies that (as a result of dispossession and subsequent history) have not maintained the bulk of their traditions. Arguments for a continued attachment to land in those parts of Australia where dispossession has been most complete have been strengthened by indigenous groups demonstrating their active participation in the management of land and its indigenous heritage. But such arguments will also be bolstered by the creation of 'conjectural histories' of social and cultural landscapes in the nineteenth and twentieth centuries that can serve to chart the lives of Aboriginal people during those times when they were of little interest to white Australia.

I have already mentioned that these histories will be the product of integrations of data and perspectives derived from traditional sources such as anthropology, oral history, ethnohistory and detailed documentary research, and from newer sources such as studies of contact and postcontact landscapes, that integrate specifically archaeological and historical data. The techniques of landscape (physical, social, cultural, symbolic) reconstruction are already fundamentally in place, deriving from a more widespread application of GIS software to create complex maps with a wide variety of spatiotemporal scales (see for example Zipfel 2002). At the same time, approaches similar to those used to map the shape and context of traditional landuse in the Canadian Arctic (Robinson *et al.* 1994) are being applied alongside low-tech reconstructions of contact landscape through the use of explorers' maps (see for example Hewitt 2001). A richer history of Aboriginal communities, patterns of residence, work and social relationships, in the towns as well as in the bush, and the role of heritage sites (both recent and ancient) in the maintenance of identity are now firmly in prospect (see especially Harrison, this volume). The same applies to interactions between the black and white communities in those areas that form the core of 'shared' histories and 'shared' identities.

Of course landscape archaeology in itself will never be enough to create 'conjectural histories'. Detailed archaeological analysis of Aboriginal places integrated into a diversity of histories – both indigenous and non-indigenous – is also essential, but so too are theory and perspective (again indigenous and non-indigenous) as sources of conjectures.

I stress the conjectural nature of such histories because Aboriginal histories, which are a rich source of data and perspective, in the main continue to
be essentially unintegrated with archaeological studies, and archaeologists
will have to struggle to convince many historians about whether archaeological data or perspectives have much to add. Such scepticism is not
completely unfounded because the archaeological characterisation of postcontact indigenous societies (even at the level of material culture, not to mention issues of gender, power or identity) continues to challenge us. Of course
there is abundant evidence of the strong interest indigenous people have in
charting the histories of their communities, and archaeology obviously has a
role to play here. However we also have the chance to reveal the significance
of archaeological data and perspectives for the creation of histories that will
address our general need to understand the experiences of indigenous societies during a period of great transformation. The shape and composition of
such histories, and the meanings of archaeological data that will both shape
and be integrated into them, are still to be determined.

I have previously made the point that the *Native Title Act* is, among other
things, the product of indigenous politics and academic research that took
place before the 1990s. I have also discussed the challenges raised by the
long struggle of the Yorta Yorta people for land justice with respect to the
provisions of that Act – especially those elements that deal with tradition
and continuity. Clearly the disappointment experienced by the Yorta Yorta
(and other communities in similar contexts) is best remedied by changing the ways in which tradition and continuity are interpreted, so that we
can acknowledge that such communities have transformed in order to survive. Whether this will be resolved by making ILUAs or will require the
development of a third iteration of the *Native Title Act* to deal specifically
with the needs of such communities is still moot, but there seems little
doubt that non-indigenous Australians need to know a lot more about the
specific histories of indigenous communities before the power of tradition and the 'essential' Aborigine can be broken. Creating new histories of
such transformed communities has the power to engender a more complete
understanding among non-indigenous Australians about the experience of
indigenous Australians over the last 150 years. So too will the notion that such
histories are to be imagined, argued about and in essence *made* by all of us.

My final example outlines the framework of a conjectural history of the
far west of New South Wales. It will be a history built around a sense of
mutuality, but also of discovery and integration. Its point of access is the
life of George Dutton, who was born in 1888 and initiated around the turn

Fig. 10.2 George Dutton in 1964.

of the nineteenth century, as told to and interpreted by the anthropologist
Jeremy Beckett over forty years ago.

Landscapes of transformation: George Dutton

All contact landscapes are crowded and ambiguous, requiring us to re-
engage with landscapes made up of memories, official records, sites that
have been abandoned or continue in use, places with multiple meanings,
and of course lies, mistakes and ignorance. All contact landscapes are also
shared, and it is the need to describe and define the context of that sharing
that provides one of the bedrock challenges of the historical archaeology
of Aboriginal Australia. During my account of the memorialisation of the
Myall Creek massacre I discussed the value that events such as massacres
have for allowing archaeologists and historians to gain access into such
crowded and ambiguous landscapes. In this discussion of George Dutton I
very briefly explore the great value of oral history in doing the same thing.
I then describe the place such information has within the framework of
research into large-scale pastoralism in the far west of New South Wales.

Jeremy Beckett first met Dutton in 1957 by the banks of the Darling River at Wilcannia. Beckett was seeking a man with traditional knowledge, and had been directed 'to the outskirts of town where a score or so of scrap iron humpies stood scattered in the saltbush and mallee scrub' (Beckett 1978: 3) to meet Dutton, who at that time was the last surviving initiated Aboriginal man in the region (Fig. 10.2).

Some youths in cowboy hats and high heeled boots led me past the wrecked cars, over the broken glass and rusty tins, to a rough single-roomed shanty, just big enough for the two beds in which he, his small son and two daughters slept. Dutton was sitting outside playing cards, a tall emaciated half-caste of about 70, his long sallow face sunken with the loss of his teeth, under his broad-brimmed stockman's hat. (Beckett 1978: 3)

Dutton, who died in 1968, was an ethnographer's dream – intelligent, experienced, extremely knowledgeable about his culture (he knew many languages), and possessing a great sense of humour. He was proud of his craft as a stockman, but he harboured no illusions about the future, telling Beckett his songs and stories knowing that he would respect their secrecy and value them, which Dutton thought was more than his own young people could do (1978: 4).

Dutton's life forms the cornerstone of my research into the 'shared' and 'conjectural' histories of the far west for three reasons. The first is that during his lifetime the old form of large-scale pastoralism ceased, taking with it the remnants of traditional Aboriginal society in that region. The world that replaced it was a world that had little place for Dutton, but it was the world of his children and the people who live in the region today. It was also a world that was to be remade by others into something that neither Dutton nor Beckett could have foreseen in the 1960s. The second is that Dutton was a man of two worlds in parentage. Dutton's mother was a Wonggumara woman living on one of the large stations in the area, and his father was a white stockman who had moved on before George was born. Dutton was raised by his mother's Maljangagba relatives and he followed his father's occupation right across the Corner Country (see Fig. 10.3). I shall briefly discuss the third reason for my interest in Dutton at the conclusion of this chapter.

Europeans settled the far west of New South Wales in the 1860s and initial contacts between pastoralists and Aboriginal people tended to follow the same pattern as they had elsewhere – in that there was mutual interest, lack of interest, avoidance and violence. However the Aboriginal people of Dutton's parents' generation soon settled down to what the anthropologist

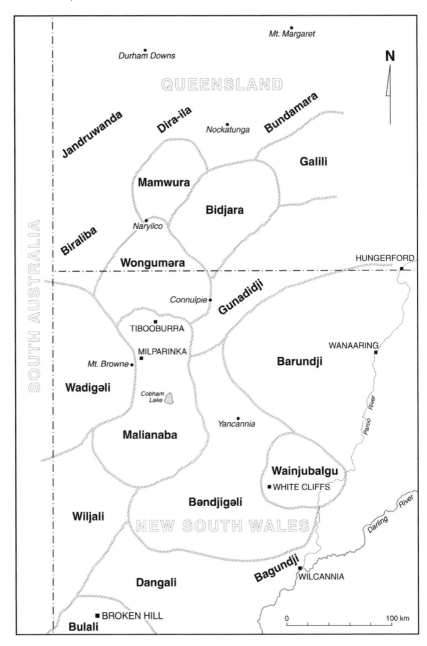

Fig. 10.3 Detail of Aboriginal language areas in north-west New South Wales.

A. P. Elkin described in the 1950s as a phase of 'intelligent parasitism' (Elkin 1951). Aborigines camped around settlements and homesteads that controlled stations typically comprising millions of hectares of grazing land. Surviving on government handouts, food and pay from casual stock work, and wild food, large populations of Aboriginal people were able to maintain culture and tradition, weaving 'station activity and certain European goods into their social and economic organisation and into their psychology without upsetting the fundamentals of their social behaviour or belief' (Elkin 1954: 324).

This pattern of life came to an end when drought, rabbit plagues and poor land management (that had already drastically reduced the productivity of marginal land) coincided with the Great Depression, and the breaking-up of large pastoral runs to provide land for soldiers returned from the First World War. Smaller family properties meant the rapid decline of available work, and Aboriginal people were evicted from many places, drifting to the outskirts of local towns and settlements, there falling under the control of government agencies, which on many occasions not only forcibly resettled them far from their country, but also took their children into care.

Dutton's life is a thread connecting these events, making them real, opening up connections with his relatives and friends so that we can gain a broader understanding of Aboriginal life in the far west during the twentieth century (see, for example, Beckett 1958, 1965). But Dutton has an additional virtue in that he moved between two worlds owing to his work and lifestyle. His work as a stockman took on a completely different aspect when he revealed to Beckett the overlap between the spiritual world of ceremony and the secular world of work.

The culture was dead, but its exponent was alive and accessible. Much of his talk was about the country he knew both in its mythological associations and as a drover. I had to send for large scale maps to follow the tracks that the dream-time heroes and he had followed. In the arid back country both Aboriginal and stockman must be able to recognize landmarks which to others seem non-descript, and they travel slowly enough for each feature to make its impression on them. I have heard drovers in bars rehearsing each step of a route, remembering what had happened here and there along the way, as though they were Aborigines 'singing the country'. The country provided the link between George Dutton's life as a stock man in white society and his life as an initiated man in black society (Beckett 1978: 4)

Of course Beckett would be the first to acknowledge that in the 1960s many like Dutton believed that his traditional culture was dead and that the future for his children as Aboriginal people was entirely uncertain. He (and Beckett) could not have expected that forty years later a revitalised culture would come to take its place (see, for example, the papers in Beckett 1988). There are many reasons for this resurgence and revitalisation, but it is worth emphasising the importance of the lives of Aboriginal people like Dutton and his friend Myles Lalor (2000) as the primary vectors of transformation and survival, and the creators of new knowledge, new sites of heritage significance and new patterns of community identification. In this sense the travels of stockmen, the waxing and waning of communities located on pastoral stations or on the edges of towns, the experience of being participants in white society but also being apart from it (whether by choice or as the result of white prejudice), have created social and cultural landscapes of adaptation and survival that reinforce the strength of Aboriginal communities in the far west.

Resurgence and revitalisation can also take on a more 'traditional' form, especially when associated with the identification and management of heritage sites or used in land claims made under the Native Title process. Nearly forty years after the conclusion of his conversations with George Dutton, Beckett participated in a major project detailing the family history of the Ngiyampaa Wangaaypuwan, whose country is close by George Dutton's (Beckett *et al*. 2003). In this project Aboriginal people and consultants sought to identify people with cultural attachments to an area of western New South Wales comprising millions of hectares. To do this the investigators collected information about language, custom and law, as well as the family histories of Ngiyampaa Wangaaypuwan groups since their dispossession during the 1860s. Such histories tend to be ones that focus on connections and disconnections from traditional lands which have become the properties of white pastoralists:

After World War II there was another round of movement in the region. In 1949, the inhabitants of the Menindee Government Station were moved once again to Murrin Bridge on the Lachlan, near Lake Cargelligo. However, the post-war labour market offered more opportunities than it had during the Depression, and the governments placed fewer restrictions on where people moved and resided. Some Ngiyampaa Wangaaypuwan people were able to work on the properties where they or their parents had been born. (Beckett *et al*. 2003: 25)

Pastoralism in the far west of New South Wales was much celebrated before the 1970s, standing, up to that time, as the near perfect exemplar of the Australian mythology of the outback as the key to what were then often touted as the essential Australian virtues of toughness, resilience, innovation and dry sense of humour (see for example Adam-Smith 1982; Hardy 1969; Idriess 1947; but quintessentially Bean 1956). However, studies that have sought to get past this veneer and to understand the process of settlement and its consequences for indigenous communities and the natural environment of the far west have not been numerous (but see for example Fokkema 1986; Goodall 1999; Hardy 1976; Heathcote 1965; Jervis 1948). None the less they have clearly established that there is much still to understand about the history of large-scale pastoralism and of the lives of those caught up in an industry that for many decades was a major contributor to the wealth of Australia.

Although it is widely accepted that the 'shared' histories of interactions with Aboriginal communities in the far west still remain largely untold (and thus remain hidden), the same very much applies to the non-Aboriginal community as well. Here, apart from the clashes between landowners and shearers over pay and conditions that were central to the early history of trade unionism in Australia, we know very little. Following the collapse of large-scale pastoralism in the far west during the 1980s and 1990s the economic and social importance of the industry rapidly eroded, leaving economically marginal communities populated by people with very little in common with the bulk of Australians living in the major urban centres on the coast. Writing the many histories of the far west, apart from promoting reconciliation with Aboriginal people, may well restore and transform the identities of the white population as well.

Much basic archaeological and historical research remains to be done. Although my conjectural history of the far west will be based on many oral histories, kilometres of microfilm, and the excavation of station and settlement occupation sites, at its core will be George Dutton's identity as a man of two worlds mediated by work and ceremony.

Concluding remarks

My brief discussion of ways in which archaeologists and historians might respond to the Yorta Yorta judgements is only a partial indication of how archaeologists might better serve the interests of reconciliation in Australia. In this I refer to the interests of all people – indigenous and immigrant. My discussion rests on the notion that understanding the history of the last 160 years of interaction in south-eastern Australia also implies a search for a kind of history which reflects the reality of Aboriginal lives in contexts where people could not continuously occupy their home territories, or maintain knowledge and ceremonies which were specifically associated with such territories. But there is more to it than this. Writing this historical archaeology also means writing the historical archaeology of non-Aboriginal people too, particularly in regional Australia, where (as we have seen at Myall Creek) memories endure and provoke very real emotional connections. No matter which way you look at it, since the first European explorers encountered Aboriginal people, ours has been a mutual history.

For much of the last century many Australians have acted as if this were not the case, and as if Aboriginal people really were invisible. This culture of forgetting, or perhaps simply not noticing, has very deep roots and has been widely practised. In my own case, growing up in the 1960s on a large pastoral holding on the Darling River close by George Dutton's country, surrounded by cases of Aboriginal artefacts collected by my great grandfather and succeeding generations (including myself), it was not until I went to university that I seriously engaged with the fact that my forebears had forcibly dispossessed the traditional owners of that land and directly or indirectly participated in the destruction of a traditional Aboriginal society. To this day I still ponder why it took so long for me to probe beneath family stories for answers to questions that would allow me to acknowledge this, and to accept that these people were a crucial part of my own history. In this sense George Dutton's story is partly mine too.

Many Australians have been profoundly shocked by the exposure of our mutual history. Massacres, the effects of disease, dispossession, the stealing of children, the abuse of people by institutions and the law, are now all there for people to see, and importantly to acknowledge that these terrible things happened. But the story of Aboriginal Australia is more than a story of death and dispossession; it is also a story of Aboriginal people making their way in the world – labouring, farming, creating communities, maintaining identity and surviving so that they remain a fundamental element of regional Australia. Archaeology has a significant role to play in telling that story.

Acknowledgements

Jeremy Beckett has been very generous in discussing his published and unpublished work on George Dutton with me. He also permitted the reproduction of his photograph of George Dutton and the adaptation of maps published by Beckett (1978). Wei Ming of the Archaeology Program at La Trobe University redrew these maps to create Figure 10.3.

Notes

1. Native Title is the formal description of the rights of Aboriginal and Torres Strait Islander peoples to land and waters in Australia in accordance with their traditional laws and customs. It was first formally recognised by the High Court of Australia in 1992 in *Mabo and Others v the State of Queensland* (No. 2) (1992) 175 CLR 1, 107 ALR 1. This decision overturned the doctrine that at time of colonisation (from 1788 onwards) Australia was *terra nullius* (an unoccupied, unowned land). Native Title was first recognised in the *Native Title Act* 1993, which was amended in 1998, and further refined and clarified in subsequent case law made by the Federal Court of Australia and the High Court of Australia. The process of making decisions about claims to Native Title is defined in the Act and may include negotiation, mediation and (more frequently) the making of Indigenous Land Use Agreements (ILUAs) that resolve competing interests in the use of land.

2. Accessible recent surveys of Australian indigenous archaeology include Flood 1995 and Mulvaney and Kamminga 1999. However, these works tend not to reflect too deeply on the consequences of high (or indeed higher) human antiquity in Australia. The best example of this kind of reflection is O'Connell and Allen 1998.

3. The viability of social, cultural or economic 'intensification' as an explanation for change in the last 5000 years in Australia is much debated. Examples of arguments against 'intensification' can be found in Murray and White 1985.

Bibliography

Abul el Haj, N., 2001, *Facts on the Ground: Archaeological Practice and Territorial Self-fashioning in Israeli Society*, Chicago: University of Chicago Press.

Acheson, S. R. 1998, 'In the wake of the ya'aats" xaatgaay ["Iron People"]: a study of changing settlement strategies among the Kunghit Haida', Oxford: BAR *International Series* 711.

Adam-Smith, P., 1982, *The Shearers*, Melbourne: Nelson.

Adams, Gary, 1981, 'Fur trade archaeology in western Canada: a critical evaluation and bibliography', *Saskatchewan Archaeology* 2–1&2: 39–53.

Adams, William Hampton, 1993, 'Historical archaeology strove for maturity in the mid-1980s', *Historical Archaeology* 27, 1: 23–32.

AJHR 1863–65, *Appendices to the Journals of the House of Representatives*: 1863, D-8; 1865, E-12.

Akerman, Kim, 1979, 'Material culture and trade in the Kimberleys today', in R. M. and C. M. Berndt (eds.), *Aborigines of the West: Their Past and Their Present*, pp. 243–51, Nedlands: University of Western Australia Press.

Alexander, R., 1998, 'Afterword: toward an archaeological theory of culture contact', in J. Cusick (ed.), *Studies in Culture Contact: Interaction, Culture, Change and Archaeology*, pp. 476–95, Carbondale: Southern Illinois University, Centre for Archaeological Investigations, Occasional Paper 25.

Allen, F. J. 1969, 'Archaeology, and the history of Port Essington', unpublished PhD thesis, Australian National University, Canberra.

    1980, 'Head on: the early nineteenth-century British colonization of the Top End', in R. Jones (ed.), *Northern Australia: Options and Implications*, pp. 33–9, Canberra: Research School of Pacific Studies, Australian National University.

Anderson, B., 1982, *Imagined Communities: Reflections on the Origin and Spread of Nationalism*, London: Verso.

Anonymous Missionary, 1801, 'The Missionaries' Journale in the Royal Admiral from Port Jackson to Matavai, Taheiti.' Microfilm of typescript copy of original MS, microfilm L.M.S 328, Auckland University Library.

Arthurs, David, 1980, 'The historical identification of Wapiscogamy House', in C. S. Reid, (ed.), *Northern Ontario Fur Trade Archaeology: Recent Research*, pp. 189–218, Toronto: Historical Planning and Research Branch, Ontario Ministry of Culture and Recreation.

Atkinson, A., 1985, 'The evidence of murder', *The Push from the Bush* 21: 58–88.

Atkinson, Geoffrey, 1920, *The Extraordinary Voyages in French Literature before 1700*, New York: Columbia University Press.

Attwood, Bain, 1989a, 'Writing the Aboriginal past. An interview with John Mulvaney', *Overland* 114: 6–8.

1989b, *The Making of the Aborigines*, St Leonards, NSW: Allen and Unwin.

1990, 'Review article. Aborigines and academic historians: some recent encounters', *Australian Historical Studies* 24: 123–35.

1992, 'Introduction', in B. Attwood and J. Arnold (eds.), *Power, Knowledge and Aborigines*, pp. i–xvi, Bundoora: La Trobe University Press.

2003, *Rights for Aborigines*, Sydney: Allen and Unwin.

Attwood, B. and Foster, S. (eds.), 2003, *Frontier Conflict: The Australia Experience*, Canberra: National Museum of Australia.

Attwood, B. and Markus, A., 1997, *The 1967 Referendum, or, When Aborigines Didn't Get the Vote*, Canberra: Australian Institute of Aboriginal and Torres Strait Islander Press.

Axtell, James, 1978, 'The ethnohistory of early America: a review essay', *William and Mary Quarterly* 25: 110–44.

1988, *After Columbus: Essays in the Ethnohistory of Colonial North America*, New York and Oxford: Oxford University Press.

1992, 'Columbian encounters beyond 1992', *William and Mary Quarterly* 49: 335–60.

Bailey, Geoff, 1981a, 'Concepts of resource exploitation: continuity and discontinuity in palaeoeconomy', *World Archaeology* 13: 1–15.

1981b, 'Concepts, time-scales and explanations in economic prehistory', in A. Sheridan and G. Bailey (eds.), *Economic Archaeology*, Oxford: BAR International Series 96.

1983, 'Concepts of time in Quaternary prehistory', *Annual Review of Anthropology* 12: 165–92.

Bairstow, Damaris, 1993, 'With the best will in the world: some records of early white contact with the Gampignal on the Australian Agricultural Company's estate at Port Stephen', *Aboriginal History* 17: 5–16.

Baker, R., 1999, *Land Is Life from Bush to Town: The Story of the Yanyuwa People*, St Leonards, Sydney: Allen and Unwin.

Barbeau, C. M., no date, 'Northwest Coast Files', Ottawa: Canadian Centre for Folk Culture Studies, Canadian Museum of Civilization.

Barrelet, James, 1953, *La Verrerie en France de l'époque gallo-romaine à nos jours*, Paris: Librairie Larousse.

Bartel, Brad, 1984, 'Comparative historical archaeology and archaeological theory', in S. Dyson (ed.), *Comparative Studies in the Archaeology of Colonialism*, pp. 8–37, Oxford: BAR International Series 233.

Bartlett, J., no date, 'Remarks on Board the Ship *Massachuset's* Capt. Joab Prince from Boston, Towards Canton', typescript of manuscript, Special Collections Division, University of British Columbia Library.

1925, 'A narrative of events in the life of John Bartlett of Boston, Massachusetts, in the years 1790–93, during voyages to Canton and the Northwest Coast of North America', in Elliot Snow (ed.), *The Sea, the Ship and the Sailor*, Salem, MA: Marine Research Society.

Baudrillard, Jean, 1968, *Le Système des objets*, Paris: Denoël/Gonthier.

Bazin, Jean and Bensa, Alban, 1994, 'Des objets à la chose', *Genèses* 17: 4–7.

Beaglehole, J. C. (ed.), 1955, *The Journals of Captain James Cook*, Vol. 1: *The Voyage of the Endeavour 1768–1771*, Hakluyt Society, Cambridge: Cambridge University Press.

Bean, C. E. W., 1956, *The Dreadnought of the Darling*, Sydney: Angus and Robertson.

Beard, J. S., 1979, *Vegetation Survey of Western Australia: Kimberley 1:1,000,000 Vegetation Series Explanatory Notes to Sheet 1*, Nedlands: University of Western Australia Press.

Beauchamp, William M., 1901, *Wampum and Shell Articles Used by the New York Indians*, Albany: University of the State of New York.

Beaudry, Mary (ed.), 1988, *Documentary Archaeology in the New World*, Cambridge: Cambridge University Press.

Beckett, J., 1958, 'Marginal men: a study of two half cast Aborigines', *Oceania* 29: 91–108.

1965, 'Kinship, mobility and community among part-Aborigines in rural Australia', *International Journal of Comparative Sociology* 6: 7–23.

1978, 'George Dutton's country: portrait of an Aboriginal drover', *Aboriginal History* 2, 1: 1–31.

Beckett, J. (ed.), 1988, *Past and Present: The Construction of Aboriginality*, Canberra: Aboriginal Studies Press.

Beckett, J., Donaldson, T., Steadman, B. and Meredith, S., 2003, Yapapunakirri, *Let's Track Back: The Aboriginal World around Mount Grenfell*, Sydney: Office of the Registrar, Aboriginal Land Rights Act, 1983 (NSW).

Bedford, S. H., 1994, 'Tenacity of the traditional: a history and archaeology of early European Maori contact, Puriri, Hauraki Plains', unpublished MA thesis, Anthropology Dept, University of Auckland.

1996, 'Post-contact Maori – the ignored component in New Zealand archaeology', *Journal of the Polynesian Society* 105, 4: 411–39.

Bedford, S. H. and Allen, H., 1992, 'Report on the 1991 and 1992 investigations on the Puriri River', Report for the Waikato Regional Council, Auckland: Uniservices.

1993, 'When is a shell midden not just a shell midden? Excavations on the Puriri River, Hauraki Plains', *Archaeology in New Zealand* 36, 3: 120–34.

Belich, J., 1986, *The New Zealand Wars and the Victorian Interpretation of Racial Conflict*, Auckland: Auckland University Press.

Bell, James, 1992, 'Universalisation in archaeological explanations', in L. Embree (ed.), *Meta-archaeology: Reflections by Archaeologists and Philosophers*, Boston Studies in the Philosophy of Science 147, pp. 143–63, Dordrecht: Kluwer Academic Publishers.

Bender, T. (ed.), 2002, *Rethinking American History in a Global Age*, Berkeley: University of California Press.

Berndt, Ronald and Berndt, Catherine, 1988, *The World of the First Australians*, 5th revised edition, Canberra: Aboriginal Studies Press (originally published in 1967).

Best, E., 1974, *The Stone Implements of the Maori*. Wellington: Dominion Museum Bulletin 4, Government Printer.

   1977, *Fishing Methods and Devices of the Maori*, Wellington: Dominion Museum Bulletin 12, Government Printer.

   1979, 'Site Survey Report, Lower Waihou River, Hauraki Plains', Wellington: Report for the New Zealand Historic Places Trust.

   1980, 'Oruarangi Pa: past and present investigations', *New Zealand Journal of Archaeology* 2: 65–91.

Best, S. and Allen, H., 1991, 'Report on the 1991 Investigations, Oruarangi Pa (Site N49/28)', Report for Department of Conservation, Waikato Conservancy, Auckland: Uniservices.

Bideaux, Michel (ed.), 1986, *Jacques Cartier. Relations.* Montreal: Presses de l'Université de Montréal.

Biggar, Henry P., 1922–36, *The Works of Samuel de Champlain*, 6 vols., Toronto: The Champlain Society.

Bintliff, J., 1991, 'The construction of an Annalist / structural history approach to archaeology', in J. Bintliff (ed.), *The Annales School in Archaeology*, pp. 1–33, London: Leicester University Press.

Birmingham, Judy, 1992, *Wybalenna: The Archaeology of Cultural Accommodation in Nineteenth Century Tasmania*, Sydney: The Australian Society for Historical Archaeology Incorporated.

Bishop, C., 1967, *The Journal and Letters of Captain Charles Bishop on the North-West Coast of America, in the Pacific and in New South Wales 1794–1799*, ed. Michael Roe, Hakluyt Society, Second Series, CXXXI, Cambridge: Cambridge University Press.

Biskup, Peter, 1982, 'Aboriginal history', in G. Osborne and W. Mandle (eds.), *New History: Studying Australia Today*, pp. 11–31, Sydney: George Allen and Unwin.

Blainey, Geoffrey, 1975, *Triumph of the Nomads: A History of Ancient Australia*, Melbourne: Macmillan Company (revised edition).

Boismier, W. and Gamble, C. (eds.) 1989, *Ethnoarchaeological Approaches to Mobile Campsites: Hunter-Gatherer and Pastoralist Case Studies*, Ann Arbor, MI: International Monographs in Prehistory.

Boit, J., 1981, *Log of the 'Union' 1794–1796*, ed. Edmund Hays, Massachusetts Historical Society/Oregon Historical Society.

Bonwick, James, 1967, *Daily Life and Origin of the Tasmanians*, New York: Johnson Reprint Corporation (originally published in 1870 by Sampson, Low, Son and Marston, London).

1970, *The Lost Tasmanian race*, New York: Johnson Reprint Corporation (originally published in 1884 by Sampson, Low, Marston, Searle and Rivington, London).

Boucher, François, 1996, *Histoire du costume en Occident des origines à nos jours*, Paris: Flammarion.

Bowdler, S. and O'Connor, S., 1991, 'The dating of the Australian Small Tool Tradition, with new evidence from the Kimberley, W.A.', *Australian Aboriginal Studies* 1: 53–61.

Bowes, R. G., 1977, 'New direction for historical parks', *Recreation Research Review* 5, 3: 20–3.

Boyd, Robert T., 1991, 'Demographic history, 1774–1874', in W. Suttles (ed.), *Handbook of North American Indians*, Vol. 7: *Northwest Coast*, pp. 135–48, Washington, DC: Smithsonian Institution.

Bradley, James, 1983, 'Blue crystals and other trinkets: glass beads from sixteenth and early seventeenth century New England', in C. F. Hayes III (ed.), *Proceedings of the 1982 Glass Trade Bead Conference*, pp. 29–40, Rochester: Rochester Museum and Science Center.

1987, *Evolution of the Onondaga Iroquois: Accommodating Change, 1500–1655*, Syracuse: Syracuse University Press.

Bradley, James and Childs, S. Terry, 1991, 'Basque earrings and panthers' tails: the form of cross-cultural contact in sixteenth-century Iroquoia', in R. M. Ehrenreich (ed.), *Metals in Society: Theory beyond Analysis*, pp. 7–17, Philadelphia: MASCA: The University Museum of Archaeology and Anthropology, University of Pennsylvania.

Brasser, Theodore J., 1978, 'Early Indian–European Contacts', in B. Trigger (ed.), *Northeast, Handbook of North American Indians*, Vol. 15, pp. 78–88, William Sturtevant, general editor, Washington: Smithsonian Institution.

Braudel, Fernand, 1989 (translated by S. Reynolds), *The Identity of France*, Vol. 1: *History and Environment*, London: Fontana Press (originally published in 1986 as *L'Identité de la France* by Les Editions Arthaud, Paris).

Brink, Y., 1992, 'Places of discourse and dialogue: a study in the material culture of the Cape during the rule of the Dutch East India Company, 1652–1795', PhD thesis, University of Cape Town.

'Figuring the cultural landscape: land, identity and material culture at the Cape in the eighteenth century', *South African Archaeological Bulletin* 52 (1997), 105–12.

Broome, Richard, 1982, *Aboriginal Australians* (1st edition), St Leonards, NSW: Allen and Unwin.

1994, *Aboriginal Australians* (2nd edition), St Leonards, NSW: Allen and Unwin.

Brumby, S., 1996, 'Wanjugawu? Gurlana na warirr yan.gu wan.gula nyinawurra' [You can't go back south to live], in Kimberley Language Resource Centre (ed.), *Moola Bulla: In the Shadow of the Mountain*, pp. 66–69, Broome, Magabala Books.

Brown, Jennifer, 1980, *Strangers in Blood: Fur Trade Company Families in Indian Country*, Vancouver: University of British Columbia Press.

    1990, 'The blind men and the elephant: fur trade history revisited', in P. A. McCormack *et al.*, *Proceedings of the Fort Chipewyan Fort Vermilion Bicentennial Conference*, pp. 15–19, Edmonton: Boreal Institute for Northern Studies.

Brumfiel, Elizabeth and Earle, Timothy, 1987, 'Introduction', in E. Brumfiel and T. Earle (eds.), *Specialization, Exchange, and Complex Societies*, pp. 1–9, Cambridge: Cambridge University Press.

Bruyn, Abraham de, 1581, *Habits de diverses nations de l'Europe, Asie, Afrique et Amerique*, Anvers: Abraham de Bruyn.

Buchanan, G., 1933, *Packhorse and Waterhole*, Sydney: Angus and Robertson.

Bureau of Meteorology, 1996, *Climatic Survey January 1996 – Kimberley*, Canberra: Australian Government Publishing Service.

Burley, David B., 1984, 'Prehistoric hunter/gatherer site development in Western Canada, Program Status and Constraints', *ASCA Report* 11, 3&4: 3–22.

Burley, David and Dalla Bona, Luke, 1988, 'Palisades and function: understanding construction variability in the western fur trade', paper presented at the 21st Canadian Archaeological Association Meeting, Whistler: British Columbia, 1988.

Burley, David V. and Hamilton, J. Scott, 1990, 'Rocky Mountain Fort: archaeological research and the late eighteenth-century North West Company expansion into British Columbia', *BC Studies* 88: 3–20.

    1991, 'Environmental impact of the 19th century Peace River fur trade: evidence from the archaeological record', paper presented at the Sixth North American Fur Trade Conference, MacKinac Island, Michigan.

Burley, David V., Hamilton, J. Scott and Fladmark, Knut, 1996, *Prophecy of the Swan: The Upper Peace River Fur Trade of 1794–1823*, Vancouver: University of British Columbia Press.

Burn, David, 1973, *A Picture of Van Diemen's Land*, Hobart, Tasmania: Cat and Fiddle Press (originally published in 1840–41).

Butlin, N. G., 1993, *Economics of the Dreamtime*, Cambridge: Cambridge University Press.

Byrne, D., 1996, 'Deep nation: Australia's acquisition of an indigenous past', *Aboriginal History* 20: 82–107.

    1998, *In Sad but Loving Memory: Aboriginal Burials and Cemeteries of the Last 200 Years in NSW*, Hurstville, NSW: NSW National Parks and Wildlife Service.

    2003, 'The ethos of return, erasure and reinstatement of Aboriginal visibility in the Australian historical landscape', *Historical Archaeology* 37, 1: 73–86.

Byrne, D., Brayshaw, H. and Ireland, T., 2001, *Social Significance: A Discussion Paper*, Hurstville, NSW: NSW National Parks and Wildlife Service.

Calder, J., 1972, *Some Account of the Wars, Extirpation, Habits, etc. of the Native Tribes of Tasmania*, Hobart: Fullers Bookshop Publishing Division (first published in 1875).

Campbell, I. C., 1997, 'Culture contact and Polynesian identity in the European age', in *Journal of World History* 8: 29–55.

Canada Census, no date, 'Federal Census Returns, 1881', Victoria: Microfilm copy, British Columbia Archives and Records Service.

Capone, Patricia H., 1995, 'Mission Pueblo ceramic analyses: implications for proto-historic interaction networks and cultural dynamics', PhD dissertation, Harvard University, Ann Arbor: University Microfilms Inc.

Carmack, Robert, 1972, 'Ethno-history: a review of its development, definitions, methods and aims', *Annual Review of Anthropology* 1: 227–46.

Ceci, Lynn, 1989, 'Tracing wampum's origins: shell bead evidence from archaeological sites in western and coastal New York', in C. F. Hayes III (ed.), *Proceedings of the 1986 Shell Bead Conference*, pp. 63–80, Rochester, Rochester Museum and Science Center.

1990, 'Native wampum as a peripheral resource in the seventeenth-century world-system', in L. M. Hauptman and J. D. Wherry (eds.), *The Pequots in Southern New England: The Rise and Fall of an American Indian Nation*, pp. 48–63, Norman and London: University of Oklahoma Press.

Champ, Joan, 1991, 'Arthur Silver Morton: beating the bounds on the Saskatchewan', *Saskatchewan History* 43, 2: 41–51.

Chapdelaine, Claude, 1988, *Le Site Mandeville à Tracy*, Montreal: Recherches Amérindiennes au Québec.

Chapman, Graham, 1997, 'On wholeness, reflexive complexity, hierarchies, structures and social dynamics', in S. Van der Leeuw and J. McGlade (eds.), *Time, Process and Structured Transformation in Archaeology*, pp. 396–425, London: Routledge.

Christianson, David, 1980, 'New Severn of Nieu Savanne: the identification of an early Hudson Bay fur trade post', MA thesis, McMaster University.

Clark, Manning, 1962, *A History of Australia: From Earliest Times to the Age of Macquarie*, Melbourne: Melbourne University Press.

Clarke, A., 2002, 'The ideal and the real: cultural and personal transformations of archaeological research on Groote Eylandt, northern Australia', *World Archaeology* 34, 2: 249–64.

Clarke, David, 1978, *Analytical Archaeology*, 2nd edition revised by B. Chapman, London: Methuen and Co. Ltd. (first published in 1968).

Cleland, Charles, 1988, 'Questions of substance, questions that count', *Historical Archaeology* 22: 13–17.

1993, 'The first half decade: the foundation of the Society for Historical Archaeology, 1967–1972', *Historical Archaeology* 27, 1: 12–14.

Clement, C., 1988, 'Pre-settlement intrusion into the east Kimberley', East Kimberley Impact Assessment Report, Working Paper 24, Canberra: East Kimberley Impact Assessment Project.

Clement, C. and Bridge, P., 1991, *Kimberley Scenes: Sagas of Australia's Last Frontier*, Carlisle, WA: Hesperian Press.

Cline, Howard, 1972, 'Introduction: reflections on ethno-history', in H. Kline (ed.), *Handbook of Middle American Indians*, Vol. 12 (part 1): *A Guide to Ethno-historical Sources*, pp. 3–16, Texas: University of Texas Press.

Clinton, E., no date, 'Journal on the Ship *Vancouver*, August 4, 1804 to September 6, 1806', Yale University: Beinecke Library.

Coetzee, C., 1994, 'Visions of disorder and profit: the Khoikhoi and the first years of the Dutch East India Company at the Cape', *Social Dynamics* 20, 2: 35–66.

Coetzee, J., 1989, 'Idleness in South Africa', in N. Armstrong and L. Tennenhouse (eds.), *The Violence of Representation: Literature and the History of Violence*, pp. 119–39, London: Routledge.

Cohen, Bernard, 1981, 'Anthropology and history in the 1980s', *Journal of Interdisciplinary History* 12: 227–52.

Cohen, Jack and Stewart, Ian, 1994, *The Collapse of Chaos: Discovering Simplicity in a Complex World*, London: Viking Press (Penguin Group).

Colenso, W., 1881, 'On the fine perception of colours possessed by the ancient Maori', *Transactions of the New Zealand Institute* 14: 49–76.

Collison, W. H., no date, 'Letterbook, 1876–1880', Church Missionary Society Records, Ottawa: National Archives of Canada.

1915, *In the Wake of the War Canoe*, London: Seeley, Service & Co.

1940, *The Journal of Captain James Colnett Aboard the 'Argonaut' from April 26, 1789 to Nov. 3, 1791*, ed. F. W. Howay, Toronto: The Champlain Society.

Comaroff, Jean and Comaroff, John, 1991, *Of Revelation and Revolution*, Vol. 1: *Christianity, Colonialism, and Consciousness in South Africa*, Chicago and London: University of Chicago Press.

1997, *Of Revelation and Revolution*, Vol. 2: *The Dialectics of Modernity on a South African Frontier*, Chicago and London: University of Chicago Press.

Cook, Ian and Crang, Philip, 1996, 'The world on a plate: culinary culture, displacement and geographical knowledge', *Journal of Material Culture* 1, 1: 131–53.

Cook, Ramsay, 1993, *The Voyages of Jacques Cartier*, Toronto, Buffalo and London: University of Toronto Press.

Corrozet, Gilles, 1997, *L'Hecatongraphie et Les emblèmes du tableau de Cebes*, 1543 Facsimile reproduction and critical edition by Alison Adams, Geneva.

Costin, Cathy L., 1991, 'Craft specialization: issues in defining, documenting, and explaining the organization of production', in M. Schiffer (ed.), *Archaeological Method and Theory*, Vol. 3, pp. 1–56, Tucson: University of Arizona Press.

Cotgrave, Randle, 1968, *A Dictionarie of French and English Tongue*, London: Menston (first published in 1611).

Coutts, Peter, 1981, *Victoria's First Official Settlement, Sullivans Bay, Port Phillip*, Melbourne: Victoria Archaeological Survey, Ministry for Conservation.

Coutts, P., Witter, D. and Parsons, D., 1977, 'Impact of European settlement on Aboriginal society in western Victoria', *Records of the Victoria Archaeological Survey* 4: 17–58.

Coutts, Robert, 1992, 'York Factory as a native community: public history research, commemoration and the challenge to interpretation', *Prairie Forum* 17, 2: 275–93.

Coveney, P. and Highfield, R., 1990, *The Arrow of Time*, London: W. H. Allen Inc.

Cowlishaw, Gillian, 1992, 'Studying Aborigines: changing canons in anthropology and history', in B. Attwood and J. Arnold, (eds.), *Power, Knowledge and Aborigines*, pp. 20–31, Bundoora: La Trobe University Press.

Crais, C., 1994, 'Slavery and emancipation in the Eastern Cape', in N. Worden and C. Crais (eds.), *Breaking the Chains: Slavery and Its Legacy in the Nineteenth Century Cape*, pp. 272–87, Johannesburg: Witwatersrand University Press.

Cribbin, J., 1984, *The Killing Times*, Sydney: Fontana/Collins.

Crosby, A. W., 1986, *Ecological Imperialism: The Biological Expansion of Europe, 900–1900*, Cambridge: Cambridge University Press.

1994, *Germs, Seeds and Animals: Studies in Ecological History*, Armonk, New York: M. E. Sharpe.

Crosby, A. and Loughlin, S., 1991, 'Site Survey Report, West Bank of the Lower Waihou River', Wellington: Historic Places Trust.

Cross, D., no date, 'Journal of a voyage round the world in the brig *Rob Roy* in the years 1821, 1822, 1823, 1824', Nantucket, MA: Nantucket Historical Society.

Curr, E., 1883, *Recollections of Squatting in Victoria*, Melbourne: George Roberston.

1886–87, *The Australian Race*, 4 vols., Melbourne: Victorian Government Printer.

Curthoys, A., 2003, 'Constructing national histories', in B. Attwood and S. Foster (eds.), *Frontier Conflict: The Australian Experience*, pp. 185–200, Canberra: National Museum of Australia.

Curtis, Edward S., 1916, 'The Haida', in *The North American Indian*, Vol. 11, Norwood, IL: Norwood Publishing.

Cusick, J., 1998, 'Historiography of acculturation: an evaluation of concepts and their application in archaeology', in J. Cusick (ed.), *Studies in Culture Contact: Culture, Change and Archaeology*, pp. 126–45, Southern Illinois University: Centre for Archaeological Investigations, Occasional Paper 25.

Dalzell, K. E., 1968, *The Queen Charlotte Islands 1774–1966*, Terrace: C. M. Adam.

Daunton, M. and Halpern, R. (eds.), 1999, *Empire and Others: British Encounters with Indigenous Peoples, 1600–1850*, Philadelphia: University of Pennsylvania Press.

Davidson, D. S., 1934, 'Australian spear-traits and their derivations', *Journal of the Polynesian Society* 43: 41–72, 143–62.

Davidson, I., Lovell-Jones, C. and Bancroft, R., 1995, *Archaeologists and Aborigines Working Together*, Armidale, NSW: University of New England Press.

Davidson, J., 1984, *The Prehistory of New Zealand*, Auckland: Longman Paul.

1880, *Report on the Queen Charlotte Islands, 1878*, Ottawa: Geological Survey of Canada Report of Progress for 1878–79, 4.

Deagan, Kathleen, 1982, 'Avenues of inquiry in historical archaeology', in M. B. Schiffer (ed.), *Advances in Archaeological Method and Theory 5*, pp. 151–77, New York: Academic Press.

1983, *Spanish St Augustine: The Archaeology of a Colonial Creole Community*, New York: Academic Press.

1988, 'Neither history nor prehistory: the questions that count in historical archaeology', *Historical Archaeology* 22: 7–12.

1991, 'Historical archaeology's contributions to our understanding of early America', in L. Falk (ed.), *Historical Archaeology in Global Perspective*, pp. 97–112, Washington DC: Smithsonian Institution Press.

1993, 'Retrospective on the Society for Historical Archaeology, 1977–1982', *Historical Archaeology* 27, 1: 19–22.

1997, 'Cross-disciplinary themes in the recovery of the colonial middle period', *Historical Archaeology* 31, 1: 4–8.

1998, 'Transculturation and Spanish American ethnogenesis: the archaeological legacy of the Quincentenary', in J. Cusick (ed.), *Studies in Culture Contact: Interaction, Culture Change and Archaeology*, pp. 23–43, Carbondale: Southern Illinois University, Centre for Archaeological Investigations, Occasional Paper 25.

Deakin, A., 1992, 'Early settlement', in B. Shaw (ed.), *When the Dust Come in Between: Aboriginal Viewpoints in the East Kimberley Prior to 1982*, pp. 123–34, Canberra: Aboriginal Studies Press.

de Bourdeille, dit Brântome, Pierre, *Recueil des dames, poésies et tombeaux*, 1655, reprinted 1899, Paris: Gallimard, 1991.

Dee, H. D. (ed.), 1944a, 'The Journal of John Work, 1835: being an account of his voyage northward from the Columbia River to Fort Simpson and return in the Brig Lama, January–October, 1835', *British Columbia Historical Quarterly* 8, 2, April.

1944b, 'The Journal of John Work, 1835: being an account of his voyage northward from the Columbia River to Fort Simpson and return in the Brig Lama, January–October, 1835', *British Columbia Historical Quarterly* 8, 3, July.

1944c, 'The Journal of John Work, 1835: being an account of his voyage northward from the Columbia River to Fort Simpson and return in the Brig Lama, January–October, 1835', *British Columbia Historical Quarterly* 8, 4, October.

Deetz, James, 1963, 'Archaeological investigations at La Purisima Mission', in *Archaeological Survey Annual Report 5*, pp. 161–241, London: UCLA.

1977, *In Small Things Forgotten*, New York: Doubleday.

1988, 'Material culture and worldview in colonial Anglo-America', in M. Leone and P. B. Parker (eds.), *The Recovery of Meaning: Historical Archaeology in the Eastern United States*, Washington DC: Smithsonian Institution Press.

1991, 'Archaeological evidence of sixteenth and seventeenth-century encounters', in L. Falk (ed.), *Historical Archaeology in Global Perspective*, pp. 1–10, Washington DC: Smithsonian Institution Press.

De Farce, Louis, 1890, *La Broderie du 11e siècle à nos jours,* Angers: Bel Homme.

de la Pérouse, J. F. G., 1798, *A Voyage Round the World, in the Years 1785, 1786, 1787 and 1788, Published Conformably to the Decree of the National Assembly, of the 22nd of April, 1791 and edited by M. L. A. Milet-Mureau* (translated from the French), 3 vols., London: Printed for J. Johnson, St Paul's Church Yard.

Denholm, D., 1981, 'The Myall Creek massacre', *The Push from the Bush* 9: 72–86.

D'Entremont, Clarence J., 1982, *Nicolas Denys, sa vie et son œuvre*, Yarmouth, Nova Scotia: Imprimerie Lescarbot.

Departmental Archives of Charentes-Maritimes (La Rochelle), 3E Notaries (DACM).

Departmental Archives of Gironde (Bordeaux), 3E Notaries (DAG).

Derrida, J., 1977, *Of Grammatology*, trans. G. Spivak, Baltimore: Johns Hopkins University Press.

Desainliens, Claude, 1970, *A Dictionarie of French and English*, London: Menston (first published in 1593).

Diderot, Denis and Lerond d'Alembert, Jean, 1751–65, *Encyclopédie ou dictionnaire raisonné des sciences, des arts et des métiers*, Paris: Briasson.

Dietler, M., 1995, 'The Cup of Gyptis: rethinking the colonial encounter in early-Iron-Age Western Europe and the relevance of world systems models', *Journal of European Archaeology* 3: 89–111.

    1998, 'Consumption, agency and cultural entanglement: theoretical implications of a Mediterranean colonial encounter', in J. Cusick (ed.), *Studies in Cultural Contact: Interaction, Culture Change and Archaeology*, pp. 288–315, Carbondale: Southern Illinois University, Centre for Archaeological Investigation, Occasional Paper 25.

Dixon, G., 1789, *A Voyage Round the World; but more particularly to the North-West Coast of America: performed in 1785, 1786, 1787, and 1788, in the* King George *and* Queen Charlotte. London: Geo. Goulding.

Dodd, C., no date, 'Letter to Board of Management, Western Department, Hudson's Bay Company, 26 October 1857', Winnipeg: Hudson's Bay Company Archives, B 226/c/1, Archives of Manitoba.

Dortch, C. E., 1977, 'Early and late stone industrial phases in Western Australia', in R. V. S. Wright (ed.), *Stone Tools as Cultural Markers*, pp. 104–32, Canberra: Australian Institute of Aboriginal Studies.

Douglas, J., no date, 'Private Papers, Second Series 1853.' A/B/40/D75.4, Victoria: British Columbia Archives and Records Service.

Doxtator, Deborah, 1988, 'The home of Indian culture and other stories in the museum', *MUSE* Autumn: 26–8.

Drewal, Henry John and Mason, John, 1998, *Beads, Body and Soul: Art and Light in the Yoruba Universe*, Los Angeles: UCLA Fowler Museum of Cultural History.

Drouin, Catherine, 1993, 'Les perles des premiers contacts entre Européens et Amérindiens aux XVIe et XVIIe siècles: une étude exploratoire', Paper presented at the Annual Meeting of the Canadian Archaeological Association, Montreal.

Duff, Wilson, 1964, *The Impact of the White Man: The Indian History of British Columbia, Victoria*, Anthropology in British Columbia, Memoir 5.

Duncan, Alexander, no date a, 'Letter, Alexander Duncan to John McLoughlin, Fort Simpson, March 6, 1834', Hudson's Bay Company Archives, B.223/c/1 fo. 30.

no date b, 'Letter, Alexander Duncan to Chief Factors and Chief Traders, Fort Simpson, March 6, 1834', Hudson's Bay Company Archives B.223/c/1.

Duncan, B. 1996, 'Teistem olawei lilbit [Tasting it slowly]', in Kimberley Language Resource Centre (ed.), *Moola Bulla: In the Shadow of the Mountain*, pp. 62–4, Broome: Magabala Books.

Dunnell, R. C., 1991, 'Methodological impacts of catastrophic depopulation on American archaeology and ethnology', in D. H. Thomas (ed.), *Columbian Consequences*, Vol. 3: *The Spanish Borderlands in Pan-American Perspective*, pp. 561–86, Washington DC: Smithsonian Institution Press.

Durack, M., 1959, *Kings in Grass Castles*, London: Constable.

Durack, M. and Durack, E., 1935, *All-About: The Story of a Black Community on Argyle Station, Kimberley*, Perth: R. S. Sampson.

Durack, P. M., 1933, 'Pioneering the East Kimberleys', *Journal of the Historical Society of Western Australia* 2, 14: 1–46.

Dutens, Louis, 1776, *Des Pierres précieuses et des pierres fines avec les moyens de les connaître et de les évaluer*, Paris: Firmin Didot.

Dyke, C., 1990, 'Strange attraction, curious liaison: Clio meets chaos', *The Philosophical Forum* 21: 369–92.

Eddy, J. and Schreuder, D. M., 1988, *The Rise of Colonial Nationalism: Australia, New Zealand, Canada and South Africa First Assert Their Nationalities 1880–1914*, London: Unwin.

Edmunds, M. and Smith, D., 2002, *Guide to Mediation and Agreement Making under the Native Title Act*, Perth: National Native Title Tribunal.

Elkin, A., 1951, 'Reaction and interaction: a food gathering people and European settlement in Australia', *American Anthropologist* 53, 2: 164–86.

1954, *The Australian Aborigines: How to Understand Them*, 3rd edition, Sydney: Angus and Robertson.

Elphick, R., 1977, *Kraal and Castle*, New Haven: Yale University Press.

Elphick, R. and Malherbe, V., 1989, 'The Khoisan to 1828', in R. Elphick and H. Giliomee (eds.), *The Shaping of South African Society, 1652–1840*, pp. 3–65, Cape Town: Maskew Miller Longman.

Elton, G., 1984, *The Practice of History*, London: Fontana Paperbacks (originally published 1967).

Eley, G. and Suny, R. (eds.), 1996, *Becoming National*, Oxford: Oxford University Press.

Farnsworth, P. (ed.), 2001, *Island Lives: Historical Archaeologies of the Caribbean*, Tuscaloosa: University of Alabama Press.

Farriss, Nancy, 1986, 'Indians in colonial northern Yucatan', in R. Spores (ed.), *Supplement to the Handbook on the Middle American Indians*, Vol. 4: *Ethnohistory*, pp. 88–102, Austin: University of Texas Press.

FCA 1606, 1998, 'Members of the Yorta Yorta Aboriginal Community vs. Victoria and Others', Federal Court of Australia, 18th December 1998.

FCA 45, 2001, 'Members of the Yorta Yorta Aboriginal Community vs. Victoria and Others', Federal Court of Australia, 8th February 2001.

Fenton, William N., 1985, 'Structure, continuity, and change in the process of Iroquois treaty making', in Francis Jennings (ed.), *The History and Culture of Iroquois Diplomacy*, Syracuse: Syracuse University Press.

1998, *The Great Law and the Longhouse: A Political History of the Iroquois Confederacy*, Norman: University of Oklahoma Press.

Ferguson, Leland, 1977a, 'Historical archaeology and the importance of material things', in L. Ferguson (ed.), *Historical Archaeology and the Importance of Material Things*, pp. 5–8, Special Publications Series 2, Lansing, MI: The Society for Historical Archaeology.

(ed.), 1977b, *Historical Archaeology and the Importance of Material Things*, Special Publication Series 2, Lansing, MI: Society for Historical Archaeology.

Ferguson, L. and Green, S., 1983, 'Recognizing the American Indian, African and European record of colonial South Carolina', in A. Ward (ed.), *Forgotten Places and Things: Archaeological Perspectives on American History*, pp. 275–81, Albuquerque: Centre for Anthropological Studies.

Fieldhouse, D. K., 1982, *The Colonial Empires: A Comparative Survey from the Eighteenth Century*, London: Macmillan.

1999, *The West and the Third World: Trade, Colonialism, Dependence and Development*, Oxford: Blackwell.

Fisher, Robin, 1977, *Contact and Conflict*, Vancouver: University of British Columbia Press.

Fitting, James E., 1977, 'The structure of historical archaeology and the importance of material things', in Leland Ferguson (ed.), *Historical Archaeology and the Importance of Material Things*, pp. 63–7, Special Publication Series 2, Lansing, MI: Society for Historical Archaeology.

Fitzgerald, William, 1990, 'Chronology to cultural process: Lower Great Lakes Archaeology, 1500–1650', PhD, McGill University.

Fitzgerald, William, 1979, 'The Hood Site: longhouse burials in an historic neutral village', *Ontario Archaeology* 32: 43–60.

Fitzgerald, William, Knight, Dean and Bain, Allison, 1995, 'Untanglers of matters temporal and cultural: glass beads and the early contact period Huron Ball Site', *Canadian Journal of Archaeology* 19: 117–38.

Fitzhugh, W. (ed.), 1985, *Cultures in Contact*, Washington DC: Smithsonian Institution Press.

Fladmark, Knut, 1980, 'British Columbia archaeology in the 1970s', *B.C. Studies* 48: 11–20.

Fletcher, Roland, 1992, 'Time perspectivism', in B. Knapp (ed.), *Archaeology, Annales and Ethno-history*, pp. 35–49, Cambridge: Cambridge University Press.

Fleurieu, C. P. C., 1801, *A Voyage Round the World Performed during the Years 1790, 1791 and 1792, by Etienne Marchand*, 2 vols., London: T. N. Longman and O. Rees.

Flood, J., 1995, *Archaeology of the Dreamtime*, 3rd revised edition, Sydney: Angus and Robertson.

Fokkema, G., 1986, *Wilcannia: Portrait of an Australian Town*, Sydney: Harper and Rowe.

Foley, R. (1981), 'A model of regional archaeological structure', *Proceedings of the Prehistoric Society* 47: 1–17.

Forrest, K., 1996, *The Challenge and the Chance: The Colonization and Settlement of North West Australia 1861–1914*, Carlisle: Hesperian Press.

Forsman, Michael R. A., 1983, 'The early fur trade artifact pattern', in S. South, *The Conference on Historic Site Archaeology Papers 1980*, Vol. 15, pp. 71–90, Columbia: Institute of Anthropology and Archaeology, University of South Carolina.

Fowler, Don D., 1987, 'Uses of the past: archaeology in the service of the state', *American Antiquity* 52, 2: 229–48.

Fowler, William, 1991, 'The political economy of Indian survival in sixteenth-century Isalco, El Salvador', in D. Hurst Thomas (ed.), *Columbian Consequences*, Vol. 3: *The Spanish Borderlands in Pan-American Perspective*, pp. 37–71, Washington DC: Smithsonian Institution Press.

Francis, Daniel, 1982, *Battle for the West: Fur Traders and the Birth of Western Canada*, Edmonton: Hurtig.

  1992, *The Imaginary Indian: The Image of the Indian in Canadian Culture*, Vancouver: Arsenal Pulp Press.

Furey, L., 1996, *Oruarangi: The Archaeology and Material Culture of a Hauraki Pa*, Auckland: Bulletin of the Auckland Institute and Museum 17.

Furgerson, S., no date, 'Journal of a Voyage from Boston to the North-West Coast of America, in the Brig *Otter*, Samuel Hill Commander, March 31, 1809 to March 24, 1811', MS, Yale University, Beinecke Library.

Galois, R. W., 1993, 'From Laxwallams to Fort Simpson: organizing the fur trade in the Lower Skeena/Nass Region, 1830–1860', Paper presented at the Columbia Department Fur Trade Conference, University of Victoria.

Gero, Joan, 1985, 'Socio-politics and the woman-at-home ideology', *American Antiquity* 50, 2: 342–50.

Gibson, James R., 1992, *Otter Skins, Boston Ships and China Goods: The Maritime Fur Trade of the Northwest Coast, 1785–1841*, Montreal: McGill-Queen's University Press.

Giliomee, H., 1979, *Die Kaap Tydens die Eerste Britse Bewind 1795–1803*, Cape Town: HAUM.

Gill, N., 1997, 'The contested domain of pastoralism: landscape, work and outsiders in central Australia', in D. Rose and A. Clarke (eds.), *Tracking Knowledge in North Australian Landscapes: Studies in Indigenous and Settler Ecological Knowledge Systems*, pp. 50–67, Canberra and Darwin: North Australia Research Unit, School of Pacific and Asian Studies, The Australian National University.

Glen, Jean de, 1601, *Des habits, moeurs, cérémonies et façons de faire anciens et modernes du monde avec des portraict des habits taillés,* Liège: Jean de Glen.

Godefroy, Frédéric, 1982, *Dictionnaire de l'ancienne langue française et de tous ses dialectes du IXe au XVe siècle,* Geneva: Slatkine.

Goldfrank, Esther (ed.), 1970, *Isleta Paintings*, with an introduction by Elsie Clews Parsons, Washington, DC: Smithsonian Institution Press.

Golson, J., 1959, 'Culture change in prehistoric New Zealand', in J. D. Freeman and W. R. Geddes (eds.), *Anthropology in the South Seas*, pp. 29–74, New Plymouth: Avery.

Goodall, H., 1999, 'Contesting on the Paroo and its sister rivers', in R. T. Kingsford (ed.), *A Free-Flowing River: The Ecology of the Paroo River*, pp. 179–200, Sydney: NSW National Parks and Wildlife Service.

Gough, B. M., 1982, 'New Light on Haida Chiefship: The Case of Edenshaw 1850–1853', *Ethnohistory* 29, 2: 131–139.

Gould, Richard and Schiffer, Michael B. (eds.), 1981, *Modern Material Culture: The Archaeology of Us*, New York: Academic Press.

Graeber, David, 1996, 'Beads and money: notes toward a theory of wealth and power', *American Ethnologist* 23, 1: 4–24.

Graham, Elizabeth, 1991, 'Archaeological insights into colonial period Maya life at Tipu, Belize', in D. Hurst Thomas (ed.), *Columbian Consequences*, Vol. 3: *The Spanish Borderlands in Pan-American Perspective*, pp. 319–35, Washington DC: Smithsonian Institution Press.

Green, J. S., 1915, *Journal of a Tour on the Northwest Coast of America in the Year 1829*, New York: Frederick Heartman.

Green, N., 1995, *The Forrest River Massacres,* South Fremantle: Fremantle Arts Centre Press.

Greer, S., 1995, 'The accidental heritage: archaeology and identity in northern Cape York', unpublished PhD thesis, Department of Anthropology and Archaeology, James Cook University, Townsville, Queensland.

Greer, S., Harrison, R. and McIntyre-Tamwoy, S., 2002, 'Community-based archaeology in Australia', *World Archaeology* 34, 2: 265–87.

Greimas, Algirdas Julien, 1992, 'La Renaissance', *Dictionnaire de l'ancien français*, Paris: Larousse.

Griffiths, T., 1996, *Hunters and Collectors: The Antiquarian Imagination in Australia*, Cambridge: Cambridge University Press.

1997, 'Ecology and empire towards an Australian history of the world', in
    T. Griffiths and L. Robbin (eds), *Ecology and Empire: Environmental History of
    Settler Societies*, pp. 1–16, Melbourne: Melbourne University Press.

Griffiths, T. and Robin, L. (eds.), 1997, *Ecology and Empire; Environmental History
    of Settler Societies*, Melbourne: Melbourne University Press.

Groube, L. M., 1964, 'Settlement pattern in prehistoric New Zealand', unpublished
    MA thesis, Department of Anthropology, University of Auckland.

Gullason, Lynda, 1990, 'The Fort George–Buckingham House Site Plantation (1792–
    1800): native–European contact in the fur trade era', PhD thesis, University of
    Alberta.

Guthe, Carl E., 1925, *Pueblo Pottery Making: A Study at the Village of San Ildefonsos*,
    New Haven: Yale University Press.

Haebich, Anna, 1992, *For Their Own Good: Aborigines and Government in the South
    West of Western Australia 1900–1940*, 2nd edition, Nedlands: University of
    Western Australia Press for the Charles and Joy Staples South West Regional
    Publications Fund (originally published in 1988).

Hall, Martin, 1986, 'The role of cattle in African agro-pastoralist societies: more
    than bones alone can tell', *South African Archaeological Bulletin Goodwin Series*
    5: 83–7.

    1993, 'The archaeology of colonial settlement in southern Africa', *Annual Reviews
    of Anthropology* 22: 177–200.

    1999a, 'Subaltern voices? Finding the spaces between things and words', in
    P. Funari, M. Hall and S. Jones (eds.), *Historical Archaeology: Back from the
    Edge*, pp. 193–203, London: Routledge.

    1999b, 'Virtual colonization', *Journal of Material Culture* 4, 1: 39–55.

    2000, *Archaeology and the Modern World*, London: Routledge.

Hall, R., 1999, *A Return to the Brink*, Sydney: Currency Press.

Hamel, Nathalie, 1995, 'Les perles de verre du site du Palais de l'Intendant à Québec',
    Mémoires Vives 9: 10–16.

Hamell, George R., 1977, 'Report on the Alhart Site radiocarbon dates', Rochester,
    Manuscript on file at the Rochester Museum and Science Center, 1977.

    1983, 'Trading and metaphors: the magic of beads', in Charles F. Hayes III (ed.),
    Proceedings of the 1982 Glass Trade Bead Conference, pp. 5–28, Rochester:
    Rochester Museum and Science Center.

    1992, 'The Iroquois and the world's rim: speculations on color, culture, and
    contact', *American Indian Quarterly* 26, 4: 451–69.

    1996, 'Wampum', in Alexandra van Dongen (ed.), *One Man's Trash Is Another's
    Man's Treasure*, pp. 41–51, Rotterdam: Museum Boymans-van Beuningen.

Hamilton, James Scott, 1990, 'Fur trade social inequality and the role of non-verbal
    communication', unpublished PhD thesis, Simon Fraser University.

Hardy, B., 1969, *West of the Darling*, Adelaide: Rigby.

    1976, *Lament of the Barkindji: The Vanished Tribes of the Darling River Region*,
    Adelaide: Rigby.

Harrison, B., 1978, 'The Myall Creek Massacre', in I. McBryde (ed.), *Records of Times Past: Ethnohistorical Essays on the Culture and Ecology of the New England Tribes*, pp. 17–51, Canberra: Australian Institute of Aboriginal Studies.

Harrison, C., 1925, *Ancient Warriors of the North Pacific*, London: H. F. and G. Witherby.

Harrison, R., 2000, 'Challenging the authenticity of antiquity: contact archaeology and Native Title in Australia', in I. Lilley (ed.), *Native Title and the Transformation of Archaeology in a Postcolonial World*, Oceania Monograph 50, pp. 35–53, Sydney: Oceania Publications, University of Sydney.

2002a, 'Archaeology and the colonial encounter: Kimberley spear points, cultural identity and masculinity in the north of Australia', *Journal of Social Archaeology* 2, 3: 352–77.

2002b, 'Australia's Iron Age: Aboriginal post-contact metal artefacts from Old Lamboo Station, Southeast Kimberley, Western Australia', *Australasian Historical Archaeology* 20: 67–76.

2002c, 'Shared histories and the archaeology of the pastoral industry in Australia', in R. Harrison and C. Williamson (eds.), *After Captain Cook: The Archaeology of the Recent Indigenous Past in Australia*, pp. 37–58, Sydney: Archaeological Computing Laboratory, University of Sydney.

Harrison, R. and Frink, D., 2000, 'The OCR carbon dating procedure in Australia: new dates from Wilinyjibari rockshelter, Southeast Kimberley, Western Australia', *Australian Archaeology* 51: 6–15.

Harrison, R. and Williamson, C. (eds.), 2002, *After Captain Cook: The Archaeology of the Recent Indigenous Past in Australia*, Sydney: Archaeological Computing Laboratory, University of Sydney.

Haswell, R., no date, 'A Voyage on Discoveries in the Ship *Columbia Rediviva* by Robert Haswell with Remarks on board the Sloop *Adventure*', photocopy of manuscript, Special Collections Division, University of British Columbia Library.

Head, L. and Fullagar, R., 1997, 'Hunter-gatherer archaeology and pastoral contact: perspectives from the northwest Northern Territory, Australia', *World Archaeology* 28, 3: 418–28.

Heathcote, R. L., 1965, 'Back of Bourke: a study of land appraisal and settlement in semi-arid Australia', Melbourne: Melbourne University Press.

Heidenreich, Conrad, 1990, 'History of the St. Lawrence–Great Lakes Area to A.D. 1650', in Chris J. Ellis and Neal Ferris (eds.), *The Archaeology of Southern Ontario to A.D. 1650*, pp. 475–92, London, Ontario: Occasional Publication of the London Chapter.

Helms, Mary W., 1988, *Ulysses' Sail: An Ethnographic Odyssey of Power, Knowledge, and Geographical Distance*, Princeton: Princeton University Press.

Herst, DiAnn, 1994, 'Reply', *Canadian Journal of Archaeology* 18: 103–8.

Hewitt, G., 2001, 'Bayunga Waters, an archeology of the Goulburn River within Strathbogie Shire', MA dissertation, La Trobe University.

Hill, W. W., 1982, *An Ethnography of Santa Clara Pueblo, New Mexico*, Albuquerque, NM: University of New Mexico Press.

Hodder, I., Shanks, M., Alexandri, A., Buchili, B., Carman, J., Last, J. and G. Lucas (eds.), 1995, *Interpreting Archaeology*, London: Routledge.

Hoskins, J., no date, 'The Narrative of a Voyage to the North West Coast of America and China on Trade and Discoveries by John Hoskins Performed in the Ship *Columbia Rediviva* 1790, 1791, 1792 & 1793', copy of manuscript, Special Collections Division, University of British Columbia Library.

Houston, Capt. W., 1854, 'Journal and Letterbook of H.M. Ship *Trincomalle*, 1852–1854', OA 20.5, T731 H, Victoria, British Columbia Archives and Records Service.

Howard, Catherine, 1998, 'Wrought identities: the Waiwai expeditions in search of the "unseen tribes" of Amazonia', PhD thesis, University of Chicago.

Howay, F. W., 1925, 'Indian attacks upon maritime fur traders of the North-West Coast, 1785–1805', *Canadian Historical Review* 6: 287–309.

   1929a, 'The Ballad of the Bold Northwestman: an incident in the life of Captain John Kendrick', *Washington Historical Quarterly* 20: 114–23.

   1929b, 'Potatoes: records of some early transactions at Fort Simpson, B.C.', *The Beaver* outfit 259: 155–6.

   1930, 'A list of trading vessels in the maritime fur trade, 1785–1794', *Transactions of the Royal Society of Canada* 3rd ser., 24, 2: 111–34.

   1931, 'A list of trading vessels in the maritime fur trade, 1795–1804', *Transactions of the Royal Society of Canada* 3rd ser., 25, 2: 117–49.

   1933, 'A list of trading vessels in the maritime fur trade, 1815–1819', *Transactions of the Royal Society of Canada* 3rd ser., 27, 2: 119–47.

   1941, *Voyages of the 'Columbia' to the Northwest Coast, 1787–1790 and 1790–1793*, Boston: Massachusetts Historical Society.

Howe, K. R., 1973, 'The Maori responses to Christianity in the Thames–Waikato region 1833–1840', *New Zealand Journal of History* 7, 1: 28–46.

Howes, David, 1996, 'Commodities and cultural borders', in David Howes (ed.), *Cross-Cultural Consumption: Global Markets, Local Realities*, pp. 1–16, London and New York: Routledge.

Huddleston, J. 1996, 'Roun taka an roun will' [My own food and my own free will], in Kimberley Language Resource Centre (ed.), *Moola Bulla: In the Shadow of the Mountain*, pp. 87–9, Broome: Magabala Books.

Hudson's Bay Company, no date a, 'Fort Simpson Journals, 1832–1866', Hudson's Bay Company Archives, B 201/a/1-9, Winnipeg: Archives of Manitoba.

Huffman, T., 1981, 'Snakes and birds: expressive space at Great Zimbabwe', *African Studies* 40: 131–50.

Huguet, Edmond, 1961, *Dictionnaire de la langue française du XVIe siècle*, Paris: Didier.

Hutchison, D. and Mitchem, J., 2001, 'Correlates of contact: epidemic disease in archeological context', *Historical Archaeology* 35, 2: 58–72.

Idriess, I. L., 1947, *The Cattle King: The Story of Sir Sidney Kidman*, Sydney: Angus and Robertson.

Ingraham, J., 1971, *Voyage to the Northwest Coast of North America 1790–1792*, ed. Mark Kaplanoff, Massachusetts: Imprint Society.

Innis, Harold, 1956, *The Fur Trade in Canada*, Toronto: University of Toronto Press.

Inskip, G. H., no date, 'Journal of a Voyage from England to the Pacific including the Northwest Coast of North America, Master of H. M. S. *Virago*, 1851–1855', Add. Mss. 805, 2 vols., Victoria: British Columbia Archives and Records Service.

Jervis, J., 1948, 'The West Darling Country: its exploration and settlement', *Journal of the Royal Australian Historical Society* 34: Parts 2, 3 and 4.

Jordan, S. and Schrire, C., 2002, 'Material culture and the roots of colonial society at the Southern African Cape of Good Hope', in C. Lyons and J. Papadopoulos (eds.), *The Archaeology of Colonialism*, pp. 241–72, Santa Monica, CA: Getty Research Institute.

Kaberry, P., 1939, *Aboriginal Woman: Sacred and Profane*, London: Routledge.

Karklins, Karlis, 1992, *Trade Ornament Usage among the Native Peoples of Canada: A Source Book,* Ottawa: National Historic Parks Service, Studies in Archaeology, Architecture and History.

Kelly, K. G., 1997, 'The archaeology of African–European interaction: investigating the social roles of trade, traders, and the use of space in the seventeenth- and early eighteenth-century *Hueda* Kingdom, Republic of Benin', *World Archaeology* 28, 3: 351–69.

Kenyon, Ian T., 1986, 'Sagard's *Rassade Rouge* of 1624', in William A. Fox (ed.), *Studies in Southwestern Ontario Archaeology*, pp. 53–9, London, Ontario: Occasional Publication of the London Chapter.

Kenyon, Ian T. and Fitzgerald, W., 1986, 'Dutch glass beads in the Northeast: an Ontario perspective', *Man in the Northeast* 32: 1–34.

Kenyon, Ian T. and Kenyon, T., 1983, 'Comments on seventeenth century glass trade beads from Ontario', in Charles F. Hayes III (ed.), *Proceedings of the 1982 Glass Trade Bead Conference*, pp. 59–74, Rochester: Rochester Museum and Science Center.

Kerruish, V. and Perrin, C., 1999, 'Awash in colonialism', *Alternative Law Journal* 42, 1: 3–7, 29.

Kidd, Kenneth E., 1953, 'The excavation and historical identification of a Huron ossuary', *American Antiquity* 18, 14: 359–79.

1979, *Glass Bead-Making from the Middle Ages to the Early 19th Century*, Ottawa: National Historic Parks, Environment Canada.

Kidd, Kenneth E. and Kidd, Martha A., 1970, 'A classification system for glass beads for the use of field archaeologists', *Canadian Historic Sites 1*, Ottawa: Environment Canada.

Kimberley Language Resource Centre (ed.), 1996, *Moola Bulla: In the Shadow of the Mountain*, Broome: Magabala Books.

Klimko, Olga, 1982, 'The archaeology and history of Fort Pelly 1: 1824–1856', MA thesis, University of Saskatchewan.

1994, 'The archaeology of land based fur trade posts in western Canada: a history and critical analysis', PhD thesis, Simon Fraser University.

1998, 'Nationalism and the growth of fur trade archaeology in western Canada', in P. J. Smith and D. Mitchell (eds.), *Bringing Back The Past: Historical Perspectives on Canadian Archaeology*, pp. 203–13, Ottawa: Canadian Museum of Civilization: Mercury Series, Archaeological Survey of Canada, Paper 158.

Kuhn, Robert D. and Funk, Robert E., 1994, 'Mohawk interaction patterns during the sixteenth century', in Charles F. Hayes III (ed.), *Proceedings of the 1992 People to People Conference*, pp. 77–84, Rochester: Rochester Museum and Science Center.

Kuper, A., 1980, 'Symbolic dimensions of the Southern Bantu homestead', *Africa* 50: 8–23.

Lach, Donald F., 1970, *Asia in the Making of Europe*, Vol. 2: *A Century of Wonder*, Chicago and London: University of Chicago Press.

Laenen, Marc, 1989, 'Looking for the future through the past', in D. Uzzell (ed.), *Heritage Interpretation*, Vol. 1: *The Natural and Built Environment*, pp. 88–9, London: Belhaven Press.

Lafitau, Joseph-François, 1977, *Customs of the American Indians Compared with the Customs of Primitive Times*, 2 vols., trans. William N. Fenton and Elizabeth L. Moore, Toronto: University of Toronto Press.

Lalor, M., 2000, *Wherever I Go: Myles Lalor's 'Oral History'*, ed., with an introduction and afterword by Jeremy Beckett, Melbourne: Melbourne University Press.

Lamb, W. K. (ed.), 1942, 'Four letters relating to the cruise of the Thetis, 1852–53', *British Columbia Historical Quarterly* 6: 189–206.

Lanigan, Manga, 1996, 'Stil Buruja Buruja' [Still run away], in Kimberley Language Resource Centre (ed.), *Moola Bulla: In the Shadow of the Mountain*, pp. 44–7, Broome: Magabala Books.

Last, Jonathan, 1995, 'The nature of history', in I. Hodder, M. Shanks, *et al.* (eds.), *Interpreting Archaeology*, pp. 141–57, London: Routledge.

Laurie, B., 1992, 'Station times', in B. Shaw (ed.), *When the Dust Come in Between: Aboriginal Viewpoints in the East Kimberley Prior to 1982*, pp. 93–119, Canberra: Aboriginal Studies Press.

Lennox, Paul A. and Fitzgerald, W. A., 1990, 'The cultural history and archaeology of the neutral Iroquoians', in Chris J. Ellis and Neal Ferris (eds.), *The Archaeology of Southern Ontario to A.D. 1650*, pp. 405–56, London, Ontario: Occasional Publication of the London Chapter.

Leonard, Robert, 1993, 'The persistence of an explanatory dilemma in contact period studies', in J. D. Rogers and S. Wilson (eds.), *Ethno-history and Archaeology: Approaches to Post Contact Change in the Americas*, pp. 31–43, New York: Plenum Press.

Leone, Mark, 1988, 'The relationship between archaeological data and the documentary record: 18th century gardens in Annapolis, Maryland', *Historical Archaeology* 22: 29–35.

Leone, Mark and Potter, P. B. (eds.), 1988, *Recovery of Meaning: Historical Archaeology in the Eastern United States*, Washington DC: Smithsonian Institution Press.

Lescarbot, Marc, 1612, *Histoire de la Nouvelle-France*, Paris: Jean Millot.
  1914, *The History of New France*, Publication 11, Vol. 3, Toronto: The Champlain Society.

Lespinasse, René de, 1888–97. *Les Métiers et corporations de la ville de Paris (XIVe–XVIIIe siècle)*, 2 vols., Paris: Imprimerie Nationale.

Lewis-Williams, D., 1981, *Believing and Seeing: Symbolic Meanings in Southern African Rock Art*, London: Academic Press.

Lightfoot, K. G., 1995, 'Culture contact studies: redefining the relationship between prehistoric and historical archaeology', *American Antiquity* 60, 2: 199–217.

Lightfoot, K. G. and Martinez, A., 1995, Frontiers and boundaries in archaeological perspective, *Annual Reviews of Anthropology* 24: 471–92.

Lilley, I., 2000, *Native Title and the Transformation of Archaeology in the Postcolonial World*, Oceania Monographs 50, Sydney: Oceania Publications, University of Sydney.

L'Incarnation, Marie de, 1971, *Correspondance*, ed. Dom Guy Oury, Solesmes: Abbaye Saint-Pierre.

Lipe, William D., 1984, 'Value and meaning in cultural resources', in Henry Cleere, *Approaches to the Archaeological Heritage*, pp. 1–11, Cambridge: Cambridge University Press.

Litchfield, J., 2001, *Mabo and Yorta Yorta: Two Approaches to History and Some Implications for the Mediation of Native Title Issues*, Perth: National Native Title Tribunal.

Loos, Noel, 1982, *Invasion and Resistance*, Canberra: Australian National University Press.

Lorenzo, José L., 1981, 'Archaeology south of the Rio Grande', *World Archaeology* 13, 2: 190–207.

Lourandos, H., 1985, 'Intensification and Australian prehistory', in T. D. Price and J. A. Brown (eds.), *Prehistoric Hunter-Gatherers: The Emergence of Cultural Complexity*, pp. 385–423, London: Academic Press.

Love, J. R. B., 1936, *Stone-Age Bushmen of Today: Life and Adventure among a Tribe of Savages in North-Western Australia*, London and Glasgow: Blackie and Son Ltd.

Lukin-Watson, P., 1998, *Frontier Lands and Pioneer Legends: How Pastoralists Gained Karawali Land*, St Leonards, NSW: Allen and Unwin.

Lydon, J., 2000 'Regarding Coranderrk: photography at Coranderrk Aboriginal Station, Victoria', unpublished PhD dissertation, Australian National University, Canberra.

Lytwyn, Victor, 1991, 'These Canadians trade the beaver with them where they kill them; Indian responses to extreme fur trade competition in the Little North, 1970–1810', paper presented at the Sixth North American Fur Trade Conference, Mackinac Island, Michigan.

McClosky, Donald, 1991, 'History, differential equations, and the problem of narration', *History and Theory* 30: 21–36.

McConnell, K. and O'Connor, S., 1997, '40,000 year record of food plants in the Southern Kimberley Ranges, Western Australia', *Australian Archaeology* 45: 20–31.

MacDonald, G. F., 1983, *Haida Monumental Art: Villages of the Queen Charlotte Islands*, Vancouver: University of British Columbia Press.

MacDonald Holmes, J., 1963, *Australia's Open North*, Sydney: Angus and Robertson.

McGlade, James, 1995, 'Archaeology and the eco-dynamics of human-modified landscapes', *Antiquity* 69: 113–32.

  1997, 'The limits of social control: coherence and chaos in a prestige-goods economy', in S. Van der Leeuw and J. McGlade, eds., *Time, Process and Structured Transformation in Archaeology*, pp. 298–330, London: Routledge.

McGlade, James and Van der Leeuw, Sander, 1997, 'Introduction: archaeology and non-linear dynamics – new approaches to long-term change', in S. Van der Leeuw and J. McGlade (eds.), *Time, Process and Structured Transformation in Archaeology*, pp. 1–31, London: Routledge.

McGrath, Ann, 1983, '"We grew up the stations", Europeans, Aborigines and cattle in the Northern Territory', unpublished PhD thesis, Bundoora, La Trobe University.

  1987, *Born in the Cattle*, St Leonards, NSW: Allen and Unwin.

MacIntyre, Stuart, 1990, 'Introduction', in S. Janson and S. MacIntyre (eds.), *Through White Eyes*, pp. x–xvi, Sydney: Allen and Unwin in conjunction with Australian Historical Studies.

MacKenzie, I., 1980, 'European incursions and failures in northern Australia', in Rhys Jones (ed.), *Northern Australia: Options and Implications*, pp. 43–72, Canberra: Research School of Pacific Studies, Australian National University.

McLeod, K. David, 1981, 'Preliminary investigations at the St. Anne Trading Post, St. Anne, Manitoba', Winnipeg: Historic Resources Branch.

McNiven, I. and David, B., 1989, *Excavations at the Lightning Brothers site (Yiwarlalay), near Katherine, Northern Territory, Australia, Report on the Earthwatch Lightning Brothers Project 1988–89*, Canberra: The Lightning Brothers Project.

Magee, B., no date, 'Log of the *Jefferson*', photocopy held by the Special Collections Division, University of British Columbia Library.

Maggs, T., 1980, 'The Iron Age sequence south of the Vaal and Pongola Rivers', *Journal of African History* 21: 1–15.

Malloy, Mary, 1998, *'Boston Men' on the Northwest Coast: The American Maritime Fur Trade 1788–1844*, ed. R. A. Pierce, Kingston: The Limestone Press.

Manne, R. (ed.), 2003, *Whitewash: On Keith Windschuttle's Fabrication of Aboriginal History*, Melbourne: Black Inc Press.

Markus, Andrew, 1977, 'Review article. Through a glass darkly: aspects of contact history', *Aboriginal History* 1: 170–80.

Marshall, Y., 2002, 'What is community archaeology?', *World Archaeology* 34, 2: 211–19.

Martain, W., no date, 'Log of the Ship *Hamilton* 1820–1822', Salem, MA: Essex Institute Library.

Mauss, Marcel, 1973, 'Essai sur le don: forme et raison de l'échange dans les sociétés archaïques', in, *Sociologie et anthropologie*, with an introduction by Claude Lévi-Strauss, Paris: Presses Universitaires de France.

Meares, J., 1790, *Voyages Made in the Years 1788 and 1789, from China to the North West Coast of America. To Which are Prefixed an Introductory Narrative of a Voyage performed in 1786, from Bengal, in the Ship 'Nootka'; Observations on the Probable Existence of A North West Passage and Some Account of the Trade between the North West Coast of America and China; and the Latter Country and Great Britain*, London: Logographic Press.

Meehan, B. and Jones, R. (eds.), 1988, *Archaeology with Ethnography: An Australian Perspective*, Canberra: Research School of Pacific Studies, Australian National University.

Melville, Henry, 1967, *The History of Van Diemen's Land from the Year 1824 to 1835 Inclusive*, Adelaide: Libraries Board of South Australia (originally published in 1835).

Mera, H. P., 1933, *A Proposed Revision of the Rio Grande Glaze Paint Sequence*, Santa Fe, NM: Laboratory of Anthropology Technical Series, Bulletin 5.

Merrell, James, 1989, 'Some thoughts on colonial historians and American Indians', *William and Mary Quarterly* 46: 94–119.

Meskell, L. (ed.), 1998, *Archaeology under Fire: Nationalism, Politics and Heritage in the Eastern Mediterranean and the Middle East*, London: Routledge.

Mester, Ann M., 1989, 'Marine shell symbolism in Andean culture', in Charles F. Hayes III (ed.), *Proceedings of the 1986 Shell Bead Conference*, pp. 157–67, Rochester: Rochester Museum and Science Center.

Miller, Christopher L. and Hamell, G. R., 1986, 'A new perspective on Indian–White contact: cultural symbols and colonial trade', *Journal of American History* 73, 2: 311–28.

Miller, Daniel, 1998, 'Why some things matter', in Daniel Miller (ed.), *Material Cultures*, pp. 3–21, Chicago: University of Chicago Press.

Miller, H., Hamilton, D., Honerkamp, H., Pendery, S., Pope, P. and Tuck, J. (eds.), 1996, *The Archaeology of Sixteenth and Seventeenth-Century British Colonization in the Caribbean, United States and Canada*, Guide to Historical Archaeology Literature 4, Bethlehem, PA: Society for Historical Archaeology.

Miller, H., Pogue, D. J. and Smolek, M. A., 1983, 'Beads from the seventeenth century Chesapeake', in Charles F. Hayes III (ed.), *Proceedings of the 1982 Glass Trade Bead Conference*, pp. 127–44, Rochester: Rochester Museum and Science Center.

Monks, Gregory G., 1992, 'Architectural symbolism and non-verbal communication at Upper Fort Garry', *Historical Archaeology* 26, 2: 37–57.

Moodie, D. (ed.), 1960, *The Record: Or a Series of Official Papers Relative to the Condition and Treatment of the Native Tribes of South Africa*, Cape Town: A. A. Balkema.

Moore, Henrietta, 1987, 'Problems in the analysis of social change: an example from the Marakwet', in I. Hodder (ed.), *Archaeology as Long Term History*, pp. 85–104, Cambridge: Cambridge University Press.

Moreau, Jean-François, 1994, 'Des perles de la protohistoire au Saguenay-Lac Saint-Jean?', *Recherches Amérindiennes au Québec* 24, 1–2: 31–48.

Morris, Barry, 1989, *Domesticating Resistance: The Dhan-Gadi Aborigines and the Australian State*, Oxford: Berg.

Morris, Ian, 1997, 'Archaeology as cultural history', *Archaeological Review from Cambridge* 14, 1: 3–16.

Morton, Arthur S., 1973, *A History of the Canadian West to 1870–71*, 2nd edition, Toronto: University of Toronto Press.

Morwood, M. J., 1987, 'The archaeology of social complexity in south-east Queensland', *Proceedings of the Prehistoric Society* 53: 337–50.

Moziño, J. M., 1970, *Noticias de Nutka: An Account of Nootka Sound in 1792*, ed. and trans. I. H. Wilson, Seattle: University of Washington Press.

Mulvaney, D. J., 1975, *The Prehistory of Australia*, revised edition, Melbourne: Penguin Books (originally published in 1969 by Thames and Hudson).

   1986, 'A sense of making history: Australian Aboriginal studies 1961–1986', *Australian Aboriginal Studies* 2: 48–56.

   1989, *Encounters in Place: Outsiders and Aboriginal Australians 1606–1985*, St Lucia, Queensland: University of Queensland Press.

   1990a, 'The Australian Aborigines 1606–1929. Opinion and fieldwork', in S. Janson and S. MacIntyre (eds.), *Through White Eyes*, pp. 1–44, Sydney: Allen and Unwin in conjunction with Australian Historical Studies (originally published in 1958).

   1990b, 'Afterword: a view from the window', in S. Janson and S. MacIntyre (eds.), *Through White Eyes*, pp. 155–67, Sydney: Allen and Unwin in conjunction with Australian Historical Studies.

Mulvaney, D. J. and Kamminga, J., 1999, *Prehistory of Australia*, 3rd revised edition, Sydney: Allen and Unwin.

Murdock, G. P., 1934, 'The Haidas of British Columbia', in *Our Primitive Contemporaries*, pp. 221–63, New York: Macmillan.

   1936, 'Rank and potlatch among the Haida', *Yale University Publications in Anthropology* 13: 1–20.

Murray, Tim, 1992a, *An Archaeological Perspective on the History of Aboriginal Australia*, Working Papers in Australian Studies 80, Sir Robert Menzies Centre for Australian Studies, London: Institute of Commonwealth Studies.

   1992b, 'Tasmania and the constitution of "the dawn of humanity"', *Antiquity* 66: 730–43.

1992c, 'Aboriginal (pre)history and Australian archaeology: the discourse of Australian prehistoric archaeology', in B. Attwood and J. Arnold (eds.), *Power, Knowledge and Aborigines*, pp. 1–19, Bundoora: La Trobe University Press.

1993, 'The childhood of William Lanne: contact archaeology and Aboriginality in Tasmania', *Antiquity* 67: 504–19.

1996a, 'Contact archaeology: shared histories? Shared identities?', in Museum of Sydney (ed.), *Sites. Nailing the Debate: Archaeology and Interpretation in Museums*, pp. 199–213, Glebe: Historic Houses Trust of New South Wales.

1996b, 'Towards a post-Mabo archaeology of Australia', in B. Attwood (ed.), *In the Age of Mabo*, pp. 73–87, Sydney: Allen and Unwin.

1997, 'Dynamic modeling and new social theory of the mid- to long term', in S. Van der Leeuw and J. McGlade (eds.), *Time, Process and Structured Transformation in Archaeology*, pp. 49–463, London: Routledge.

2000a, 'Conjectural histories: some archaeological and historical consequences of indigenous dispossession in Australia', in I. Lilley (ed.), *Native Title and the Transformation of Archaeology in the Postcolonial World*, pp. 65–77, Sydney: Oceania Monographs 50.

2000b, 'Digging with documents, understanding intention and outcome in north-west Tasmania 1825–1835', in A. Anderson and T. Murray (eds.), *Australian Archaeologist: Collected Papers in Honour of Jim Allen*, pp. 145–60, Canberra: Coombs Academic Publishing.

2002, 'Epilogue: an archaeology of indigenous/non-indigenous Australia from 1788', in R. Harrison and C. Williamson (eds.), *After Captain Cook*, pp. 213–23, Sydney: Archaeological Computing Laboratory, University of Sydney.

Murray, Tim (ed.), 1999, *Encyclopedia of Archaeology: The Great Archaeologists*, 2 vols., Santa Barbara: ABC – CLIO Press.

Murray, T. and White, J. P. (eds.), 1985, 'Trends towards social complexity in Australia and New Guinea', *Archaeology in Oceania* 20: 2 and 3.

Murray, T. and Williamson, C., 2003, 'Archaeology and history', in R. Manne (ed.), *Whitewash: On the Fabrication of Aboriginal History*, pp. 311–33, Melbourne: Black Inc Press.

Newman, Peter C., 1985, *The Company of Adventurers*, New York: Viking.

1987, *Caesars of the Wilderness*, New York: Viking.

Niblack, A. P., 1890, 'The Coast Indians of southern Alaska and northern British Columbia; based on the collections in the United States National Museum and on the personal observations of the writer in connection with a survey of Alaska in the seasons of 1885, 1886 and 1887', *Annual Report of the United States National Museum for the Year Ending June 30, 1888*, pp. 225–386, Washington DC.

Nunkiarry, G., Gardiya, 1996a, 'Booty' [Booty], in Kimberley Language Resource Centre (ed.), *Moola Bulla: In the Shadow of the Mountain*, pp. 41–2, Broome: Magabala Books.

1996b, 'No bel riingin' [No bell ringing], in Kimberley Language Resource Centre (ed.), *Moola Bulla: In the Shadow of the Mountain*, pp. 36–9, Broome: Magabala Books.

O'Connell, J. and Allen, J., 1998, 'When did humans first arrive in Greater Australia and why is it important to know?', *Evolutionary Anthropology* 6, 4: 132–46.

O'Connor, S., 1995, 'Carpenter's Gap Rockshelter 1: 40,000 years of Aboriginal occupation in the Napier Ranges, Kimberley, W.A.', *Australian Archaeology* 40: 58–9.

Opper, Marie-José and Opper, Howard, 1991, 'French beadmaking: an historical perspective emphasizing the 19th and 20th centuries', *Beads* 3: 47–59.

Ortiz, Alfonso, 1969, *The Tewa World*, Chicago: University of Chicago Press.

Palissy, Bernard, 1844, *Œuvres complètes*, Paris: Dubochet.

Parkington, J., 1984, 'Soaqua and Bushmen: hunters and robbers', in C. Schrire (ed.), *Past and Present in Hunter Gatherer Studies*, pp. 151–74, New York: Academic Press.

Parkington, J. and Mills, G., 1989, 'From space to place: the architecture and social organisation of Southern African mobile communities', in W. Boismier and C. Gamble (eds.), *Ethnoarchaeological Approaches to Mobile Campsites: Hunter-Gatherer and Pastoralist Case Studies*, pp. 355–70, Ann Arbor, MI: International Monographs in Prehistory.

Parsons, Elsie Clews, 1932, 'Isleta, New Mexico', *47th Annual Report of the Bureau of American Ethnology for 1929–30*, pp. 193–466, Washington, DC.

Patterson, A., 2000, 'Confronting the sources: the archaeology of culture-contact in the south-western Lake Eyre Basin', unpublished PhD dissertation, University of Sydney.

Payne, Michael B., 1991a, 'The political sub-text of fur trade history: fur trade sites and fur trade research', paper presented at the Canadian Historical Association Annual Meetings, Kingston, Ontario.

1991b, 'Summary report: fur trade and native history workshop', *Rupert's Land Research Newsletter* 7, 1: 7–21.

Paynter, Robert and McGuire, Randall H., 1991, 'The archaeology of inequality: material culture, domination, and resistance', in R. McGuire and R. Paynter (eds.), *The Archaeology of Inequality*, pp. 1–27, Oxford: Blackwell.

Peña, Elizabeth, 1990, 'Wampum production in New Netherland and colonial New York: the historical and archaeological context', PhD thesis, Boston University.

Pendergast, James, 1989, 'The significance of some marine shell excavated on Iroquoian archaeological sites in Ontario', in Charles F. Hayes III (ed.), *Proceedings of the 1986 Shell Bead Conference*, pp. 97–106, Rochester: Rochester Museum and Science Center.

Penney, Jan and Rhodes, David, 1990, *Lake Condah Project: Post-contact Archaeological Component*, Occasional Report 35, Melbourne: Victoria Archaeological Survey, Department of Conservation and Environment.

Petch, Virginia P., 1983, 'Whitefish Lake Trading Post', manuscript on file with the Ministry of Culture and Communications, Thunder Bay.

Phillips, C., 1986, 'Excavations at Raupa Pa (N53/37) and Waiwhau Village (N53/198), Paeroa, New Zealand', *New Zealand Journal of Archaeology* 8: 89–113.

    1988, 'University of Auckland Field School excavations at Waiwhau', *New Zealand Journal of Archaeology* 10: 53–72.

    1994, 'The archaeology of Maori occupation along the Waihou River, Hauraki', unpublished PhD dissertation, University of Auckland.

    2000, *Waihou Journeys: The Archaeology of 400 Years of Maori Settlement*, Auckland: Auckland University Press.

Phillips, C. and Green, R. C., 1991, 'Further archaeological investigations at the settlement of Waiwhau, Hauraki Plains', *Records of the Auckland Institute and Museum* 28: 147–83.

Phillipson, D., 1977, *The Later Prehistory of Southern Africa*, London: Heinemann.

Physiologus, 1979, *The Very Ancient Book of Beasts, Plants and Stones*, trans. Michael J. Curley, Austin, University of Texas Press.

Pool, I., 1991, *Te Iwi Maori: A New Zealand Population, Past, Present and Projected*, Auckland: Auckland University Press.

Poole, Francis, 1872, *Queen Charlotte Islands: A Narrative of Discovery and Adventure in the North Pacific*, London: Hurst and Blackett.

Prager, Gabriella, 1980, 'Behavioural implications of cultural formation processes: an example from fur trade archaeology', MA thesis, Simon Fraser University.

Preucel, Robert, 1995, 'The postprocessual condition', *Journal of Archaeological Research* 3, 2: 147–73.

Prevost, James C., 1853, Report to Rear-Admiral Fairfax Moresby, 23 July 1853, enclosure in Adm. 1/5630, Admiralty Papers, Public Record Office, London.

Prickett, N., 1990, 'Archaeological investigations at Raupa: the 1987 season', *Records of the Auckland Institute and Museum* 27: 73–153.

    1992, 'Archaeological investigations at Raupa: the 1988 season', *Records of the Auckland Institute and Museum* 29: 25–101.

Prigogine, Ilya and Stengers, Isabelle, 1984, *Order Out of Chaos: Man's New Dialogue with Nature*, London: Heinemann.

Pyszczyk, Heinz, 1978, 'The Fort Victoria faunal analysis: considerations of subsistence change of the fur trade era in north central Alberta', MA thesis, University of Manitoba.

    1987, 'Economic and social factors in the consumption of material goods in the fur trade of western Canada', PhD thesis, Simon Fraser University.

    1989, 'The archaeology of the recent past: research in historical archaeology in western Canada', *Saskatchewan Archaeology* 10: 3–27.

    1992, 'Archaeological investigations at Fort Edmonton V, 1992: legislative grounds', manuscript on file with the Provincial Museum of Alberta, Edmonton.

Quinn, David B., 1977, *North America from Earliest Discovery to First Settlements: The Norse Voyages to 1612*, New York: Norton.

Rae-Ellis, Vivienne, 1981, *Trucanini: Queen or Traitor?*, Canberra: Australian Institute of Aboriginal Studies.

Ramenofsky, A. F., 1987, *Vectors of Death: The Archaeology of European Contact*, Albuquerque: University of New Mexico Press.

    1991, 'Historical science and contact period studies', in D. H. Thomas (ed.), *Columbian Consequences*, Vol. 3: *The Spanish Borderlands in Pan-American Perspective*, pp. 437–52, Washington DC: Smithsonian Institution Press.

Ramsden, Peter, 1990, 'The Hurons: archaeology and culture history', in Chris J. Ellis and Neal Ferris (eds.), *The Archaeology of Southern Ontario to A.D. 1650*, pp. 361–84, London, Ontario: Occasional Publication of the London Chapter.

    1993, 'The Huron-Petun: current state of knowledge', paper presented at the Canadian Archaeological Association Annual Meeting, Montreal.

Ray, Arthur J., 1974, *Indians in the Fur Trade*, Toronto: University of Toronto Press.

Reece, R. H. W., 1974, *Aborigines and Colonists: Aborigines and the Colonial Society in New South Wales in the 1830s*, Sydney: Sydney University Press.

    1979, 'The Aborigines in Australian historiography', in J. Moses (ed.), *Historical Disciplines and Culture in Australasia*, pp. 253–81, Queensland: University of Queensland Press.

Reid, James Murray, 1853, 'Affidavit concerning loss of Brigantine Vancouver, 1853', A C 205, Y27m., Victoria, British Columbia Archives and Records Service.

Renfrew, A. Colin, 1977, 'Alternative models for exchange and spatial distribution', in T. K. Earle and J Ericson (eds.), *Exchange Systems in Prehistory*, pp. 71–89, New York: Academic Press.

Reynolds, Henry, 1972, *Aborigines and Settlers*, Stanmore, NSW: Cassell.

    1984, *The Breaking of the Great Australia Silence: Aborigines in Australian Historiography 1955–1983*, London: Australian Studies Centre, University of London.

    1990a, *The Other Side of the Frontier: Aboriginal Resistance to the European Invasion of Australia*, revised edition, Ringwood, VIC: Penguin.

    1990b, *With the White People*, Ringwood, VIC: Penguin.

    1998, *This Whispering in Our Hearts*, St Leonards, NSW: Allen and Unwin.

Rhodes, David, 1986, 'The Lake Condah Aboriginal mission dormitory: an archaeological and historical investigation', unpublished MA (Preliminary) thesis, Bundoora, La Trobe University.

Rich, E. E., 1958, *The History of the Hudson's Bay Company: 1670–1763*, The Hudson's Bay Record Society Volume XXI.

Riches, L., 2003, 'True places: native title and the archaeology of Aboriginal land', unpublished PhD dissertation, La Trobe University.

Ritchie, G., 1990, 'Dig the herders/display the Hottentots: the production and presentation of knowledge about the past', MA thesis, University of Cape Town.

Roberts, Mary Nooter and Roberts, A. F., 1996, 'Memory: Luba art and the making of history', *African Arts* (Winter) 23–35.

Robinson, M. P., Garvin, T. and Hodgson, G., 1994, *Mapping How We Use Our Land Using Participatory Action Research*, Calgary: Arctic Institute of North America.

Rogers, J. D., 1990, *Objects of Change: The Archaeology and History of Arikara Contact with Europeans*, Washington DC: Smithsonian Institution Press.

Rogers, J. D. and Wilson, S. M. (eds.), 1993, *Ethnohistory and Archaeology: Approaches to Postcontact Change in the Americas*, New York: Plenum.

Rooney, Matthew, 1853, 'Capture of the American Schooner, Susan Sturgis', *Illustrated News*, New York, 9 April, p. 240.

Ross, H. and Bray, E., 1989, *Impact Stories of the East Kimberley*, East Kimberley Working Paper 28, Canberra: East Kimberley Impact Assessment Project.

Ross, R., 1994, *Beyond the Pale: Essays on the History of Colonial South Africa*, Johannesburg: Witwatersrand University Press.

Roth, H. Ling, 1899, *The Aborigines of Tasmania*, 2nd edition, Halifax: F. King and Sons Printers and Publishers (facsimile edition by Fullers Bookshop Pty. Ltd., Hobart).

Roth, Paul and Ryckman, Thomas, 1995, 'Chaos, Clio and scientistic illusions of understanding', *History and Theory* 34: 30–44.

Roth, W. E., 1905, 'Royal Commission on the Conditions of the Natives', *Votes and Proceedings of the Legislative Council* 1 (5), Perth: Western Australia Government Printer.

Rowland, W., no date, 'Correspondence Outward', A/C/20/R79, Victoria, British Columbia Archives and Records Service.

Rowley, C. D., 1970, *Aboriginal Policy and Practice*, Vol. 1: *The Destruction of Aboriginal Society*, Canberra: Australian National University Press.

Rowley, C. D., 1971, *Aboriginal Policy and Practice*, Vol. 3: *The Remote Aborigines*, Canberra: Australian National University Press.

Rowley, C. D., 1972, *Aboriginal Policy and Practice*, Vol. 2: *Outcasts in White Australia*, Canberra: Australian National University Press (first published in 1970).

Rowse, T., 1987, 'Were you ever savages? Aboriginal insiders and pastoralists' patronage', *Oceania* 58, 1: 81–99.

1998, *White Flour, White Power: From Rations to Citizenship in Central Australia*, Cambridge, New York and Melbourne: Cambridge University Press.

1988, 'Middle Australia and the noble savage: a political romance'. in J. Beckett (ed.), *Past and Present*, pp. 161–77, Canberra: Aboriginal Studies Press.

Ruhl, D. and Hoffman, K., 1997, 'Preface', *Historical Archaeology* 31: 1–3.

Rumley, H. and Toussaint, S., 1990, 'For their own benefit? A critical overview of Aboriginal policy and practice at Moola Bulla, East Kimberley, 1910–1955', *Aboriginal History* 14, 1: 80–103.

Rusden, G. W., 1883, *A History of Australia*, London.

Russell, Dale, 1982, 'Initial European contacts and the fur trade to 1767 on the Saskatchewan River', in D. Burley and D. Meyer (eds.), *Nipawin Reservoir Heritage Study*, Vol. 2, pp. 90–115, Saskatoon: Saskatchewan Research Council Publication C-805-25-E-82.

Russell, L., 2001, *Colonial Frontiers: Indigenous–European Encounters in Settler Societies*, Manchester: Manchester University Press.

Ryan, Lyndall, 1975, 'The Aborigines of Tasmania 1800–1974 and their problems with the Europeans', unpublished PhD thesis, Macquarie University.

   1996, *The Aboriginal Tasmanians*, 2nd edition, St Leonards, NSW: Allen and Unwin.

Sadr, K., Smith, A., Plug, J., Orton, J. and Mütti, B., 2003, Herders and foragers on Kasteelberg: interim report on excavations 1999–2000. *South African Archaeological Bulletin* 58, 177: 27–37.

Sagard, Gabriel, 1632, *Dictionnaire de la langue huronne*, Paris: Denys Moreau.

   1866, *Histoire du Canada et voyages que les Frères mineurs Recollets y ont faicts*, Vol. 1, Paris: Tross (originally published in 1634).

   1990, *Le grand voyage du pays des Hurons*, in Réal Ouellet and Jack Warwick (eds.), Montreal: Leméac (originally published in 1632).

Sahlins, Marshall D., 1961, 'The segmentary lineage: an organization of predatory expansion', *American Anthropologist* 63, 2: 322–43.

   1972, *Stone Age Economics*, New York: Aldine Publishing Co.

   1993, 'Goodbye to *Tristes tropiques*: ethnography in the context of modern world history', in *Journal of Modern History* 65: 1–25.

Saunders, Nicholas J., 1998, 'Stealers of light, traders in brilliance: Amerindian metaphysics in the mirror of conquest', *Res* 33: 225–52.

Scaramelli, F. and Scaramelli, K., 1999, 'Beads: meaning and value in the colonial context of Middle Orinoco, Venezuela', paper presented at the Symposium *Colonialism and Material Culture*, Society for American Archaeology Annual Meeting, Chicago.

Schiffer, Michael, 1999, *The Material Life of Human Beings: Artefacts, Behavior and Communication*, London and New York: Routledge.

Schmidt, Peter R. and Patterson, Thomas C., 1995, 'Introduction: from constructing to making alternative histories', in P. Schmidt and T. Patterson (eds.), *Making Alternative Histories: The Practice of Archaeology and History in Non-Western Settings*, pp. 1–24, Santa Fe: School of American Research Press.

Schoeman, K., 1997, *Dogter van Sion: Machtelt Smit en die 18de-eeuse Samelewing aan die Kaap, 1749–1799*, Cape Town: Human and Rousseau.

Schrire, C., 1980, 'An enquiry into the evolutionary status of San hunter-gatherers', *Human Ecology* 8: 9–32.

   1991, 'The historical archaeology of the impact of colonialism in seventeenth-century South Africa', in L. Falk (ed.), *Historical Archaeology in Global Perspective*, pp. 69–96, Washington DC: Smithsonian Institution Press.

Schrire, C. and Deacon, J., 1989, 'The indigenous artifacts from Oudepost I, a colonial outpost of the VOC at Saldanha Bay, Cape', *South African Archaeological Bulletin* 44: 105–13.

Schubert, L. A., 1992, *Kimberley Dreaming: The Century of Freddie Cox*, Mandurah: L. A. Schubert.

Schuyler, Robert L., 1976, 'Images of America: the contribution of historical archaeology to national identity', *Southwestern Lore* 42, 4: 27–39.

(ed.), 1978, *Historical Archaeology: A Guide to Substantive Theoretical Contributions*, Farmingdale: Baywood.

1988, 'Archaeological remains, documents, and anthropology: a call for a new culture history', *Historical Archaeology* 22: 36–42.

Sciama, Lidia D., 1998, 'Gender in the making, trading and uses of beads: an introductory essay', in Lidia D. Sciama and Joanne B. Eicher (eds.), *Beads and Bead Makers: Gender, Material Culture and Meaning*, pp. 1–45, Oxford and New York: Berg.

Scouler, J., 1841, 'Observations on the indigenous tribes of the N.W. coast of America', *Journal of the Royal Geographical Society of London* 11: 215–50.

Sempowski, Martha L., 1989, 'Fluctuations through time in the use of marine shell at Seneca Iroquois sites', in Charles F. Hayes III (ed.), *Proceedings of the 1986 Shell Bead Conference*, pp. 81–96, Rochester: Rochester Museum and Science Center.

Shanks, M. and Hodder, Ian, 1995, 'Processual, postprocessual and interpretive archaeology', in I. Hodder, M. Shanks, *et al.* (eds.), *Interpreting Archaeology*, pp. 3–29, London: Routledge.

Shanks, M. and Tilley, C., 1987, *Social Theory and Archaeology*, Cambridge: Polity Press.

1992, *Re-constructing Archaeology: Theory and Practice*, London: Routledge.

Shaw, B. (ed.), 1986, *Countrymen: The Life Histories of Four Aboriginal Men as Told to Bruce Shaw*, Canberra: Australian Institute of Aboriginal Studies.

(ed.), 1992, *When the Dust Come in Between: Aboriginal Viewpoints in the East Kimberley Prior to 1982*, Canberra: Aboriginal Studies Press.

Shermer, Michael, 1995, 'Exorcising Laplace's demon: chaos and anti-chaos, history and meta-history', *History and Theory* 34: 59–83.

Simonds Muñoz, Peggy, 1992, *Myth, Emblem, and Music in Shakespeare's Cymbeline: An Iconographic Reconstruction*, Newark: University of Delaware Press.

Simpson, George, no date, 'Letter, George Simpson to the Governor and Committee of the H.B.C., June 10, 1835', Hudson's Bay Company Archives, D.4/102 fo. 28.

Skull, Gideon, 1967, *Voyages of Peter Esprit Radisson*, New York: Burt Franklin.

Smith, I., 1990, 'Historical archaeology in New Zealand: a review and bibliography', *New Zealand Journal of Archaeology* 12: 5–27.

1992, *Pastoralism in Africa: Origins and Development Ecology*, Johannesburg: Witwatersrand University Press.

Smith, A., Sadr, K., Gribble, J. and Yates, R., 1991, 'Excavations in the South Western Cape, South Africa, and the archaeological identity of prehistoric hunter gatherers within the last 2000 years', *South African Archaeological Bulletin* 46: 71–91.

Smith, Marvin and Good, Mary E., 1982, *Early Beads in Spanish Colonial Trade*. Greenwood, MS: Cottonlandia Museum Publications.

Snow, Dean, 1994, *The Iroquois*, Oxford: Blackwell.

    1995, *Mohawk Valley Archaeology: The Sites*, University Park, PA: Matson Museum of Anthropology.

South, Stanley, 1977, *Method and Theory in Historical Archaeology*, New York: Academic Press.

    1993, 'Strange fruit: historical archaeology, 1972–1977', *Historical Archaeology* 27, 1: 15–18.

Sparrow, Kathy D., 1998, Correcting the record: Haida oral tradition in anthropological narratives, *Anthropologica* 40: 215–22.

Spencer-Wood, Suzanne M. (ed.), 1987, *Consumer Choice in Historical Archaeology*, New York: Plenum Press.

Spores, Ronald, 1980, 'New world ethno-history and archaeology, 1970–1980', *Annual Review of Anthropology* 9: 575–603.

Stanner, W. E. H., 1969, *After the Dreaming*, 1968 Boyer Lecture, Sydney: Australian Broadcasting Commission.

Stasiulis, D. and Yuval-Davis, N. (eds.), 1995, *Unsettling Settler Societies: Articulations of Gender, Race, Ethnicity and Class*, London: Sage.

Stewart, Ian, 1992, *Does God Play Dice? The Mathematics of Chaos*, Boston, MA: Blackwell Publishers (first published in 1989).

Stewart, Susan, 1993, *On Longing: Narratives of the Miniature, the Gigantic, the Souvenir, the Collection*, Durham and London: Duke University Press.

Sturgis, W., no date a, 'My first Voyage: Remarks on Voyage of *Eliza* 1798 to Feb. 19th 1799', photocopy of original journal, Special Collections Division, University of British Columbia Library.

    no date b, 'Journal of the *Eliza*, February–May 1799, of a voyage to the NW Coast of N.A. and China', photocopy of original, Special Collections Division, University of British Columbia Library.

    No date c, 'Three lectures', Boston, MA, Massachusetts Historical Society.

    1978, *The Journal of William Sturgis*, ed. S. W. Jackman, Victoria: Sono Nis Press.

Sturma, M., 1985, 'Myall Creek and the psychology of mass murder', *Journal of Australian Studies* 16: 62–70.

Sullivan, J., 1983, *Banggaiyerri: The Story of Jack Sullivan as Told to Bruce Shaw*, Canberra: Australian Institute of Aboriginal Studies.

Sullivan, P., 1996, *All Free Man Now: Culture, Community and Politics in the Kimberley Region, North-Western Australia*, Canberra: Australian Institute of Aboriginal and Torres Strait Islander Studies.

Swanton, J. R., no date, 'Haida notebooks, 1900–01', 2 vols., National Anthropological Archives, Washington DC, Smithsonian Institution.

1905a, *Contributions to the Ethnology of the Haida*, Memoir of the American
Museum of Natural History 5, Pt 1, New York: American Museum of Natural
History.

1905b, 'Social organization of the Haida', in *Proceedings of the International
Congress of Americanists*, 13th Session, 1902, New York, Vol. 13, pp. 327–34.

Tavernier, Jean Baptiste, 1678, *The Six Voyages of John Baptiste Tavernier a Noble
Man of France, through Turky into Persia, and the East Indies*, translation into
English by J. Phillips, London: R.L. and M.P.

Taylor, C. J., 1990, *Negotiating the Past: The Making of Canada's National Historic
Parks and Sites*, Montreal: McGill-Queen's University Press.

Taylor, C. J. and Payne, M. B., 1992, 'The invention of traditions of invention at
fur trade sites: animated adventures in the skin trade', paper presented at the
Rupert's Land Conference, Winnipeg.

Tervarent, Guy de, 1997, *Attributs et symbols dans l'art profane: dictionnaire d'un
langage perdu (1450–1600)*, Geneva: Droz.

Thom, H. (ed.), 1952, *Journal of Jan Van Riebeeck*, Vol. 1: *1651–1655*, Cape Town:
Van Riebeeck Society.

Thomas, D. H., 1989, *Columbian Consequences*, Vol. 1: *Archaeological and Historical
Perspectives on the Spanish Borderlands West*, Washington DC: Smithsonian
Institution Press.

1990, *Columbian Consequences*, Vol. 2: *Archaeological and Historical Perspectives
on the Spanish Borderlands East*, Washington DC: Smithsonian Institution
Press.

1991, *Columbian Consequences*, Vol. 3: *The Spanish Borderlands in Pan-American
Perspective*, Washington DC: Smithsonian Institution Press.

Thomas, J., 1996, *Time, Culture and Identity: An Interpretive Archaeology*, London:
Routledge.

Thomas, N., 1991, *Entangled Objects: Exchange, Material Culture and Colonialism
in the Pacific*, Cambridge, MA, and London: Harvard University Press.

1999, *Possessions: Indigenous Art, Colonial Culture*, New York: Thames and
Hudson.

2002, 'Colonizing cloth: interpreting the material culture of nineteenth-century
Oceania', in C. Lyons and J. Papadopoulos (eds.), *The Archaeology of Colonialism*, pp. 182–98, Santa Monica, CA: The Getty Research Institute.

Thwaites, Reuben G., 1896–1901, *The Jesuit Relations and Allied Documents*, 73 vols.,
New York: Pageant Book Company.

Tilley, Christopher, 1990a, 'Michel Foucault: towards an archaeology of archaeology', in C. Tilley (ed.), *Reading Material Culture*, pp. 281–347, Oxford:
Blackwell.

1990b, 'On modernity and archaeological discourse', in I. Bapty and T. Yates
(eds.), *Archaeology after Structuralism*, pp. 128–52, London: Routledge.

Tillyard, Eustache Mandeville, 1965, *The Elizabethan World Picture*, New York: Vintage.

Todorov, Tzvetan, 1986, 'Le croissement des cultures', *Communications* 43: 1–22.

Torrence, R. and Clarke, A. (eds), 2000a, *The Archaeology of Difference: Negotiating Cross-Cultural Engagements in Oceania*, One World Archaeology Series 38, London: Routledge.

Torrence, R. and Clarke, A., 2000b, 'Negotiating difference: practice makes theory for contemporary archaeology in Oceania', in R. Torrence and A. Clarke (eds.), *The Archaeology of Difference: Negotiating Cross-cultural engagements in Oceania*, pp. 1–31, One World Archaeology Series 38, London: Routledge.

Townsend, N., 1985, 'Masters and men at the Myall Creek massacre', *The Push from the Bush* 20: 4–34.

Tremblay, Roland, 1998, 'Le site de l'anse à la vache et le mitan du Syvicole Supérieur dans l'estuaire du St-Laurent', in Roland Tremblay (ed.), *L'Eveilleur et l'ambassadeur: essais archéologiques et ethnohistoriques en hommage à Charles Martijn*, pp. 91–126, Montreal: Recherches Amérindiennes au Québec.

Trigger, Bruce, 1976, *The Children of Aataentsic: A History of the Huron People to 1660*, Montreal and Kingston; McGill-Queen's University Press.

1978a, 'Early Iroquoian contacts with Europeans', in Bruce Trigger (ed.), *Northeast Handbook of North American Indians*, Vol. 15, pp. 344–56, William Sturtevant, general editor, Washington DC: Smithsonian Institution.

1978b, *Time and Traditions: Essays in Archaeological Interpretation*, Edinburgh: Edinburgh University Press.

1980, 'Archaeology and the image of the American Indian', *American Antiquity* 45, 4: 662–76.

1983, 'American archaeology as native history: a review essay', *William and Mary Quarterly* 40: 413–52.

1984, 'Alternative archaeologies: nationalist, colonialist, imperialist', *Man* 19: 355–70.

1985, *Natives and Newcomers: Canada's 'Heroic Age' Reconsidered*, Kingston and Montreal: McGill-Queen's University Press, 1985.

1986, 'Prehistoric archaeology and American society', in D. Meltzer, D. Fowler and J. Sabloff (eds.), *American Archaeology Past and Future*, pp. 187–215, Washington DC: Smithsonian Institution Press.

1991a, 'Early native North American responses to European contact: romantic versus rationalistic interpretations', *The Journal of American History* 77, 4: 1195–1215.

1991b, 'Distinguished lecture in archaeology: constraint and freedom – a new synthesis for archaeological explanation', *American Anthropologist* 93: 551–69.

Trivellato, Francesca, 2001, 'Entrepreneurial strategies and technological change: the case of Venetian glass manufacturing in the 17th and the 18th centuries', in L. Bergeron, G. Fontana, R. Leboutte and D. Woronoff (eds.), *Mobilité du capital humain et industrialisation régionale en Europe: entrepreneurs, techniciens et main-d'œuvre spécialisée (XVIème–XXème siècles)*, Padua and Paris: CLEUP-Publications de la Sorbonne.

Tunbridge, J. E. and Ashworth, G. J., 1996, *Dissonant Heritage*, Chichester: John Wiley.

Turgeon, Laurier, 1997, 'The tale of the kettle: odyssey of an intercultural object', *Ethnohistory* 44, 1: 1–29.

1998, 'French fishers, fur traders, and Amerindians during the sixteenth century: history and archaeology', *William and Mary Quarterly* 60, 4: 585–610.

Turner, Terrance, 1995, 'Social body and embodied subject: bodiliness, subjectivity, and sociality among the Kayapo', *Cultural Anthropology* 10, 2: 143–70.

Tyrrell, I., 2002, 'Beyond the view from Euro-America. Environment, settler societies, and the internationalization of American history', in T. Bender (ed.), *Rethinking American History in a Global Age*, pp. 168–91, Berkeley: University of California Press.

Urry, James, 1979, 'Beyond the frontier: European influence, Aborigines and the concept of traditional culture', *Journal of Australian Studies* 5: 2–16.

Vachon, André, 1970–71, 'Colliers et ceintures de porcelaine chez les Indiens de la Nouvelle France', *Les Cahiers de Dix* 35: 251–78; 36: 179–92.

Van der Leeuw, Sander, 1998, 'Multidisciplinarity, policy-relevant research and non-linear paradigm', in S. Van der Leeuw (ed.), *The Archaeomedes Project: Understanding the Natural and Anthropogenic Causes of Land Degradation and Desertification in the Mediterranean Basin*, Vol. 1: *Synthesis*, pp. 25–41, Luxembourg: Office for Official Publications of the European Communities.

Van der Leeuw, Sander and McGlade, James, 1997, 'Structural change and bifurcation in urban evolution: a non-linear dynamical perspective', in S. Van der Leeuw and J. McGlade (eds.), *Time, Process and Structured transformation in Archaeology*, pp: 331–72, London: Routledge.

Van Dommelen, P., 2002, 'Ambiguous matters: colonialism and local identities in Punic Sardinia', in C. Lyons and J. Papadopoulos (eds.), *The Archaeology of Colonialism*, pp. 121–47, Santa Monica, CA: Getty Research Institute.

Van Ossel, Paul, 1991, *Les Jardins du Carroussel à Paris: fouilles 1989–1990*, Paris: Service Régional de l'Archéologie d'Ile-de-France, Ministère de la Culture, de la Communication et des Grands Travaux.

Vecellio, Cesare, 1860, *Costumes anciens et modernes*, French edition by Firmin Didot, Paris: Didot Frères (first published in 1590).

Walbran, John T., 1909, *British Columbia Coast Names, 1592–1906*, Ottawa: Government Printing Bureau.

Walker, W., no date, 'Log-Book of the Brig *Lydia* on a Fur-Trading Voyage from Boston to the Northwest Coast of America 1804–1805, with the return Voyage by way of The Sandwich Islands and Canton Aboard the Ships *Atahualpa* and *Swift* 1805–1807', MS, Yale University, Beinecke Library.

Walton, J., 1995, *Cape Cottages*, Cape Town: Intaka.

Watson, R., 1991, *The Slave Question: Liberty and Property in South Africa*, Johannesburg: Witwatersrand University Press.

Webby, E., 1980, 'Reactions to the Myall Creek massacre', *The Push from the Bush* 8: 1–13.

Webster, S., 1993, 'Islands of culture: the post-modernisation of the Maori', *Sites* 26: 2–26.

Weed, Charles E., 1868, 'Narrative of Charles E. Weed', in *The Early History*, The Washington Standard, Olympia, May 16, 2.

Weik, T., 1997, 'The archaeology of maroon societies in the Americas: resistance, cultural continuity and transformation in the African diaspora', *Historical Archaeology* 31, 2: 81–92.

Weiner, J., Godwin, L. and L'Oste-Brown, S., 2002, *Australian Aboriginal Heritage and Native Title: An Example of Contemporary Indigenous Connection to Country in Central Queensland*, Perth, WA: National Native Title Tribunal.

West, John, 1971, *The History of Tasmania*, Sydney: Angus and Robertson, published in association with the Royal Australian Historical Society (originally published in 1852 by Henry Dowling, Launceston).

Whitbread, Ian K., 1989, 'A proposal for the systematic description of thin sections towards the study of ancient ceramic technology', in Y. Maniatis, *Archaeometry: Proceedings of the 25th International Symposium*, pp. 127–38, Proceedings of the 25th International Symposium, Amsterdam: Elsevier.

Whitehead, Ruth, 1993, *Nova Scotia: The Protohistoric Period, 1500–1630*, Halifax: Nova Scotia Museum.

Williams, Glyndwr, 1970, 'Highlights of the first 200 years of the Hudson's Bay Company', *The Beaver*, Outfit 301.

Wilson, B., 1985, 'Edward Denny Day's investigations at Myall Creek', *The Push from the Bush* 20: 35–57.

Wilson, S. M., 1993, 'Structure and history. Combining archaeology and ethnohistory in the contact period Caribbean', in J. Rogers and S. Wilson (eds.), *Ethnohistory and Archaeology: Approaches to Postcontact Change in the Americas*, pp. 19–30, New York: Plenum.

Wilson, Samuel and Rogers, J. Daniel, 1993, 'Afterword', in J. Rogers and S. Wilson (eds.), *Ethnohistory and archaeology: Approaches to Post Contact Change in the Americas*, pp. 223–7, New York: Plenum Press.

Windschuttle, K., 2002, *The Fabrication of Aboriginal History*, Vol. 1: *Tasmania*, Paddington, NSW: Macleay Press.

Winship, George Parker (ed.), 1905, *Sailors' Narratives of Voyages along the New England Coast, 1524–1624*, Boston: Houghton, Mifflin.

Witthoft, John, 1966, 'Archaeology as a key to the colonial fur trade', *Minnesota History* 40, 4: 203 9.

Wolf, Eric R., 1982, *Europe and the People without History*, Los Angeles: University of California Press.

Wolters, Natacha, 1996, *Les Perles: au fil du textile*, Paris: Syros.

Wood, Raymond, 1990, 'Ethno-history and historical method', *Archaeological Method and Theory* 2: 81–110.

Worden, N. and Crais, C., (eds.), 1994, *Breaking the Chains: Slavery and Its Legacy in the Nineteenth Century Cape*, Johannesburg: Witwatersrand University Press.

Work, J., no date, 'Diary of a Trip of Chief Factor John Work in 1851 from Fort Simpson to Queen Charlotte Islands to investigate reported Gold discoveries', Special Collections Division, University of British Columbia Library.

    1945, 'The Journal of John Work, January to October, 1835', Victoria, *Archives of British Columbia Memoir* no. X.

Wray, Charles F., 1983, 'Seneca glass trade beads, c. A.D. 1550–1820', in Charles F. Hayes (dir.), *Proceedings of the 1982 Glass Trade Bead Conference*, p. 42, Rochester, NY: Rochester Museum and Science Center Research Record 16.

Wray, Charles F., Sempowski, M. L. and Saunders, L. P., 1991, *Tram and Cameron: Two Early Contact Era Seneca Sites*, Rochester, New York: Rochester Museum and Science Center.

Wray, Charles F., Sempowski, M. L., Saunders, L. P. and Cervone, G. C., 1987, *The Adams and Culbertson Sites*, Rochester, NY: Rochester Museum and Science Center.

Wyckoff, Lydia L., 1985, *Designs and Factions: Politics, Religion, and Ceramics on the Hopi Third Mesa*, Albuquerque: University of New Mexico Press.

Wylie, Alison, 1992, 'Rethinking the Quincentennial: consequences for past and present', *American Antiquity* 57, 4: 591–4.

    1993, 'Facts and fictions: writing archaeology in a different voice', *Canadian Journal of Archaeology* 17: 5–12.

Zipfel, C., 2002, 'Linking places. Constructing an Aboriginal social landscape in the Wimmera region of north-western Victoria', unpublished BA thesis, La Trobe University.

Index